Donald R. Cruickshank

has held several positions that have enabled him to know teachers and teaching. A former teacher himself, he has also been a principal and a teacher of teachers. He is currently a professor in the Faculty of Educational Foundations and Research, The Ohio State University. Cruickshank has conducted several national studies of teacher concerns and has published two multimedia kits on teacher problems—"The Teaching Problems Laboratory" and "The Inner-City Simulation Laboratory."

And Associates

Jane Applegate, Franklin County Teacher Center, Columbus, Ohio
John Holton, The Ohio State University, Columbus, Ohio
Gerald Mager, Syracuse University, Division for the Study of Teaching
Betty Myers, Syracuse University, Division for the Study of Teaching
Charles Novak, Wittenberg College, Springfield, Ohio
Katherine Tracey, Sarasota, Florida

Illustrator

Kathy Cruickshank

The **Applied Education** Series offers books based on sound principles of education drawn from the areas of philosophy, pedagogy, learning psychology, human development, and interpersonal relations. The aim is to present useful and meaningful ways for the readers to apply the principles of education to their teaching situation, whatever the setting. The authors build on their personal experiences as well as on the rich body of modern educational theory and research.

Series Editor: Ronald T. Hyman
Rutgers University

Donald R. Cruickshank
And Associates

TEACHING IS TOUGH

Prentice-Hall, Inc., Englewood Cliffs, New Jersey 07632   A SPECTRUM BOOK

Library of Congress Cataloging in Publication Data

Cruickshank, Donald R
   Teaching is tough.

   (A Spectrum Book)
   Includes bibliographies and index.
     1. Teaching.   2. Classroom management.   3. Problem solving.   I. Title.
LB1025.2.C68   371.1'02   80-14625
ISBN 0-13-893495-9
ISBN 0-13-893487-8 (pbk.)

*To my daughter Carol
and all her colleagues who are beginning teaching careers*

Editorial/production supervision by Betty Neville
Chapter and part opening design by Christine Gehring Wolf
Cover design by Kay Ritta
Manufacturing buyer: Cathie Lenard

© 1980 by Prentice-Hall, Inc., Englewood Cliffs, New Jersey 07632

A SPECTRUM BOOK

All rights reserved.
No part of this book may be reproduced
in any form or by any means
without permission in writing from the publisher.

10 9 8 7 6 5 4 3 2 1

Printed in the United States of America

Prentice-Hall International, Inc., London
Prentice-Hall of Australia Pty. Limited, Sydney
Prentice-Hall of Canada, Ltd., Toronto
Prentice-Hall of India Private Limited, New Delhi
Prentice-Hall of Japan, Inc., Tokyo
Prentice-Hall of Southeast Asia Pte. Ltd., Singapore
Whitehall Books Limited, Wellington, New Zealand

contents

PREFACE   vii

ACKNOWLEDGMENTS   ix

INTRODUCTION / WHY IDENTIFY AND STUDY TEACHER PROBLEMS?
Donald R. Cruickshank

PART I / PROBLEMS AND PROBLEM SOLVING

ONE / What Are the Problems of Classroom Teachers?   7
Donald R. Cruickshank

TWO / What Are Your Teaching Problems?   31
Donald R. Cruickshank

THREE / How Can Teacher Problems Be Lessened?   45
Donald R. Cruickshank

FOUR / Lessening One of Your Problems   63
Donald R. Cruickshank

PART II / HELP RELATED TO YOUR PROBLEMS

FIVE / Affiliation   75
Katherine Tracey

SIX / Control   113
Charles Novak

SEVEN / Parent Relationships and Home and Community Conditions   153
Gerald Mager

EIGHT / Student Success   199
John Holton

NINE / Time   257
Jane Applegate

PART III / TEACHER PROBLEMS AND TEACHER PERSONALITY

TEN / Relationships between Classroom Problems and Personality or Place of Work   303
Betty Myers

PART IV / SUPPLEMENTS

ONE / Some Problems of Practice   324
Donald R. Cruickshank

TWO / The Development of the Teacher Problems Checklist   330
Donald R. Cruickshank and Betty Myers

INDEX   339

preface

Teaching is tough! It is difficult to think of many occupations as demanding intellectually, physically, and psychologically. Who else but teachers must keep well informed in one or more disciplines, must organize and manage one or more groups of workers (students) and provide for both their success and satisfaction? Who else must be concerned not only with the client but with maintaining good relationships with the client's family? Who else gets blamed when vandalism and crime increase and when scores on college entrance examinations drop? What other occupational group is subjected to so much national criticism in barrages from books like *Why Johnny Can't Read* and *Crisis in the Classroom?* Who else is constantly second-guessed by nearly everyone about what to do and how to do it?

Yes, teaching is tough, and that is why teachers have so many legitimate concerns or problems. The purpose of this book is to help teachers address those problems and show them how to lessen or resolve them. *Teaching Is Tough* can be used in a variety of contexts. In preservice teacher education it has a place in early experience programs, in introduction to teaching, and in general and special methods of teaching courses. Further it should be invaluable during student teaching. In graduate teacher education it can provide a foundation for courses such as supervision which focus upon improving life in classrooms and the solving problems of teachers. In in-service education it has the most natural audience since it was written to assist the practicing teacher. Parents should find it useful, too, especially those who take an active interest in school improvement.

acknowledgments

The idea for the "writing" of this book began when I was a public school teacher. The motivation to produce it increased when, as a supervisor and principal, I worked with so many teachers as they strove to meet the many demands of teaching.

Its gestation period was long because so much needed to be done. First, numerous studies had to be conducted to determine what were the real problems of classroom teachers. Next, those problems had to be examined with an eye toward developing a helpful problem-solving procedure. Finally, the literature had to be searched to locate information teachers would find useful for resolving the problems.

Along the way, many people contributed. Thousands of classroom teachers from scores of school districts across the United States provided daily detailed reports of their concerns. Over the years many colleagues helped me to analyze the data that the classroom teachers provided. Among those who provided substantial help were Frank Broadbent and Betty Myers of Syracuse University, James Leonard of Kansas State University, and John Kennedy, a colleague at The Ohio State University. Hundreds of teachers, most of them enrolled in graduate classes at Ohio State University, have examined the problems with me. As we worked toward their resolution, we conceived of the problem-solving process which is so central to this book. Finally, six collaborators provided some of the finishing touches as they worked with me to locate and present the "knowledge of most worth" related to the areas of teaching problems that had been uncovered.

Now the gestation period is over, and for the sake of classroom teachers we hope the result is worth the effort.

Donald R. Cruickshank
The Ohio State University
November 1979

Figure 5-7 on page 98 is from *Realities of Teaching: Explorations with Video Tape* by Raymond S. Adams and Bruce J. Biddle. Copyright © 1970 by Holt, Rinehart and Winston, Inc. Reprinted by permission of Holt, Rinehart and Winston.

Figure 6-1 on page 147 is reprinted by permission of Associates for Behavior Change.

The poem on page 227 is reprinted from *The Cherry Tree* by Geoffrey Grigson by permission of the publisher, Vanguard Press, Inc. Copyright © 1959; Copyright © renewed 1970 by Geoffrey Grigson.

Excerpts from *The Art of Teaching* by Gilbert Highet, copyright © 1950, are used by permission of Alfred A. Knopf, Inc.

The excerpts from *How to Get Control of Your Time and Your Life*, by Alan Laken—copyright © 1973 by Alan Laken—are reprinted by permission of the David McKay Company, Inc.

The excerpt from *Toward a Psychology of Being,* 2nd edition by Abraham H. Maslow—© 1968 by Litton Educational Publishing, Inc.—is reprinted by permission of Van Nostrand Reinhold Company.

The problems on pages 22-27 are from *Problem Solving and Creativity in Individuals and Groups* by N.R.F. Maier. Copyright © 1970 by Wadsworth, Inc. Reprinted by permission of the publisher, Brooks/Cole Publishing Company, Monterey, California.

introduction

why identify and study teacher problems?

DONALD R. CRUICKSHANK

There are three reasons why teacher concerns or problems should be identified and studied. First, there is a need to respond to the long-standing admonition of many teachers, their national professional associations, and school administrators that *teacher education must be related more directly to the everyday needs of practitioners.* Hill noted this failure over a decade ago when he wrote: "For too long we have been lining up teachers and having them undergo courses, seminars, and institutes for the wrong reasons. . . . It is time to determine which problems or types of problems require a greater degree of skills than teachers on the scene can provide."[1] So far as practitioners are concerned, teacher education is still guilty of this charge.

---

1. Warren G. Hill. "The Dynamic Duo," in *Seattle Conference: The Role of the State Department of Education in Teacher Education* (Olympia, Wash.: State Superintendent of Public Instruction, 1967), p. 11.

Second, *teacher concerns or problems do not go away with the accumulation of teaching experience.* A teacher is not likely to be much better at achieving classroom control after ten years than after five. Practice per se does not necessarily make perfect. Practice is only effective when learners receive adequate knowledge of how well they perform. If a part of the teacher preparation program provides meaningful practice in solving teacher problems, then the likelihood of such problems being lessened is considerably greater.

Third, *teacher satisfaction is important!* Teachers count too! Unfortunately, some would argue that the teachers don't count or at least they don't count very much. I still recall my first principal, who said to us, "God comes first, the children come second, and teachers come last." That statement has always troubled me. Leaving God out for the moment, I would suggest an equally viable statement, "Teachers come first, students come second." For *unless there is a satisfied teacher in the classroom, students will count not at all.* It simply is impossible for teachers to achieve personal and professional satisfaction until their problems are acknowledged and sources are brought to bear that will reduce or eliminate them. If teacher preparation accepts that teacher satisfaction is important, then it must focus in part on teacher concerns arising out of practice.

It is logical that teacher concerns should be a focus in all three arenas of professional education: undergraduate, graduate, and in-service or continuing education. In other words, education students should study classroom problems as part of their course work and certified teachers should study them in graduate courses or as part of their in-service work. Unfortunately, such is not the case. The problem areas of teachers tend, at best, to be sporadically mentioned and then only in passing. Furthermore, teachers get vague and sometimes seemingly contradictory advice about them. They are told, for example:

Maintain academic standards (but)
    Provide each child with success each day.

Do not interfere in the home (but)
   Hold parent conferences.
Treat each child the same (but)
   Individualize instruction.

In summary, teachers feel their preparation program does not adequately prepare them for their work. They do not necessarily improve from on-the-job experience and they are often told or made to feel they don't count. It is little wonder that Jersild, in his classic book *When Teachers Face Themselves*,[2] reported that he found teachers anxious, hostile, and lonely.

---

2. Arthur Jersild. *When Teachers Face Themselves* (New York: Teachers College Press, Columbia University, 1955).

part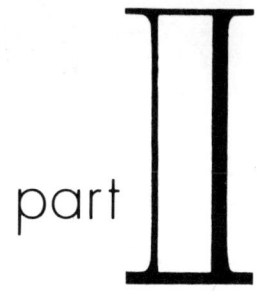

PROBLEMS AND PROBLEM SOLVING

We begin our inquiry in Chapter 1 by finding out what a problem is and what makes a problem difficult. We discover what the major problem areas are for all teachers.

In Chapter 2 we fill in the Teacher Problems Checklist to determine what teacher problems trouble us most. This helps us to find out something about ourselves and becomes a starting place for self-improvement.

Chapter 3 presents and describes a problem-solving process that has been developed to help us lessen our problems. In Chapter 4 we practice using it to reduce a teaching problem of our own.

chapter 1

what are the problems of classroom teachers?

DONALD R. CRUICKSHANK

Chapter 1 Outcomes: *After reading Chapter 1 you should be able to:*
—define what a problem is,
—list the components of a problem,
—describe what makes a problem difficult and difficult to solve,
—describe the kinds of needs teachers try to meet, and relatedly describe the five persistent areas of teacher concerns or problems.

What is a problem? What makes a problem difficult? What are teacher problems? In this chapter we present an overview of teacher problems—what they are and why they occur. The following scenario will be helpful as a point of reference.

The faculties from Central High School and two of its "feeder" schools, Grimm and Edison, have joined together because of shared concern over the high state of teacher stress and the low state of teacher morale in that attendance area. They have decided to work to identify and to think of ways to resolve the problems they share as classroom teachers. As a beginning, each teacher has written down a problem that occurred in the past week. Pat Taylor, a sixth grade teacher at Edison Elementary School, is the first to present a problem description.

> Monday morning when I went to the library to get the boys and bring them back to the room, the librarian was frantic. Even when I came into the library I saw the boys tussling, hitting each other over the head with books, and causing a general disturbance. I was so ashamed I took them back to the room and led a discussion about the library and appropriate behavior when with another teacher. When the discussion was over I asked if anyone had anything else to say. One of the boys said, "Yeah, shut up." When I asked him to whom he was talking he said, "You!"

Arthur Daniels, a teacher from Grimm Junior High School, was next.

> One of my students who has never really tried very hard in the past has recently been doing all her homework and classwork and seems to be working to the best of her ability. Today was test day and she failed. When she turned in her paper she appeared most pleased with herself for having done her best. We are told to treat students as individuals. If I were to do this and pass her with a low grade, the other students would accuse me of being unfair. And don't think they don't know each other's business. However, if I don't pass her, she will believe all her work was in vain and go back to not caring.

WHAT IS A PROBLEM?

Both of the above classroom vignettes seem to satisfy psychological and lay definitions of what a problem is. Such definitions include the following criteria:

What Are the Problems of Classroom Teachers? 9

A problem exists when an organism (for example, a teacher) is motivated toward some goal and there is no ready way to achieve it.
A problem is an expression of an unmet need or unfulfilled goal.
A problem arises when we want something and cannot have it.

Visually a problem can be depicted as in Figure 1-1.

From the illustration and the definitions, it is assumed that a problem has three components: an object or goal, a person who is motivated or who wants the goal, and something that impedes or stands in the way of goal achievement.

Pat Taylor's problem was caused because Pat wanted to have rapport with the librarian and felt that the boys were interfering with that goal. A second problem developed because Pat also wanted to have rapport with the class and at least one pupil was putting that in jeopardy.

On the other hand, Arthur Daniels' problem resulted because Arthur wanted a particular pupil to succeed and thus continue to be motivated toward learning. The obstacle was the pupil's failure of a test, an event Arthur would have liked to overlook but couldn't.

A PROBLEM EXISTS WHEN WE WANT TO ACHIEVE A GOAL AND CANNOT

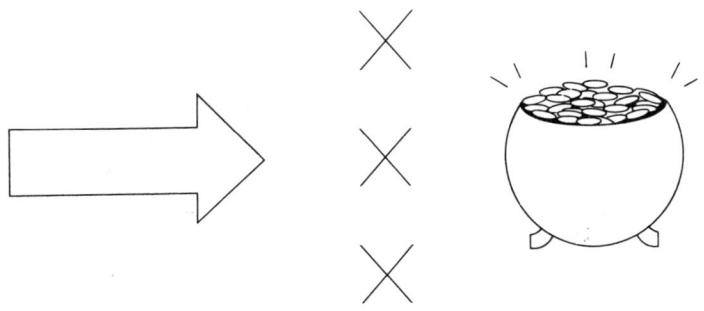

FIGURE 1-1.

WHAT MAKES A PROBLEM DIFFICULT AND DIFFICULT TO SOLVE?

Some teacher problems are easy to resolve. Other problems almost defy resolution. For example, it is a simple matter to clean the chalkboards when they are left dirty. On the other hand, it is a complex matter to deal with classroom control or motivation. Such problems are complex and difficult because of personal or environmental impediments. There are at least four *personal* impediments to problem solving.

Lack of sufficient mental, physical, or social ability makes solving problems more difficult. The most difficult classroom problems severely tax or even overtax our mental, physical, or social abilities. Since we vary in these abilities, some of us will have more or different kinds of problems than will others. For example, the problem of knowing what to do when told by a pupil to "shut up" will be more taxing to a Pat Taylor, who, compared to other teachers, (1) may be somewhat less quick and creative, (2) has less fortitude physically, and (3) does not have facility in relating well to others socially. Conversely, teachers with greater mental, physical, and social abilities will feel less perplexed in a similar situation.

Lack of related knowledge and experience makes problems difficult. Lack of related knowledge and experience is also a personal impediment to problem solving. Either knowledge of or successful experience in similar situations would most likely place the problem solver in better stead. All other things being equal, a Pat Taylor or an Arthur Daniels who has knowledge of and successful experience with similar problems would clearly have an edge over someone who has no related knowledge or experience.

Applying old solutions to new problems makes problem solving difficult. Despite the advantage of experience, overgeneralization or trying to apply old solutions to new problems can increase the difficulty when the old solution doesn't apply. Many of us have found that sometimes talking quietly with a student or a class about a problem can be very effective, at least for resolving some kinds of problems. But that solution didn't seem to work when Pat Taylor applied it following the disrupted library period.

Inability to give up or escape the goal makes problem solving difficult. Finally, inability to give up the goal or to escape from it makes a problem difficult. Suppose it is absolutely essential to Arthur Daniels for the girl to feel successful. Then, Daniels can accept nothing less!

Figure 1-2 summarizes the four personal impediments that limit the goal-directed behavior of a problem solver.

What are some of the factors within a problem's *environment* that make it difficult? There are at least five.

The availability of multiple plausible solutions makes problem solving difficult. To begin with, some problems appear to have several potentially effective solutions, thus making selec-

PROBLEM SOLVING IS ESPECIALLY DIFFICULT
WHEN PERSONAL IMPEDIMENTS EXIST.

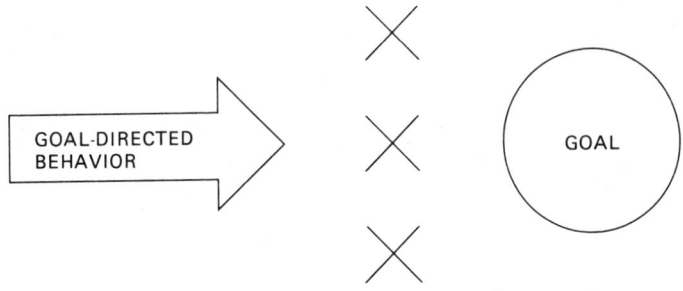

The motivated person may:

1. lack sufficient mental, physical, and social abilities
2. lack related knowledge and experience
3. try to apply old solutions to new problems
4. not be able to give up or escape the goal

FIGURE 1-2. A summary of personal impediments that can make problem solving difficult.

tion among them difficult. In vignette one, Pat Taylor probably is considering many options for dealing with the pupil who said, "Shut up!" Unfortunately, more than one appear plausible. Of course, one is a preferred solution but Pat does not know for certain which it is. The odds appear too even. Thus, any problem seems difficult when its solutions appear to be numerous, varied, and of equal value.

Absence of immediate feedback regarding the effectiveness of a solution makes problem solving difficult. A problem is also difficult when the person involved feels he or she will not know if the solution reached is effective or ineffective. In some cases it is easy to see if a problem has been solved. In other cases, feedback is not readily available. Consider the two vignettes again. In the first, no matter what solution Pat chooses, the results will be clear rather immediately. The confrontation will be resolved or it will not. Arthur Daniels' situation is different. Whatever is done will not provide Arthur with immediate feedback or knowledge of results. Suppose Arthur passes the pupil with a low grade. It may be some time before it is clear what the consequences of that decision are. In addition, the consequences could be untoward. Suppose the pupil, finding the other pupils angry, blames the teacher for the situation and rejects school learning entirely?

Problem novelty makes problem solving difficult. In addition, a problem is difficult when we must approach it in an entirely novel or different way. Because Arthur believes the pupil's motivation to be fragile or delicate, a straightforward solution seems nonexistent, making the case vexatious. Clearly this kind of problem requires creative thinking.

The presence of several competing goals makes problem solving difficult. Having more than one goal also increases problem difficulty. Suppose Pat Taylor wants both to control the situation *and* to be liked by the confronting child. It is extremely difficult to find a solution that will achieve both goals.

The presence of pressure makes problem solving difficult. Finally, problems are difficult when pressure is present. Most people respond well to pressure but each of us has a limit. If Pat Taylor has to deal with the confrontation in less than five minutes because the principal is coming in to do a classroom observation, the pressure and anxiety of trying to resolve the problem probably are heightened greatly. Altogether, five environmental impediments to problem solving have been added to the four personal impediments. Figure 1-3 shows the environmental factors that can impede classroom problem solving.

When we consider a problem to be difficult or serious, it is very likely that more than one personal and/or environmental impediment are at work. These are the most complex and vexatious kinds of problems. Unfortunately, these are the kinds of problems teachers frequently face. That is why teaching is tough.

PROBLEM SOLVING IS ESPECIALLY DIFFICULT WHEN ENVIRONMENTAL IMPEDIMENTS EXIST.

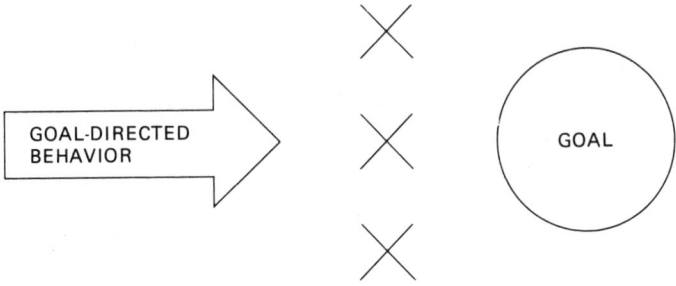

Obstacles include:

1. multiple plausible solutions
2. absence of immediate feedback regarding effectiveness of the solution
3. problem novelty
4. presence of several competing goals
5. pressure

FIGURE 1-3. A summary of environmental factors that can make problem solving difficult.

WHAT ARE TEACHER PROBLEMS?

A teaching or teacher problem is simply an example of goal-response interference that occurs during the course of a school day.

In order to understand teacher problems, it is essential to know teacher goals. Teacher goals come from two sources.

First, teachers have the same goals as other humans. Psychologists call these *general human needs* and subdivide them into two categories, *physiological* needs and *socio-psychological* needs. For example, in terms of physiological needs the organism requires food, water, and rest. The physiological needs of people can be compared loosely to the maintenance needs of a car for gas, oil and water, and no excessive abuse. The other component of general human needs, the socio-psychological category, is not inborn but learned. These needs are acquired via the process of specialization. Since socialization or child-rearing practices differ among cultures and subcultures, a particular American child (and later an American teacher) is socialized in a somewhat different way from other particular individuals. Consequently, the learned needs—achievement, social approval, status, and so forth—exhibit themselves in different forms and in different amounts in different individuals.

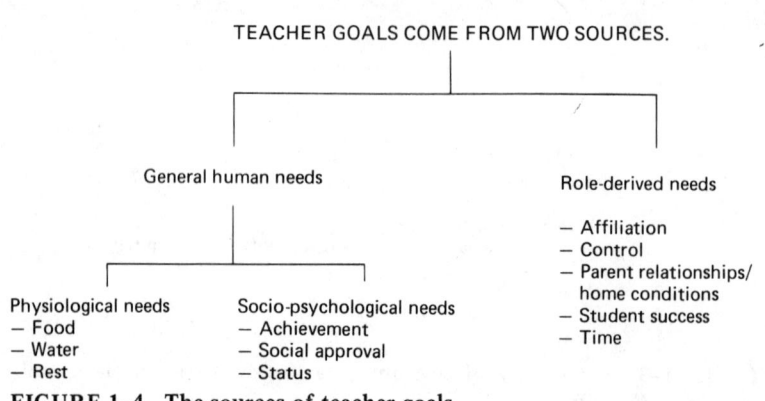

FIGURE 1-4. The sources of teacher goals.

The second source of goals arises when the individual takes on the role of teacher and assumes what has been referred to variously as *role-derived,* institutional, or nomothetical needs. Here the person-as-teacher is expected and usually expects to behave in institutionally sanctioned ways. That is, assuming the role of teacher makes one behave toward students in ways demanded by the community or the teaching profession. For example, since some communities will not tolerate one child's physically abusing another, the teacher, acting on this normative standard, must stop and prevent fighting. Furthermore, since communities believe in property rights, the teacher must try to guarantee the property rights of children and of the school and therefore control vandalism and theft. In like manner, the profession expects the teachers to individualize and personalize instruction and they feel obliged to try to do so.

In summary, teacher problems result as teachers try to meet both (1) their own human needs which are physiological or socio-psychological in nature and (2) role-derived needs that the job of teaching demands.

It seems that most classroom problems result when persons assume the teacher role and have to achieve goals that are completely new or for which they are unprepared, such as controlling and motivating. Even the person who had a propensity for controlling and motivating before becoming a teacher may find these needs greatly exacerbated and therefore more difficult to attain. What of the poor person who lands in teaching with no leanings toward controlling and motivating?

WHAT TEACHER GOALS SEEM MOST INTERFERED WITH?

Teacher goals that are most interfered with have been reported in several studies (see Related Readings at the end of the chapter). Five such goals consistently appear from study to study and therefore can be considered stable. They are *affiliation, control, parent relationships, student success,* and *time.*

Affiliation is the need on the part of a teacher to establish and maintain good relationships with others in the school, both staff and pupils. Teachers want cooperation and support from other teachers and administrators. Such support makes them feel professionally satisfied. Teachers want to have confidence in and respect for their colleagues. They also want to have good feelings about their pupils. They want to like them and to be liked and treated with respect in return.

Inability to achieve affiliation makes teachers feel lonely, ineffective, unappreciated, alienated, or even rejected. Affiliation might also be equated with social and professional acceptance or interpersonal relationships. As you will see when you read Chapter 10, teachers who do not achieve affiliation are dissatisfied with teaching.

Part of Pat Taylor's problem over the boys' behavior in the library resulted because of Pat's need for affiliation—the need to establish and maintain a good relationship with the librarian.

Following is another example of an affiliation problem, this one reported by a printing/geology teacher from Central High.

> I had a clash with my department chairman today. He is very interested in the philosophical aspects of the department and school while I believe that I am more practically oriented. In a department meeting today he was proposing all sorts of new classes for the department to be added to the present list and I kept bringing up what I thought would be the administration's response to an enormous expansion of the department for next year. He finally became quite irritated with me. I don't think it is worth the time to dream up all those new classes when the administration is planning or seems to be planning on cutting the department back. I was upset by the friction between us.

If in Chapter 2 you find out that you have affiliation problems, you will want to read Chapter 5 and the section on affiliation in Chapter 10.

Control is the need to have pupils behave appropriately. Among other things teachers want pupils to be relatively quiet, orderly, and courteous. They also expect them to display honesty and to show respect for others and for property. In general, teachers want these things because they believe they will result in more enjoyable and productive school experiences for the pupils and for themselves. When pupils don't behave in appropriate ways, teachers are faced with decisions about control. Some teachers become frustrated. As a consequence they may become hostile to the extent that they claim their pupils have learning problems when in fact they do not, or they may seek to have certain pupils removed from the class.

To some extent all humans wish to influence or control others. However, the kinds of persons entering teaching are not strongly control oriented. Rather they are attracted to teaching as a social service activity. This is an example of a goal which likely is intensified by becoming a teacher.

Pat Taylor's confrontation by the pupil who says "Shut up" is partly a problem because Pat wanted to control the class.

A music teacher at Grimm Junior High School reported the following control problem.

> I recently acquired a new seventh grade class and there is one student who is intent on disrupting the rest of the class. This particular student obviously has no interest in school. Today he was tardy for class (fourth day in a row), refused to do his work, popped gum during class, constantly disrupted me every time I tried to say something, kicked other students in the back, and when told to remain after class told me I couldn't keep him in and walked out of the room. I would like to reach every student in some way but I will not force learning; but I think students' rights end when they keep other students from learning and I feel this is the case with this particular student. I reported him to the office. I really don't feel able to get through to him.

If in Chapter 2 you find out that you have control problems, then you'll want to read Chapter 6 and the appropriate pages in Chapter 10.

Good *parent relationships and home conditions* are also goals sought by teachers. Teachers want to relate and work well with adults outside of school who are important in the lives of students. They are especially concerned about having good relationships with parents and knowing and understanding the conditions which exist within students' homes and communities. Teachers would like to be able to support the values of parents and communities and to be supported in return. Sometimes differences in values make it hard to create and maintain mutual support. Sometimes lack of mutual support and understanding results from poor or limited communication.

Although teachers know they have little influence over home and community values and conditions, they would like them to be such that they would enhance students' intellectual, emotional, and social development. Values and conditions that seem to teachers to hamper or adversely affect what they consider appropriate student development are a special source of concern for teachers.

Establishing a good relationship with a parent seems to be a problem for one American history teacher who reported the following problem.

> When report cards went out I wrote notes to several parents to try to improve understanding between parent and teacher and to try to help public relations in general. One parent answered with a very sarcastic note. Her son had been given a note stating that he had not made up any of his work that he missed during an illness. He'd been told what he missed and reminded several times. The mother seemed to think she should have been given an itemized list of this work. This is impossible to do with 153 students.

If in Chapter 2 you find out that you have problems of this sort, you'll want to read Chapter 7 and related pages in Chapter 10.

Student success matters a great deal to teachers. That is why most of them teach. They want to possess the knowledge, skills, and attitudes that will help their pupils to personal success—both academic and social. Because they care in this way, they nurture, tutor, counsel, motivate, and cajole pupils. Anything so that they do well! They may even be guilty of marking pupils too high and lowering academic standards. The institution of "social promotion" can probably be attributed to the desire on the part of school personnel to see students succeed. However, sometimes concern for student success manifests itself in negative ways. With the same goal in mind, some teachers may demand punctuality and attentiveness and become grumpy and mean when pupils do not meet these expectations.

You may remember that Arthur Daniels was concerned about student academic success. The English teacher from Central High who reported the following problem also was concerned about helping a student to be successful, in this case socially.

> I got a call from a mother whose daughter has been in several of my classes. It seems the daughter is having a very difficult time making friends here and is reacting by withdrawing more and more from her parents, which is quite unusual, as I understand. The mother was asking me to help them with the girl because they were quite concerned. I know the girl pretty well and she is really a great person but quite shy. Part of her problem is the fact that both her father and mother are quite talented people in the arts and the girl has been accepted by classmates in previous schools because of *who her parents were.* I'm trying to get her involved with other students but *without* coming on like a train wreck. How do you ask kids to befriend someone they haven't befriended in a *normal* situation? The academic is only a small part of the educational process and very few teachers either know this or can handle it.

If in Chaper 2 you find that you have student success problems, then you'll want to read Chapter 8 and appropriate pages in Chapter 10.

Wise use of *time* is the fifth goal or teacher concern. Time represents a constraint for teachers; it formulates boundaries that can be either binding or freeing. Teachers have either too much time or too little. They would like more time to plan, more time to work with students in instructional settings, more time to evaluate students' progress, and more time for themselves. On the other hand, teachers want less time when its use means coping with interruptions, attending unproductive faculty meetings, fulfilling extra duties unrelated to instruction, or having to deal with changes in the regular school routine. Teachers want to be effective managers of their personal and professional lives, but lack of time often seems to interfere.

Time was a problem for the business education teacher whose description of her day follows:

> The day was filled with interruptions. Morning classes were shortened because of the homeroom meetings. The guidance counselors called kids out of the already shortened periods to register for next year—kids were coming and going in my classes all day. Then the intercom broke in three or four times during the day to announce things that didn't pertain to my classes. Afternoon classes were supposed to be shortened so we could have an assembly—a vocal group who didn't show up. After I changed my lesson plans for the afternoon and had gotten halfway through the first class doing something different than I had originally planned, it was announced that classes would run full length after all. With so many ill-timed interruptions, I didn't have enough time to accomplish anything and I was completely exhausted by the end of the day.

If in Chapter 2 you find out that time is a problem for you, then you'll want to read Chapter 9 and the related pages in Chapter 10.

The nature of the five areas of teacher concern described above will not surprise practicing teachers. Every teacher who has lived has, from time to time, experienced difficulty with one or more of them. Very few teachers report they have no problems and when that occurs, we wonder. What should surprise America's teachers is that the five areas of concern heretofore have not been well circumscribed and studied with an eye toward their reduction or elimination. What should baffle teachers is, Why schools and school districts do not attend to any or all of these areas of concern in meaningful ways as part of staff development programs? What should bother teachers is that, in general, university professors engaged in teacher preparation have not yet accumulated and organized the knowledge that exists so that teachers have not been given help either during preservice or in-service education that would enhance their skills in solving classroom problems. What should mystify teachers is, Why state teacher certification requirements seldom, if ever, require attention be given to educating teachers as problem solvers?

Educational programs for children have the ultimate goal of helping them to solve problems. Educational programs for teachers are remiss in that they do not seem to have a similar high level outcome. The aims of teacher preparation must be adjusted to include producing better teacher problem solvers and better teacher thinkers. An aim of teacher education, both preservice and in-service, must be to help teachers respond more intelligently to life in classrooms.

SUMMARY

A problem occurs when a person wants something and cannot have it. In psychological terms a problem is an example of a goal-response interference. Whether a problem is difficult depends upon many conditions within us and within the environment that facilitate or impede achievement of our goal.

A teaching problem occurs when a teacher wants to accomplish a classroom goal and cannot. Teachers want the same things generally as all humans. In addition, because of the nature of their role, they have other needs—for example, to teach socially desirable behavior.

Problems somewhat peculiar to teachers can be grouped into five categories: *affiliation, control, parent relationships, student success,* and *time.*

Teacher problems need to be identified and studied because teachers should be helped to reach their goals.

In Chapter 2 you will have an opportunity to identify your own teaching problems.

DISCUSSION QUESTIONS

1. What is a problem?
2. What are the three components of a problem?
3. What makes a problem difficult and difficult to solve?
   What makes the same problem more difficult for one person than for another?
   Do you think there are "good problem solvers"?
   Why or why not?
4. What do you believe might help you to gain the mental, physical, or social abilities which would make you less problem-prone and a better problem solver?
5. What is a teaching or teacher problem?
6. What are the sources of teacher problems?
7. Do you think the problems of teachers really differ from the problems of people generally?
   What are some problems you think persons have, or have to an increased degree, after they assume the role of teacher?
8. Which of the five kinds of problems do you perceive to be most difficult for you?
9. Why is it important to identify teacher problems?
   Which of the reasons given appeals to you most?
10. What happens when a problem is too difficult for you?
    Give some examples from your experience.

RELATED ACTIVITIES*

Problem 1

Try to solve the problem below. As you do, consider what personal and environmental factors may be making the solution difficult.

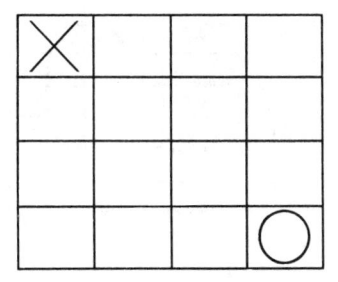

FIGURE 1-5.

Figure 1-5 is a diagram of a state prison showing each cell. It happened that Mr. Punch, the prisoner in the cell marked X, went berserk. He broke into the cell next to his and murdered that inmate. He then broke into every other cell and killed each inmate, leaving the body on the floor. Mr. Punch never went back into a cell containing a body and he never went through a cell without disposing of the inmate. Neither did he break through an outside wall or corner. By the time the guards arrived, he had just killed the last inmate in the cell marked 0. Show on the diagram a path he might have taken in order to do these things.

Factors that may make the problem difficult include:
  a. Your abilities.
  b. Lack of practice in solving similar problems.
  c. Failure of a solution to a similar problem to solve this one.
  d. Inability to give up trying to find a solution.
  e. Competition with others and awareness that some of them may be succeeding.

---

*The prisoner problem and the Changing Work Procedure Problem have been used by Maier and his associates (1970), who have done extensive work on problem solving.

Solution:

Mr. Punch began by entering an adjacent cell, killing the inmate and then returning to his own cell before proceeding to the other adjacent cell and then onward. See Figure 1-6.

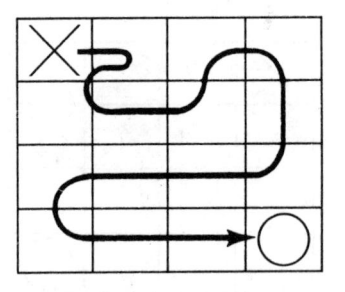

FIGURE 1-6.

Problem 2

Here is another problem. Like its predecessor, it will challenge your ability. As you try to resolve it consider what personal and environmental factors make the problem difficult. And consider how this problem differs from the first one.

Following are descriptions of the roles of four persons who work in a factory: a foreman and three assemblers. Resolve the conflict among them.

Role for Gus Thompson, Foreman:

You are the foreman in a shop and supervise the work of about 20 men. Most of the jobs are piece rate jobs and some of the men work in teams and are paid on a team piece rate basis. In one of the teams, Jack, Walt, and Steve work together. Each one of them does one of the operations for an hour and then they exchange, so that all men perform each of the operations at different times. The men themselves decided to operate that way and you have never given the plan any thought.

Lately, Jim Clark, the methods man, has been around and studied conditions in your shop. He timed Jack, Walt, and Steve on each of the operations and came up with the following facts.

	Position 1	Position 2	Position 3	Total
Jack	3 min.	4 min.	4½ min.	11½ min.
Walt	3½ min.	3½ min.	3 min.	10 min.
Steve	5 min.	3½ min.	4½ min.	13 min.
				34½ min.

He observed that with the men rotating, the average time for all three operations would be one-third of the total time or 11½ minutes per complete unit. If, however, Jack worked in the number 1 spot, Steve in the number 2 spot, and Walt in the number 3 spot, the time would amount to a daily saving of more than 80 minutes. In other words the lost production is about the same as that which would occur if the men loafed for 80 minutes in an 8-hour day. If the time were used for productive effort, production would be increased more than 20 percent.

This made pretty good sense to you so you decided to take up the problem with the men. You feel they should go along with any change in operation that is made.

Role for Jack:

You are one of three men on an assembly operation. Walt and Steve are your teammates and you enjoy working with them. You get paid on a team basis and you are making wages that are entirely satisfactory. Steve isn't quite as fast as Walt and you, but when you feel he is holding things up too much each of you can help out.

The work is very monotonous. The saving thing about it is that every hour you all change positions. In this way you get to do all three operations. You are best on the number 1 position, so when you get in that spot you turn out some extra work and so make the job easier for Steve, who follows you in that position.

You have been on this job for two years and have never run out of work. Apparently your group can make pretty good pay without running yourselves out of a job. Lately, however, the company has had some of its experts hanging around. It looks like the company is trying to work out some speed-up methods. If they make these jobs any simpler, you won't be able to stand the monotony. Gus Thompson, your foreman, is a decent guy and has never criticized your team's work.

26   PROBLEMS AND PROBLEM SOLVING

Role for Walt:

You work with Jack and Steve on a job that requires three separate operations. Each of you works on each of the three operations by rotating positions once every hour. This makes the work more interesting and you can always help out the other fellow by running a job ahead in case one of you doesn't feel so good. It's all right to help out because you get paid on a team piece rate basis. You could actually earn more if Steve were a faster worker, but he is a swell guy and you would rather have him in the group than someone else who might do a little bit more.

You find all three positions about equally desirable. They are all simple and purely routine. The monotony doesn't bother you much because you can talk, daydream, and change your pace. By working slow for a while and then fast you can sort of set your pace to music you hum to yourself. Jack and Steve like the idea of changing jobs and even though Steve is slow on some positions, the changing around has its good points. You feel you get to a stopping place every time you change positions and this kind of takes the place of a rest pause.

Lately some kind of efficiency expert has been hanging around. He stands some distance away with a stopwatch in his hand. The company could get more for its money if it put some of these guys to work. You say to yourself, "I'd like to see one of these guys try and tell me how to do this job. I'd sure give him an earful."

If Gus Thompson, your foreman, doesn't get him out of the shop pretty soon, you're going to tell him what you think of his dragging in company spies.

Role for Steve:

You work with Jack and Walt on an assembly job and get paid on a team piece rate basis. The three of you work very well together and make pretty good wages. Jack and Walt like to make a little more than you think is necessary but you go along with them and work as hard as you can so as to keep the production up where they want it. They are good fellows—often help you out if you fall behind and so you feel it is only fair to try and go along with the pace they set.

The three of you exchange positions every hour. In this way, you get to work all positions. You like the number 2 position best because it is easier. When you get in the number 3 position you can't keep up and then you feel Gus Thompson, the foreman, watching you. Sometimes Walt and

Jack slow down when you are on the number 3 spot and then the foreman seems satisfied.

Lately the methods man has been hanging around watching the job. You wonder what he is up to. Can't they leave guys alone who are doing all right?

Factors that may make the problem difficult include:
  a. Your abilities.
  b. Your lack of practice in solving similar problems.
  c. Failure of a solution to a similar problem to solve this one.
  d. Inability to give up trying to find a solution.
  e. Inability to discriminate among possible alternative solutions.
  f. Absence of immediate feedback regarding the correctness of the solutions.
  g. Competition with others to find the best solution.

Problem 2 differs from Problem 1 mainly because there is no definitely correct answer.

Solution:

Old—Retain the present worker rotation, perhaps with minor variations.

New—Have each worker work continuously on his best position with minor variations such as rest pauses or use of music to reduce boredom.

Integrative—Have Jack and Walt rotate but have Steve work only in his best position, *or* have all three men rotate between their two best positions, *or* have all three men rotate among all three positions but spend more time at their best one. . . . *or*,

Integrative solutions combine or resolve aspects of old and new solutions.

Problem 3
Figure 1-7 is a diagram showing the components of a problem.

a. Consider Problem 2 above when answering the questions.
  (1) What is the goal of Gus Thompson, the foreman?
  (2) What are three obstacles impeding goal achievement?

FIGURE 1-7.

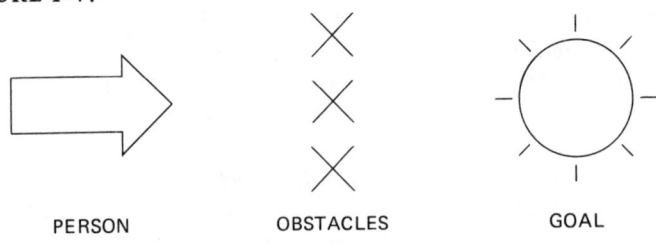

PERSON → OBSTACLES (XXX) GOAL (○)

b. Consider Pat Taylor's problem with the children being noisy in the library.
(1) What is Pat's goal?
(2) What is an obstacle to achieving it?

Answers:

a. (1) To increase production.
(2) The workers' desire to avoid monotony.
Their fear of rate cuts.
Hostility toward the time-study man.
b. (1) To maintain good relationships with other teachers including the librarian.
(2) Children's unruly library behavior.

Problem 4
Describe in writing a difficult problem you had or are having as a teacher. Next describe why it is or was difficult.

RELATED READINGS

Cruickshank, Donald R., and Frank W. Broadbent. *The Simulation and Analysis of Problems of Beginning Teachers.* U.S. Department of Health, Education and Welfare, Office of Education Cooperative Research Project No. 5-0789, Washington, D.C.: Government Printing Office, 1968. ED 024 637.

Cruickshank, Donald R., John J. Kennedy, James Leonard, and Robert Thurman. *Perceived Problems of Teachers in Schools Serving Rural Disadvantaged Populations: A Comparison with Problems Reported by Inner-City Teachers.* The NDEA National Institute for Advanced Study in Teaching Disadvantaged Youth, Occasional Paper/Five. Washington, D.C.: The American Association of Colleges for Teacher Education, 1968. ED 127 986.

Cruickshank, Donald R., John J. Kennedy, and Betty Myers. "Perceived Problems of Secondary School Teachers." *Journal of Educational Research,* 68, 4 (December, 1974), 154-59.

Cruickshank, Donald R., John J. Kennedy, and Betty Myers. "Perceived Problems of Elementary School Teachers" (in process).

Cruickshank, Donald R., and James Leonard. *The Identification and Analysis of Perceived Problems of Teachers in Inner-City Schools.* The NDEA National Institute for Advanced Study in Teaching Disadvantaged Youth, Occasional Paper/One. Washington, D.C.: The American Association of Colleges for Teacher Education, 1967. ED 026 335.

Maier, Norman, R.F. *Problem Solving and Creativity.* Belmont, Calif.: Wadsworth, 1970.

Myers, Betty, Donald R. Cruickshank, and John J. Kennedy. *Problems of Teachers Graduated from The Ohio State University as Teacher Education Curriculum Indicators.* Columbus, Ohio: College of Education, The Ohio State University, 1975.

Myers, Betty, Donald R. Cruickshank, and Victor Rentel. *Perceived Problems of Teachers of Reading: Fact and Paradox.* Washington, D.C.: ERIC Clearinghouse, August 1979.

chapter 2

what are your teaching problems?

DONALD R. CRUICKSHANK

Chapter 2 Outcomes: *As a result of reading Chapter 2 you will be able to identify the problem areas of greatest concern to you.*

In Chapter 1 we found out what a problem is, what makes a problem difficult to solve, and what are the problem areas reported consistently by teachers. In this chapter we turn to you. The purpose is to have you identify your teaching problems and to start you on the road toward their resolution.

We have learned that teacher problems or concerns can be grouped into five areas:

1. Affiliation. The need to establish and maintain good relationships with others in the school, both staff and pupils.
2. Control. The need to have pupils behave appropriately.
3. Parent relationships and home conditions. The need to relate and

work well with adults outside the school who are important in the lives of children and the need to understand home conditions.
4. Student success. The need to have pupils be successful academically and socially.
5. Time. The need to be effective managers of our professional and personal lives.

As a teacher, most likely you have concerns in one or more of these areas.

The first activity in problem solving is problem identification. Once you have identified your own teaching problems you will have gained valuable insight into your life as a teacher. Furthermore you will be in a position to do something about them either through self-help provided in this book, through preservice, in-service, or graduate education, or through personal counseling.

The Teacher Problems Checklist which follows contains 60 problems consistently reported by teachers in several research studies listed in the Related Readings at the back of Chapter 1. The development of the instrument is described in Supplement 2 in Part Four of this book. Turn to the Checklist, read the introduction and directions, respond to the 60 items by recording your answers in the Self-Scoring Answer Sheet, and then follow the directions for scoring. The result will be the identification of your personal teaching problems.

TEACHER PROBLEMS CHECKLIST (TPC)

Introduction

A problem arises when we have a goal and cannot achieve it. Everyone has problems, teachers included. Some problems are personal and similar to the problems all human share. Other problems result from the nature of the special work of teachers. It is important for teachers, school districts, teacher organizations, and teacher educators to know what teachers' problems are so that conscious, planned efforts can be made to consider and perhaps to reduce or eliminate them.

The problems on this check list have been reported by both elementary and secondary teachers. Therefore, they likely reflect problems you encounter.

Directions

Read each statement (mentally preface it with the words "I have a problem . . ."). Respond to the statement in one of the five following ways.

$\boxed{1}$ = If it is *not* a problem for you.

$\boxed{2}$ = If it is a *minor* problem for you.

$\boxed{3}$ = If it is a *moderate* problem for you.

$\boxed{4}$ = If it is a *difficult* problem for you.

$\boxed{5}$ = If it is a *serious* problem for you.

Thus if the problem is a *serious* one for you, mark an X over the boxed numeral 5 opposite the problem number on the Answer Sheet found on page 336. If it is a *minor* problem, mark an X over the boxed numeral 2.

The following shows the response of a teacher to a statement perceived to be a *difficult* problem.

"I HAVE A PROBLEM . . ."

Creating interest in the topic being taught $\boxed{1}$ $\boxed{2}$ $\boxed{3}$ $\boxed{\cancel{4}}$ $\boxed{5}$

Now locate and remove the answer sheet on page 336 and respond, in the way illustrated above, to each of the 60 problem statements in the Teacher Problems Checklist. Remember the higher the numeral you mark, the more difficult is the problem.

TEACHER PROBLEMS CHECKLIST (TPC)

"I have a problem..."

1. Liking my students.
2. Getting students to participate in class.
3. Maintaining order, quiet, or control.
4. Improving life for my students by correcting conditions both inside and outside school.
5. Having enough free time.
6. Getting my students to feel successful in school.
7. Getting students to behave appropriately.
8. Gaining professional knowledge, skills, and attitudes and using them effectively.
9. Controlling and using my professional time in the most functional, efficient way.
10. Understanding and helping the atypical or special child.
11. Getting cooperation and support from the administration.
12. Helping students who have personal problems.
13. Keeping my students away from things and people which may be a bad influence.
14. Planning instruction in different ways and for different purposes.
15. Responding appropriately to improper behavior such as obscenities.
16. Developing and maintaining student rapport, affection, and respect.
17. Assessing my students' learning.
18. Soliciting appropriate student behavior.
19. Improving conditions so that students can study better at home.
20. Having enough preparation time.

21. Extending learning beyond the classroom.
22. Controlling aggressive student behavior.
23. Getting my students to achieve competence in basic skills such as expressing themselves effectively in both writing and speaking.
24. Completing the work I have planned.
25. Promoting student self-evaluation.
26. Getting the understanding and sustenance of teachers and administrators so that I feel efficient and professional.
27. Helping students adjust socially or emotionally.
28. Establishing good relationships with parents and understanding home conditions.
29. Getting my students to value school marks and grades.
30. Enforcing considerate treatment of property.
31. Establishing and maintaining rapport with students and staff.
32. Helping students improve academically.
33. Enforcing social mores and folkways such as honesty and respect for teachers.
34. Encouraging parental interest in school matters.
35. Having enough time to teach and also to diagnose and evaluate learning.
36. Providing for individual learning differences.
37. Getting students to use their leisure time well.
38. Getting students to enjoy learning for its own sake.
39. Avoiding duties inappropriate to my professional role.
40. Getting every student to work up to his or her ability.
41. Being professional in my relationships with staff.
42. Creating interest in the topic being taught.
43. Holding worthwhile conferences with parents.
44. Having students present and on time for all classes, rehearsals, games, etc.

45. Maintaining student attention.
46. Establishing and maintaining rapport with administrators and supervisors.
47. Learning to use alternative methods of instruction.
48. Eliminating inappropriate student behavior.
49. Understanding the conditions of the homes and community in which my students live.
50. Using time wisely to get both professional and personal things accomplished.
51. Guiding my students to do the things which will help them succeed in school.
52. Removing students who are sources of frustration.
53. Knowing how to differentiate between student learning and psychological problems.
54. Teaching too many students or large classes.
55. Vitalizing my students' interest in learning and improving their achievement.
56. Developing confidence in my colleagues.
57. Overcoming a student's feelings of upset or frustration with himself.
58. Assisting parents having difficulty with their children.
59. Overcoming student apathy or outright dislike.
60. Teaching self-discipline.

DIRECTIONS FOR SCORING THE
TEACHER PROBLEMS CHECKLIST

Many previous studies of problems of teachers have indicated that teachers perceive both specific problems and areas or groups of problems. You have already identified your specific problems. Now in order to identify the areas of problems you need to follow the scoring procedure outlined below. First, consider what these problem areas are. Figure 2-1 gives their names, identifying symbols, and definitions.

PROBLEM AREA	PROBLEM AREA SYMBOLS	DEFINITIONS
Affiliation	☐	Establishing and maintaining rapport with others in the school, both staff and pupils.
Student success	○	Getting pupils to be successful academically and socially.
Control	◇	Getting pupils to behave appropriately.
Parent relationships and home conditions	△	Establishing good relationships with parents and understanding home conditions.
Time	⬡	Using time wisely to get both professional and personal things accomplished.

FIGURE 2-1.

Your responses to the specific items on the checklist, when added in the right combinations, will provide you with a personal score for each problem area.

1. The Self-Scoring Answer Sheet you have been using has fifteen rows. Row 1 across contains boxes for the answers to four questions: 1, 16, 31, and 46. Begin scoring by adding the numerals in the four boxes you have marked across the first row, but *don't* add any 1's. Write that total in the square at the far right of row 1 on the

40 PROBLEMS AND PROBLEM SOLVING

Answer Sheet. In the same way add your answers across the second row and write the total in the circle at the far right of that row. Continue to add the answers across each row, always placing the total in the symbol at the end of that row.

2. Now the numbers you have recorded in each of the symbols on the right-hand column of the Answer Sheet must be transferred to the boxes in the Answer Sorter, Figure 2-2.

Answer Sorter

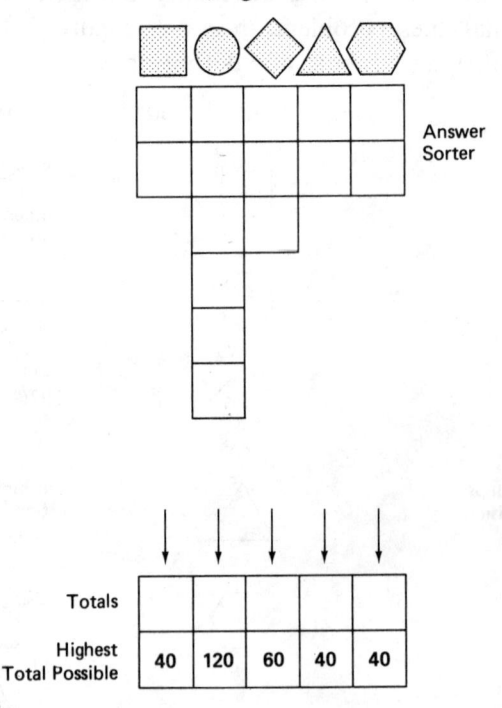

Totals					
Highest Total Possible	40	120	60	40	40

FIGURE 2-2.

Begin by taking the number you wrote in the square at the far right of the first row of the Answer Sheet and placing it in the first box under the square in the Answer Sorter.

Continue taking the numbers you wrote in the symbols on the Answer Sheet and transferring them one by one to an empty box in the corresponding column of the Answer Sorter. Since there are fifteen symbols with numbers in them, all of the boxes in the Answer Sorter will be filled with a number.

3. Finally to get a total score for each of the five areas, add the numbers downward in each column of the Answer Sorter and place that total in the corresponding Totals box below it. When you finish adding the numbers downward in each of the five columns, there will be a number for each Totals box.

4. To find out how much of a concern each problem area is, divide each number you placed in the Totals boxes by the number in the box below it (the numbers in the Highest Total Possible row). Multiply that answer by 100. Place that number in the appropriately shaped box of Your Score, Figure 2-3. The closer each score is to 100, the greater that is an area of concern for you.

Your score for each problem area

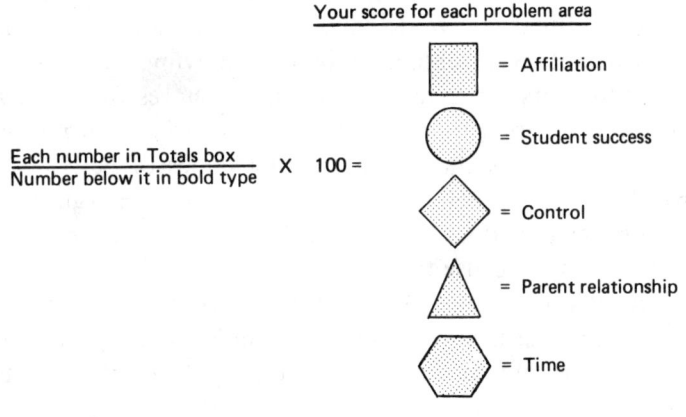

$$\frac{\text{Each number in Totals box}}{\text{Number below it in bold type}} \times 100 =$$

☐ = Affiliation
◯ = Student success
◇ = Control
△ = Parent relationship
⬡ = Time

FIGURE 2-3.

5. Finally, rank order your areas of concern.
   1.
   2.
   3.
   4.
   5.

The teaching problems you have just identified exist and are difficult for several reasons. Some were presented in Chapter 1; these were related to personal and environmental impediments. Two more are notable and interrelated. First, to a large extent you are not completely prepared for your work. Those enrolled in a typical undergraduate professional education program take surprisingly few education courses. For secondary education majors, about one-sixth of the work is in professional education. Elementary majors take a whopping one-fourth of their studies in education. This simply is not enough time to devote to preparing for the demanding business of teaching.

In addition, much of what you are studying or studied has little bearing on the problems of practice; that is, it fails to prepare you for life in classrooms. It is not the case that you didn't learn anything, but rather that you may not have learned some things that are critical to survival. Furthermore, your instructors likely admonished you to do certain things ("individual instruction") without ever telling, or better, showing, you how. As teacher educators we have been singularly successful in providing future teachers with directions regarding what to do but not how to do it. This induces personal feelings of guilt and an approach-avoidance behavior pattern. Teachers feel guilty because they cannot do what they have been admonished to do. They do not try because they are afraid of failure.

But let's not blame universities and professional educators entirely. Teaching is an enormously complex activity. It is both difficult to do and to teach about. For centuries it has defied efforts to quantify and reduce it to a science. Consequently, even our best information about teaching and learning is tenuous and tentative. There are no laws of teaching and learning. Rather teacher behavior is based mostly upon myths, folklore, and personal wisdom mixed artfully with small relatable insights adopted (sometimes erroneously) from the behavioral sciences, especially psychology.

So to begin with, if you have teaching problems, don't despair! Who doesn't? One book, one in-service program, or one graduate class cannot possibly transform us into a Mr. Chips, Mr. Tibbs, or Miss Dove, but any one or a combination of them carefully chosen can help us to move away from being an Ichabod Crane.

The purpose of this book is to overcome the general deficiencies of teacher education and the particular teaching deficiencies you have identified. In order to do this, two activities have precedence. First, using Chapters 3 and 4, you will learn and then practice the application of a problem-solving process. Then in Chapters 5 through 9 you will be provided knowledge related to your particular teaching problems. This knowledge has been carefully selected and organized so that its application to problems of practice is enhanced. Used artfully, the problem-solving process and the knowledge of the problem areas should assure you of greater teacher satisfaction.

DISCUSSION QUESTIONS

1. Which of the five areas of teacher problems are of greatest concern to you?
2. Which of the personal and/or environmental factors may make these problems difficult for you?
3. How could professional education, either preservice or in-service, do a better job of preparing you for life in classrooms?

chapter 3

how can teacher problems be lessened?

Chapter 3 Outcomes: *After reading Chapter 3 you should be able to:*
—*list the steps in the problem-solving process,*
—*elaborate on each step,*
—*describe and discriminate among "obstacles," "facilitating forces," and "lateral thinking," and*
—*apply the problem-solving process to a teaching problem.*

In Chapter 1 we found out what a problem is, what makes a problem difficult, and what teacher problems are. In Chapter 2 you responded to the Teacher Problems Checklist, identifying the individual problem areas most troublesome to you. In this chapter you will learn a problem-solving process that can be used to lessen teacher problems.

The steps in the problem-solving process can be understood most easily if we think about them in relationship to a common teaching problem such as the one revealed by the following vignette.

> You are the teacher of a sixth grade class in an inner-city school. You have assigned homework of the practice variety which is due today. When you look the assignments over, you note that Marsha's is missing.

Given this situation what could you do as a teacher using the problem-solving process?

PROBLEM IDENTIFICATION AND OWNERSHIP

Initially a set of three activities must be undertaken so that the problem can be identified and its ownership established.

First, you would state the problem. What is it?

The problem is that Marsha didn't turn in her assignment.

Second, you would identify the goal. Remember the definition of a problem: someone has a goal and cannot achieve it. What is the goal here?

The goal is to have everyone, including Marsha, do the assignment.

Third, you would identify the problem's owner. Who owns the problem? Again, remember the definition of a problem— someone who has a goal and cannot achieve it. In this case who has the goal thus who owns the problem?

> The goal belongs to me. *I* want all students to do the assignment. *I* own the problem.

VALUE CLARIFICATION

Once the problem has been identified and the goal and its ownership established, a second stage of activity occurs. This is the stage of value clarification. Herein you must decide the value of your goal. In other words, do you really care enough about the goal to continue to pursue it?

Many teachers have not had the time or opportunity to consciously establish their goals or beliefs let alone to value them. Consequently when asked why we are doing something, we sometimes are hard-pressed to come up with a reasonable answer. If this assumption is correct, then it might be said that as teachers we frequently do not know why we are doing what we are doing. Continuing with the problem-solving process . . .

Fourth, you would value the goal. After serious reflection, how valuable is it? Select one:

> The goal—getting everyone, including Marsha, to do the assignment—is of:
> a. unquestionable value. I could not under any circumstances give it up!
> b. great value to me. I intend to pursue it as best I can.
> c. value to me but I would be willing to negotiate.
> d. little value to me. I'm not really sure why I'm pursuing it.
> e. no value—really ridiculous. I've been a fool!

If you selected (a) or (b) then you have a pressing problem. That is, you have a goal that you care about a lot but that you are unable to achieve. Using the homework incident, you feel the assignment, or what it represents, is an important goal which must be reached. If you selected (c) you consider the problem to be only of relative importance. Although the goal is of some importance, you probably would negotiate it. In this case perhaps you would give Marsha additional time or let her perform an alternative task. Suppose you selected (d) or (e). In either case, upon reflection, you would decide not to pursue the goal any longer; thus this problem evaporates. Some of our goals as teachers are not well conceived and can, after reflection, be set aside easily. When the goal is set aside, the problem-solving process is over. However, consider that you value the goal very much and intend to pursue it. In that case, problem-solving goes on.

ANALYSIS OF THE PROBLEM SITUATION

During the first two stages of problem solving the problem has been identified, the goal and its ownership established, and the goal valued.

The third general stage in the problem-solving process requires that an analysis be made of the problem situation. This analysis is aimed primarily at answering the questions: What is causing goal-response interference? or What obstacles are standing in the way of achieving the goal?

Therefore, **fifth, you would identify the obstacles in the way of goal achievement.** In order to do this, you will need to know the problem situation and the persons in it more intimately.

Consider the homework assignment incident again. Several obstacles may be standing in the way of getting Marsha to complete the work. Looking into her situation reveals she has recently been caring for her sisters and brother while her mother cares for a sick aunt. This situation leaves her no time for homework. In addition, we learn that Marsha had another assignment and that between the two assignments and her home responsibilities she was frazzled. Thus, upon analysis of the problem situation we have identified two obstacles which seem to be preventing Marsha from completing her book report. Of course there may be others as well. Obviously, identifying obstacles standing in the way of the goal is only a first step.

Summarizing, so far the problem-solving process has required several activities to be undertaken.

1. The problem must be stated.
2. The goal must be identified.
3. Goal and problem ownership must be established.
4. The goal must be valued.
5. Obstacles to goal achievement must be identified.

It is possible to take Figure 1-1 in Chapter 1 and overlay most of the above activities on it. The result, Figure 3-1, is an activity sheet which can be used to guide the initial stages of problem solving.

Sixth, you would project ways by which the goal could be achieved. Once the obstacles standing in the way of goal achievement have been identified, they must be removed or overcome before the goal can be reached. This can be done in three ways.

The first and most obvious is to *remove the obstacles.* In Marsha's situation that could mean eliminating her role as a baby-sitter for her siblings and/or eliminating other homework assignments she has. Figure 3-2 presents this approach to goal achievement pictorially.

Suppose in Marsha's case that her role as baby-sitter cannot be eliminated and that her other homework assignments must also be done. In other words, the obstacles cannot be removed. When this is the case a second way to pursue the goal is possible. That way is to identify and make use of facilitating forces. A *facilitating force* is merely one that can be utilized to overcome an obstacle when the obstacle cannot be removed.

50 PROBLEMS AND PROBLEM SOLVING

FIGURE 3-1. An overview of early problem-solving activities.

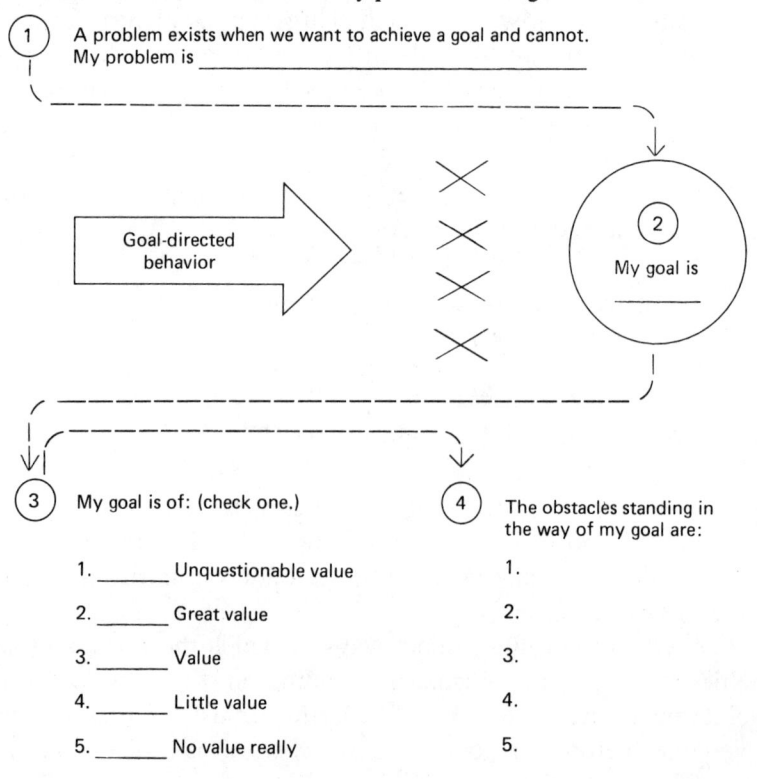

(1) A problem exists when we want to achieve a goal and cannot.
My problem is _____

Goal-directed behavior

(2) My goal is _____

(3) My goal is of: (check one.)

1. _____ Unquestionable value
2. _____ Great value
3. _____ Value
4. _____ Little value
5. _____ No value really

(4) The obstacles standing in the way of my goal are:

1.
2.
3.
4.
5.

Consider, for example, an automobile stuck in deep snow. The several persons in the auto do not have a snow shovel, so they cannot remove the snow obstacle. However, they do have the physical strength that, in combination with proper engine acceleration, can overcome the obstacle.

How might we overcome the obstacles in Marsha's case? This is more complex but still possible. For example, we could make the assignment or its completion so rewarding that Marsha will do it anyway. ("Every person has his price.") Couldn't we provide Marsha with something sufficiently personally rewarding so that she will succeed in her task? Contrarily, we could make failure to do the assignment so punishing

FIGURE 3-2. Removal of obstacles can result in goal achievement.

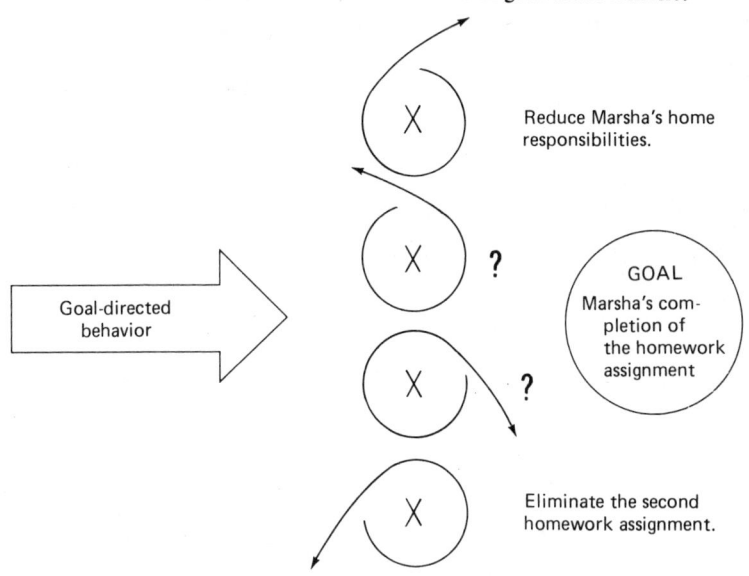

that Marsha will do it. Couldn't we let Marsha know that she will receive a failing grade for the marking period unless the work is completed? In either case we have not removed the obstacles to the goal; rather we have tried to overcome them by using facilitating forces, namely, reward and punishment.

The solutions normally projected when one is solving problems can be termed *vertical thinking solutions.* A vertical thinking solution is arrived at thoughtfully and logically. Thus, when Marsha fails to turn in her homework, we work toward a solution or solutions in sequential, justifiable steps. The carefulness of the process seems to justify the solution. "This must be a good solution because it has been arrived at so thoughtfully." In reality, the solution or solutions may be limited by the very "thoughtfulness" and "logic" used.

There is a third kind of thinking that can be employed. It is called *lateral thinking.* Lateral, as opposed to vertical thinking, proceeds by any means and in any order. It is difficult to

FIGURE 3-3. Overcoming obstacles with facilitating forces can result in goal achievement.

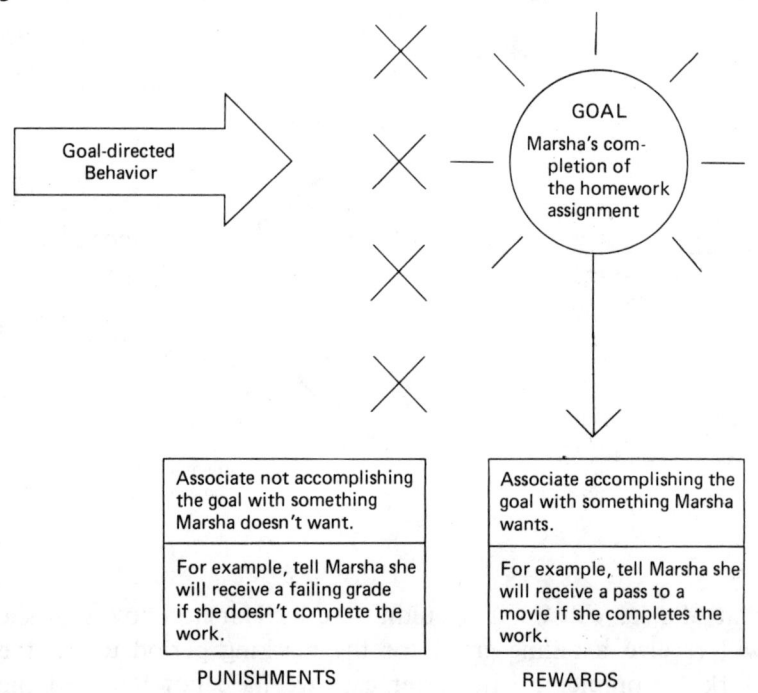

| Goal-directed Behavior → | | GOAL
Marsha's completion of the homework assignment |

PUNISHMENTS	REWARDS
Associate not accomplishing the goal with something Marsha doesn't want.	Associate accomplishing the goal with something Marsha wants.
For example, tell Marsha she will receive a failing grade if she doesn't complete the work.	For example, tell Marsha she will receive a pass to a movie if she completes the work.

define. It is imaginative, creative, and provocative. When one is engaged in it, negative judgment is suspended. All solutions are possibly correct. Lateral thinking solutions to Marsha's case include:

> Not permitting Marsha to do any homework (on the assumption that she will feel "left out" and "alienated" and thus want to do her assignments and become part of the group).
> Putting reminders in her desk, books, coat, and so forth.
> Baby-sitting or finding someone else to baby-sit for Marsha's siblings so she can complete her homework.
> Paying Marsha to do the homework.
> Helping Marsha with her other homework.

Solutions reached by lateral thinking are not necessarily better than those reached vertically. They are usually only different, because they are obtained more spontaneously and without immediate concern for their consequences. Each of them might also be obtained vertically—that is, thoughtfully—but that might take considerably more time.

As a result of this sixth step in the problem-solving process, a variety of solutions for eliminating or overcoming the obstacles to the goal have been projected and listed. Some have been related to reducing the obstacles standing in the way of achievement of the goal. Others have increased the facilitating forces in order to overcome the obstacles. Finally, a third set of lateral solutions was proposed. Obviously, not all of the proposed solutions can be employed, or at least they cannot all be employed at once.

Consequently, **seventh you would list all the projected solutions and the possible consequences of each**—consequences that the proposed solution could have for you or anyone else involved in the problem situation. Here, for illustration only, are a few proposed solutions and some possible consequences.

Proposed Solutions	*Possible Consequences*
1. I would give up the goal in relationship to Marsha.	1.1 Marsha might not learn something important.
	1.2 Marsha might learn that she doesn't have to meet the same standards as others.
	1.3 Other students might feel it is unfair.
	1.4 Other students might not turn in assignments either.
	1.5 I might feel compromised.
	1.6 Her mother might become angry. She wants her to do well in school.
2. I would call upon Marsha's mother to see if Marsha could	2.1 Her mother might not talk to me.

54 PROBLEMS AND PROBLEM SOLVING

    be relieved of any of her home duties.

3. I would offer a reward to Marsha for completing the assignment under unusual circumstances.

4. I would place cute reminders in Marsha's coat pocket, her books, desk, etc.

2.2 Her mother might be despondent or angry or embarrassed.

2.3 Marsha might be embarrassed, or she might be grateful.

3.1 Marsha might like the reward and complete the book report.

3.2 The reward might not be rewarding to Marsha.

3.3 The other students might find out and want a reward too.

3.4 Marsha might want a special reward to do everything.

3.5 Her mother might complain that Marsha is not doing her job at home.

4.1 Marsha might see I am trying to be patient and understanding and respond favorably.

4.2 Marsha might ignore me and the notes.

4.3 Marsha might say, "I'd like to do the report but I haven't any time."

4.4 Marsha's mother might find the notes and urge Marsha to comply.

CHOOSING

Now that a variety of proposed solutions and their possible consequences have been zeroed in on, some criteria must be used in order to select the "best" from among them. In short, we should know a "good" solution when we see one. This problem-solving approach accepts that *a good problem solution is one which gains the goal and has either positive or few negative side effects for others.*

In the eighth step in the problem-solving process you would rate each proposed solution. In order to make such ratings, each proposed solution must be given two scores. The first score is given for the likelihood that the solution would achieve the goal. In this case the goal is to have everyone including Marsha do the assignment. Give the solution a *3* if it would, a *2* if it's uncertain, or a *1* if it would not. The second score is given for the likelihood that the solution would have either positive or at least few negative side effects. Give the solution a *3* if it would likely have positive or few negative side effects, a *2* if it is uncertain, or a *1* if the solution probably will upset others. Again a higher score is more promising. Below are the few proposed solutions mentioned and their possible scores.

Proposed Solution	Goal Score	Side Effects Score	Combined Score
1. Give up the goal in relationship to Marsha.	1 +	1 =	2
2. Call upon Marsha's mother to see if Marsha could be relieved of her home duties.	2 +	2 =	4
3. Offer a reward to Marsha for completing the assignment under unusual circumstances.	2 +	2 =	4
4. Place reminders in Marsha's coat pocket, books, desk, etc.	2 +	3 =	5

You may or may not agree with these scores. Again, the solutions and their scoring are illustrative only. In actual practice when you use the problem-solving process, *you* provide and *you* score the solutions. As in the situation above, you will seldom find a solution which can be given a combined score of 6. Generally you'll have to be satisfied with 4's and 5's. Teaching is tough.

Use of Theory and Practice. The ability to propose solutions and to choose among them is affected by what you know. Teachers who know more should be able to propose more possible solutions and be able to judge their likely outcomes or consequences more accurately. If you knew a lot prior to reading this chapter, the problem of getting students to complete assignments was probably less of a problem for you and you found it easier to resolve. Knowledge about teaching comes from at least two sources. The first is practical experience as a teacher. The second is course work taken at a university. It is not possible to provide actual teaching practice in a book. It is possible, however, to provide knowledge about teaching. In this book the theory that is presented is the knowledge about the five problem areas identified in Chapter 1: affiliation, control, parent relationships and home conditions, student success, and time. You may have already located and read all the related theory found in Part Two of the book. If you did, you are more knowledgeable and your problem-solving ability has been enhanced. If you did not, it would be propitious to turn to it now, especially the theory related to the problem area(s) of greatest concern to you. By the way, in Marsha's case the relevant chapter in the book is Chapter 8, Student Success.

IMPLEMENTATION

Having chosen the best problem solution—the one which would presumably gain the goal and have either positive or at least few negative side effects—an implementation scheme must be developed.

Ninth, you would decide how to implement the best proposed solution and then do it. It is quite possible to have selected a promising solution yet to implement it in such a way that it fails. In Marsha's case the best solution (of those illustrated) seemed to be to place reminders to do the assignment among Marsha's possessions. Important questions have not been addressed, however. For example, what should be the content of the reminders? Where should they be placed? How? When? How many? Clearly it is not just what we do but *how* we do it that makes a difference! Thus, the implementation plan and schedule must be carefully formed. Below is an example of a plan.

> *The implementation plan* is to prepare the following personal notes and place them as follows:
> 1. "I am really looking forward to getting your assignment tomorrow." (To be taped on Marsha's desk before she arrives the next day.)
> 2. "How are you doing on the assignment? I'm sure you'll get it in tomorrow. Let me know how I can help." (To be placed in the sleeve of Marsha's coat the second day if necessary.)
> 3. "I haven't heard from you about the assignment so I guess you are getting it done all right." (To be attached to a paper to be returned to Marsha on the third day if necessary.)
> 4. "Please fill in the blank on the bottom of this so I'll know when I can expect your assignment. Thanks." (To be placed on Marsha's desk in an envelope marked "Confidential" on the fourth day if necessary.)
> 5. "I want to help you to think about getting that assignment finished. I've made arrangements for you to stay to talk about it when the class goes to gym today. See you then. I know we can get this done." (To be handed to Marsha prior to gym class on the fifth day if necessary.)

Again you may or may not agree completely with the implementation plan. It is illustrative only. In actual practice the plan will be your own. However, a few caveats are offered which often are useful when student success or control problems are being resolved.

First, *play your lower cards first.* Think of yourself as in a card game. If you can win the hand by playing a lower card, you would play it so as to save a higher card for later. Do the same thing in the classroom. Play your twos, threes, and fours whenever a little facilitating force or power will do. Hold the face cards and aces for something really big. In the implementation plan above, the problem solver used only lower cards or lower teacher power. Should the problem continue, higher power can be used. There are many more potential low cards that could have been played. You have probably thought of several.

A second caveat is to *use private power.* In this case, keep things between you and Marsha. Publicly announced hopes, requests for progress reports, and so forth can be seen by the rest of the class and Marsha as manifestations of a power struggle. Working on the problem publicly could create additional obstacles that could make the problem more difficult.

EVALUATION

The only way a problem can be solved is to either give up the goal, achieve an approximation of it, or achieve it fully. So . . .

Tenth, you would decide whether you are satisfied with your position in relation to goal attainment. If you are, then the problem is less of a problem or perhaps no problem at all.

Since teaching is so complex, it is entirely possible that your plan or the implementation of it was unsuccessful. When this occurs it's "back to the drawing boards." That this phrase is not from the field of education should give us all heart. Consider the setback momentary and a challenge. Return to "Go" and rethink each of the ten steps. Engage the help of others—teachers, supervisors, administrators, parents, the child herself. Why not ask Marsha what went wrong and what *will* work?

SUMMARY

A problem-solving process which can be used to lessen teacher problems requires ten steps.

1. State the problem.
2. Identify the goal.
3. Identify the problem's owner.
4. Value the goal.
5. Identify obstacles standing in the way of goal achievement.
6. Project alternative ways by which the goal might be achieved.
7. Consider the possible consequences of each proposed alternative solution.
8. Rate each proposed solution.
9. Decide how to implement the best proposed solution and do so.
10. Decide whether you are satisfied with your position in relation to goal attainment.

More generally speaking, when you utilize the problem-solving process and the ten steps enumerated above, problem identification and ownership are established, values are clarified, the problem situation is analyzed, you zero in on a "best" solution, you choose that best solution, you implement, and you evaluate.

In Chapter 4 you will have an opportunity to practice the problem-solving process.

DISCUSSION QUESTIONS AND RELATED ACTIVITIES

Problem 1

An obstacle interferes with or stands in the way of the attainment of a goal.

a. List as many obstacles as you can that might interfere with a teacher's desire to achieve each of the following:

(1) Establishing rapport with other staff and students.

(2) Getting students to behave appropriately.
(3) Establishing good relationships with parents and understanding home conditions.
(4) Getting students to be successful both personally and academically.
(5) Using time wisely.
b. For any one of the above (1) through (5) describe how you would reduce or eliminate the obstacles.

Problem 2

A facilitating force is a source of power which helps to overcome the obstacles to goal achievement.
a. List as many facilitating forces as you can that might be used by a teacher to overcome obstacles to each of the following:
(1) Establishing rapport with other staff and students.
(2) Getting students to behave appropriately.
(3) Establishing good relationships with parents and understanding home conditions.
(4) Getting students to be successful both personally and academically.
(5) Using time wisely.
b. For any one of the above (1) through (5) describe how you would use the forces to overcome an obstacle and achieve a goal.

Problem 3

What is a lateral solution to the following problem?

Harold is obese. He has sought the advice of friends and physicians. All of them recommend dieting. What would you recommend?
Solution for Problem 3

One possibility is: consume a large quantity of low-calorie drink before each meal.

Problem 4

What other "low cards" could you as Marsha's teacher play in order to get her to complete her assignment? What are some higher cards? Do you have an ace? The ace must win the hand. What is your ace?

RELATED READINGS

de Bono, Edward. *Lateral Thinking: Creativity Step-by-Step.* New York: Harper and Colophon Books, 1973.

Hudgins, Bryce. *Problem Solving in the Classroom.* New York: Macmillan, 1966.

Maier, Norman R.F. *Problem Solving and Creativity.* Belmont, Calif.: Wadsworth, 1970.

Morrison, Donald W. *Personal Problem Solving in the Classroom: The Reality Technique.* New York: John Wiley, 1977.

Schmuck, Richard, Mark Chesler, and Ronald Lippitt. *Problem Solving to Improve Classroom Learning.* Chicago: Science Research Associates, 1966.

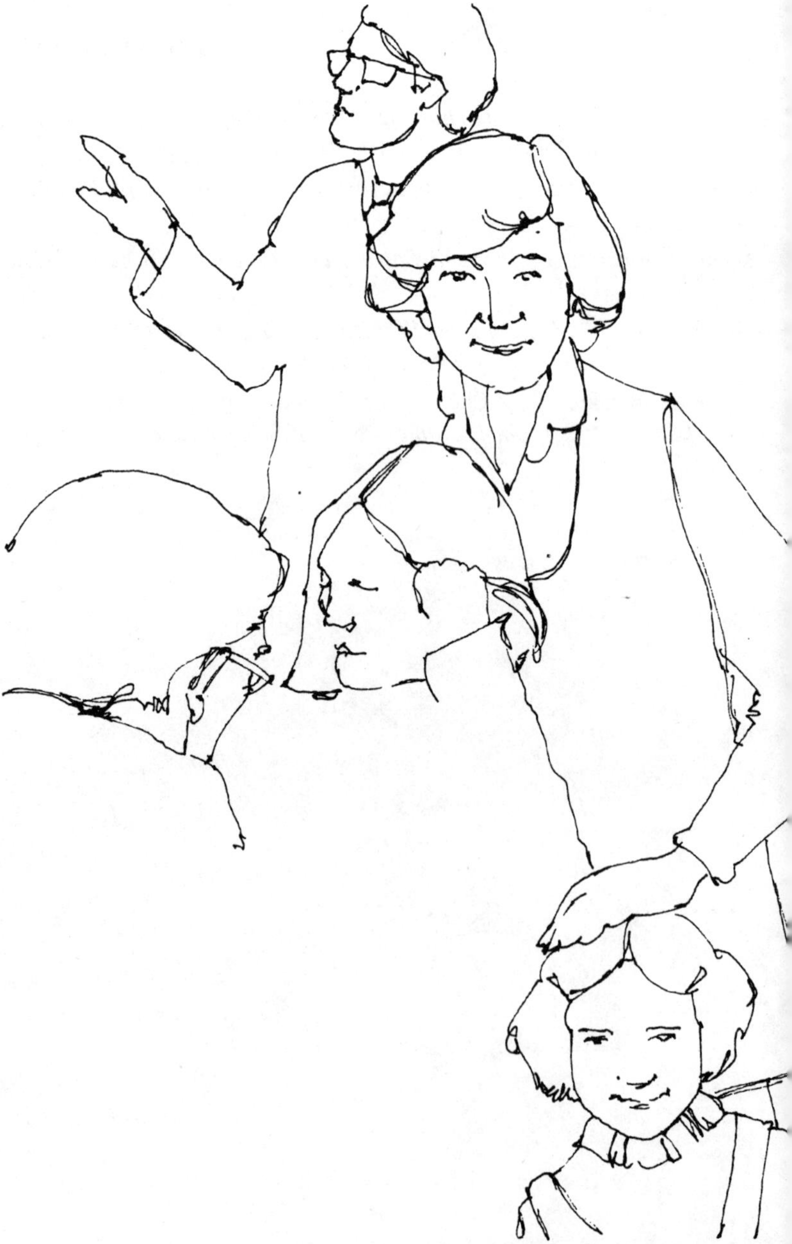

chapter 4

lessening one of your problems

DONALD R. CRUICKSHANK

Chapter 4 Outcomes: *As a result of reading Chapter 4, you will practice resolving one or more classroom problems you identify.*

Now that you are somewhat familiar with the problem-solving process presented in the preceding chapter, you should have an opportunity to practice it. In the case of solving teacher problems, practice may not "make perfect" but it will certainly help.

Obviously, the first thing to do is to identify and state a problem that bothers you. This can be done in a variety of ways. For example, at the end of the school day think back upon the instances of goal-response interference you encountered. Write out a diary-like record of one or more of them. Do this over a week's time, or longer if you wish, in order to determine a problem that not only is bothersome but occurs frequently as well. If you choose to identify problems in this way, it might be helpful to look at the beginning of Chapter 1 in order to recall how Pat Taylor and Arthur Daniels stated their concerns. A few more examples of teacher-reported problems follow.

Example 1
Sally has not been doing well in class. She daydreams, distracts other students, does not complete her assignments, including homework, and has not made up any work. I have made several attempts, after talking with Sally, to contact her parents both in writing and by telephone. Sally's mother and father have not returned any of my calls. Only once have they responded to my letters. That note to me read: "I realize that Sally is not doing well. Isn't there anything you can do. I don't know what I can do and it is hard for me to get over to school. I hope she doesn't fail. We would be disappointed. She's never been like this before."

Example 2
When the 1979–80 school year began, I was assigned a study hall in Room 125 the third period every day. There are seven periods at the high school, and therefore seven different study hall teachers are needed. When the school year started we study hall teachers held a meeting to determine how study halls would be conducted. It was a general agreement that study halls would be quiet with no card game playing or group study. About halfway through the year a few teachers let down on the rules and allowed students to play card games and move their seats around. The second period teacher allowed seats to be moved. When the period ended, not all seats were put back in their proper places. When I came in, it did not bother me because I had only 35 students and there were 90 seats, so I did not complain. However, the fourth period teacher needed all the seats in their proper places in order to take attendance. He complained to me about having seats out of order. I told him that my class was not responsible and that the second period class was to blame. He said it does not matter and that I should tell the second period teacher. I told him that I did not need all the seats in order and that *he* should tell the second period teacher. He got mad at me and went to the principal.

Example 3
Each year I have a "Hannah Hanger" who will not leave me alone. They find me, or nearly any teacher, wonderful. They will bestow all kinds of comments about how much they like me while standing so close they are stepping on my toes, running over my heels, ruining my nylons, etc. They are a real headache, especially at recess, and I want to get rid of them without being rude. They absolutely cannot take a hint. Also, most of the other students I would enjoy talking to will not even bother to try to talk to me (they've learned) when "Hannah" is around.

Example 4
As I sit down at my kitchen table to begin to work on a term paper, the phone rings. Who could this be at this time of night?

The caller is Mrs. D, mother of one of my students. In the next forty minutes a conversation which had begun with a mother's questions about her son's school program ends with a feeling of anger and frustration for both parent and teacher.

Mrs. D's son, Arnold, is one of the five students in my class of severely and profoundly mentally retarded youngsters who are referred to our program for treatment of behavior problems. Arnold is a multi-handicapped fourteen-year-old who, along with his self-abuse and severe tantruming, also has cerebral palsy, suffers a moderate to severe visual handicap, is nonambulatory, is nonverbal, and is profoundly mentally retarded. He is involved in all extremities and must be cared for exclusively by others.

Arnold is a very difficult child with whom to work but I have attempted to put my best efforts into applying suitable programming to meet his many needs. This effort has been even more demanding due to the fact that my classroom is the first formal educational program in which Arnold has ever been enrolled.

However, my extra time and patience with Arnold never seem to be sufficient to meet Mrs. D's approval. She remains very negative toward some of the classroom programs and is persistent in her attempts to pressure certain types of training (especially in mobility) which we are unable to carry out with our staff and facilities.

All in all, Mrs. D pushes my professional demeanor to the limits with her criticism, particularly when I hear it secondhand from another professional to whom she has spoken, or late at night when she decides to make one of her famous phone tirades. The situation is becoming a very frustrating and defeating one for me, and I am sure that it is not overly rewarding for Mrs. D, either.

Example 5

At Evans Junior High there seems to be little parental interest in the school or the school activities. Although we have a student population of more than 700 students, there are only 20 parents who belong to PTA. Even fewer parents come to either the concerts or the awards assembly in the spring.

This low interest in school affects the children, for it is not unusual for parents to take them out of school to visit relatives for several weeks or to keep them home to baby-sit or do housework. The children are also affected psychologically by their parents' attitudes for they adopt the view their parents hold that school has a low priority in their allocation of time and energy. As a result, not only is attendance low but academic achievement is low also, as reflected by the average reading level for the third grade.

There is also an effect on teacher morale because the indifference to education and teacher efforts displayed by both the students and their family makes the teachers feel unappreciated. This seeming lack of support and appreciation from the local community, coupled with a high incidence of behavior problems and teacher assaults, is the cause of low morale among the teachers. Cynicism and depression characterize teacher outlooks at the school.

The majority of families in the school district are of the lower socioeconomic class. The school is racially mixed, and most of the white students are of an Appalachian background. In keeping with the low socioeconomic status, many of the families are welfare and food stamp recipients. The educational level of the parents tends to be low, often to the point of functional illiteracy. The majority of parents have not completed high school.

Example 6
The problem involves two speech classes, scheduled third and fourth hours of the day. Third hour is 50 minutes long; fourth hour involves the lunch periods, and it is *never* shortened because to do so would interfere with the already minimal lunch time. Third hour classes, however, are often shortened, because of picture schedules, a morning assembly, class meetings, etc. It is just a good time of the day for a lot of things.

Because of this situation, the third class is almost always behind the fourth hour class. For several reasons, I feel the two classes should be together in content. First of all, it is easier to teach, since if the classes are even a day apart it is easy for me to forget something for one which was given to the other. In addition, the time separation causes extra work for me: either (1) I have to make extensive notes so both classes get the same thing, or (2) I find myself feeling very rushed to align the third hour with the fourth hour class, or (3) I feel I must find "extra" work for the fourth class, to slow them down.

The problem is definitely one of time (with shades of student success): how can both classes be kept together so there is not extra work for me?

A second way by which you can identify and state a problem is to turn back to Chapter 2 and look at the areas of problems you recorded on the Teacher Problems Checklist. Were the majority of them in the area of affiliation, control, parent relationships, student success, or time? One or more of the problem statements on the checklist probably will serve as the basis for triggering your memory.

Once you have identified and stated the problem, you have completed the first step in the problem-solving process and you are well on your way toward lessening it.

Here are a few additional things to keep in mind when you are practicing the problem-solving process.

1. The problem you identify should be yours. It probably

is but you may not have identified it as such. Teachers commonly make the error of stating that a certain pupil or another teacher has the problem. The fact is that if the pupil or teacher does not perceive the problem, for them it is not a problem. It is a problem only for the person who perceives it! Thus Johnny does not have a reading problem unless he perceives it as such. You likely have a problem of Student Success; that is, *you* want Johnny to read better. It is your problem!

2. When you are asked early in the problem-solving process to value your goal, you may feel at that time that it is of "unquestionable value" and that to achieve it you will go through hell and high water. However, as you work toward problem resolution and begin to see the difficulty or complexity of achieving your goal, you may want to reconsider its value. It may suddenly be negotiable. You may even decide to give it up. In such instances, don't despair! It probably is better to have some goals you value highly and to seek them even if they must later be negotiated than it is to have no goals or to be willing to doubt you can accomplish anything as a teacher. As Robert Browning said, "A man's reach should exceed his grasp, or else what's a heaven for?"

3. Try to eliminate obstacles to goal achievement and employ facilitative forces as you seek your goal. Remember, the latter are forms or kinds of power that teachers have or that they can marshal to overcome obstacles that cannot be removed. It is definitely to your advantage if you can both eliminate obstacles and organize your arsenal of facilitating forces.

4. Try to think of lateral or creative solutions to the problem. A story is told about a large manufacturer who had built a beautiful new office building. Unfortunately for management, when it was occupied, workers became disgruntled because at closing time large numbers of persons had to wait for elevators. Usual suggestions for resolving the problem included installing more elevators and staggering quitting times. The solution that was adopted was neither of these, but one that was

both imaginative and provocative. It took the minds of the workers off the problem. The company installed mirrors along the walls near the elevators and the grumbling stopped. How often have you been preoccupied with surreptitiously stealing a glance at yourself or someone else in a mirror?

5. Try to produce a large number of alternatives for reaching the goal. Problem solvers who project more alternatives, even though these may not be of uniformly high quality, eventually produce superior solutions. If you don't produce a large array of solutions, then be thankful that the few you do produce are the best. So suspend your judgment as best you can and produce!

6. Think through the consequences of each alternative most carefully. Think of everyone who could be affected. What looks like a straightforward, simple solution to the problem may, for someone, have harsh consequences that never were imagined. Try to imagine every consequence you possibly can.

7. Use knowledge which is available to you in Part Two of this book or elsewhere. What you don't know *will* hurt you! Accept that your teaching experience and university preparation can and indeed must be supplemented. In fact, either or both may be inadequate or out of date. Don't expect old wine always to taste good. Don't expect old solutions to work with new problems. Much is known about human behavior, but unfortunately the information is not all well organized for use by teachers.

8. Modify the problem-solving process to suit you. Although it has been used and revised many times, you may find that some modification of this process works best for you. Be certain, however, that you aren't merely abbreviating it to make less work. In the long run that will probably make more work since the problem may not be reduced at all.

9. Finally, don't be hesitant to ask for help in problem solving. It usually is readily available from other teachers, administrators, or staff persons. When you ask someone for help, you usually make that person feel important, and we can

all use that feeling. Besides, remember everyone has problems and many of them have problems much like yours.

Following is a problem-solving activity sheet based upon the problem-solving process presented in the last chapter. Use it now to work toward reducing or eliminating any of your teaching concerns.

PROBLEM-SOLVING ACTIVITY SHEET

Problem Identification and Ownership (see pages 46-47)
1. State the problem. What is it that is bothersome?
2. Identify the goal(s). What specifically is wanted?
3. Identify the problem's owner. Who wants the goal?

Value Clarification (see pages 47-48)
4. Value the goal. The goal is of:
   ___ unquestionable value.
   ___ great value.
   ___ value but negotiable.
   ___ little value.
   ___ no value.

Analysis of the Problem Situation (see pages 48-54)
5. Identify the obstacles standing in the way of goal achievement.
6. Project ways by which the goal might be achieved by:
   a. getting rid of obstacles standing in the way of the goal,
   b. overcoming or circumventing the obstacles, and/or
   c. brainstorming imaginative, creative solutions.
7. For each of the projected ways by which the goal might be achieved, list some possible consequences.

Choosing (see pages 54-56)
8. Rate *each* proposed solution and decide on the best one, i.e., the one most likely to get the goal and have the fewest unsatisfactory side effects.
   a. To what extent is it likely to achieve the goal? (Score it a 3 if it would, 1 if it would not, 2 if undecided)

b. To what extent is it likely to have positive or at least few negative side effects? (Score it a 3 if it would, 1 if it would not, 2 if undecided)

Implementation (see pages 56-58)
9. Decide *how* you would implement the best proposed solution and then do it.

Evaluation (see page 58)
10. Decide whether you are satisfied with your position in relation to goal attainment. Is the problem less bothersome?

part III

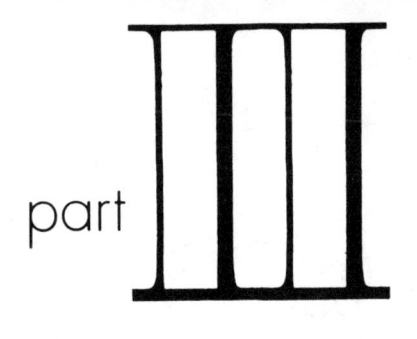

HELP RELATED TO YOUR PROBLEMS

As a result of reading Part One, you now know what a problem is and what makes a problem difficult. You also know the five major problem areas for teachers and which of them are of most concern to you. Further, you know a problem-solving process and you have practiced using it to resolve a problem of your own.

The second part of the book provides knowledge that is helpful for solving problems in any of the five areas of greatest concern to teachers.

What follows, then, is the theory or knowledge which seems to be of most worth for solving teacher problems. It includes concepts, facts, and conditional propositions (if-then statements) gathered from a variety of fields. The artistry of teaching is to skillfully and sensitively select from the knowledge that which creates the conditions necessary for teaching, learning, and their related activities to take place.

chapter 5

affiliation
KATHERINE TRACEY

PART I: INTRODUCTION

Chapter 5 Outcomes: *After reading Chapter 5 you should be able to:*
—*define affiliation,*
—*list reasons why affiliation is important,*
—*describe how expectations affect social interaction,*
—*list principles of social interaction and social competence,*
—*describe nonverbal communication and its significance to social interaction, and*
—*use a sociogram to identify patterns of social interaction.*

What is affiliation?
Affiliation is the desire expressed by teachers to like and to get along with others in the school, that is, students, other teachers, and administrators.

There are eight statements contained in the Teacher Problem Checklist related to the teacher need for affiliation. They were: I have a problem:

Liking my students.
Developing and maintaining student rapport, affection, and respect.
Establishing and maintaining rapport with students and staff.
Developing confidence in my colleagues.
Being professional in my relationships with staff.
Getting the understanding and sustenance of teachers and administrators so that I can feel efficient and professional.
Establishing and maintaining rapport with administrators and supervisors.
Getting cooperation and support from the administration.

How important is affiliation?

All primates demonstrate the need to affiliate. Strum (1975) studied baboons in their natural setting. She observed a complex society in which affiliation was a strong influence. Similarly, anthropological observations confirm that affiliation is a strong need of gorillas, orangutans, and other primates (Bourne, 1971; Hahn, 1971).

Social contact has always been recognized as a need of humans. Maslow (1968) in his hierarchy of human needs felt that it emerged as soon as physiological and safety needs were met. (Chapter 8 provides a discussion of Maslow's work.) Since antiquity one of man's greatest inhumanities to man has been the separation of a person from contact with other persons—hence imprisonment and solitary confinement. To be deprived of affiliation or to exist in a state of unsatisfactory affiliation can be very traumatic indeed. It is little wonder that teachers who report affiliation problems also report job dissatisfaction (see Chapter 10).

How important is affiliation to teachers as an occupational group?

Apparently, those who enter teaching have a stronger than average need for affiliation, or at least that need emerges during a teaching career. Super (1970) compared several occupational groups (psychologists, psychiatrists, C.P.A.'s, engineers, lawyers, teachers, and priests) by having them rank-order fifteen items that could be considered important for an ideal job. He found that there were four items that teachers valued more highly than did other occupational groups: *associate* (a value characterized by work that brings one into contact with fellow workers whom one likes), *surroundings* (a value associated with work carried out under pleasant conditions), *prestige* (associated with work that gives one standing in the eyes of others and evokes respect), and *security* (associated with work that provides one with a certainty of having a job even in hard times).

Along those same lines, Holland (1973), when studying how and why people make vocational choices, administered the Self-Directed Search inventory to a variety of occupational groups. This instrument identifies personality types (artistic, investigative, social, conventional, enterprising, and realistic). Teachers as a group ranked highest in the social area.

Thus limited evidence suggests affiliation is of greater concern to persons in teaching than in other occupational groups.

Why is affiliation of special significance and difficulty?

Affiliation is of special significance to practitioners because the role of teacher requires so much interaction with pupils, teachers, supervisors, and administrators. Furthermore, each type of interaction is different. For example, a teacher usually is in a leadership role when working with pupils, in the role of equal when working with fellow teachers, and in the role of subordinate when interacting with supervisors or administrators. The variety of teacher social interactions all requiring different interpersonal skills makes reaching the goal of affiliation complex indeed. Some teachers, for example, might be very skillful working with peers. Furthermore, certain teachers may be more skillful working with groups of children than with individuals.

What are some examples of affiliation problems reported by teachers?

The following teacher-written vignettes are examples of teacher-pupil affiliation concerns.

> I had a problem last year with a student who swore at me in front of the class. Having had this student for two years, I was disappointed with his lack of respect.

> The students in my class seem very hesitant to share their feelings. How can I help students enter into discussion and share feelings regarding their own personal views and opinions?

Both teachers desire to establish better affiliation with their students. Stating the problem and identifying the goal are the initial steps in problem solving. Think of some of your own interactions with students which represent inadequate affiliation.

The following vignettes are reports of colleague-related problems.

> Students giving oral reports in my class were disturbed by students in psychology across the hall who were acting out their problems. The noise, screams, etc. were not conducive to concentration.

> The other teachers at my grade level had their weekly meeting. Once again it was them against me. Everything was decided by them. They didn't even know I was there.

Describe an interaction with a colleage in which you did not reach your goal.

Teachers also report affiliation problems with administrators. The following vignettes illustrate two such interactions.

I have heard that my principal said to a colleague of mine that he thinks I do not work hard enough—that I should have more students and/or teach more classes. I am already working so hard. I can't believe he thinks so little of me when I work so hard.

The principal wanted me to be involved in team teaching and I felt I operated better in my own self-contained classroom. How will he react if I approach him about this?

Think of some situations in which you would like to improve or change your relationships with your administrators.

What do people in schools expect of each other to satisfy the need for affiliation?

We have said that there are a variety of social interactions in schools: teachers with students, teachers with teachers, and teachers with administrators. If we could determine the expectations each group has for the other, then we would know which conditions must be established in order to improve affiliation.

TEACHER-STUDENT EXPECTATIONS

What do pupils expect of teachers?

Pupils' expectations of teachers are affected mostly by their age, sex, and socioeconomic background. However, all pupils expect one thing in common: They expect teachers to teach. When pupils are asked to rank in importance the things teachers do, they will invariably rank teaching first. A problem arises, however, when we try to determine what it is teachers should do when they teach. Pupils disagree. Some feel teachers should lecture or tell, others believe they should be more inquiry and activity oriented. In order for a teacher to meet the variety of expectations pupils have for teaching, teachers themselves probably must exhibit great variability in teaching methods.

Taylor (1962) asked pupils to describe specific qualities that characterized good teachers: Those mentioned most frequently were helpfulness, fairness, patience, firmness, encouragement, and friendliness. Girls valued a teacher's friendliness and approachability more than boys did. Students in the high-ability groups reacted more favorably toward their teachers. The similarity of values and expectations for higher-ability students and teachers partially explains this positive relationship.

The age of the student affects his or her view of the teacher's role. During the early elementary years school is viewed as an extension of parenting. Later, as adolescents attempt to become more independent, they sometimes may rebel against all authority figures including teachers. What expectations of teachers do your pupils hold? Think about the influence their age, sex, socioeconomic background, and ability have on these expectations.

What impact do pupil expectations have?

Teachers whom students reported they did not get along with were those who did not follow the established rules or norms. By not meeting student expectations, teachers may also fail to establish the classroom rapport they desire.

The lone teacher trying to innovate within a traditional setting is probably perceived as a rule breaker and is not apt to be very successful at initiating change. In contrast, changes initiated by the majority group of teachers probably can overcome the existing student expectations and create new ones.

Knowing something about the expectations of pupils and then determining what particular pupils expect of school and of their teacher can help us to understand the dynamics of the teacher-student relationship. Problems occur because expectations on either side are not being met or are in conflict. In order to determine if the goal of affiliation is of great value in a particular problem situation, we must be aware of the expectations of all the people involved and we must answer two questions:

1. How important is it for me to meet my expectations?
2. How much am I willing to invest (time, energy, risk) to try to achieve this?

What expectations might be present in a teacher-pupil affiliation problem?

The following is a teacher-reported problem dealing with student affiliation.

> For a young teacher like myself, trying to justify rights and wrongs of the adult world is difficult. Today a student confronted me, wanting me to explain why it is right for me to smoke but very wrong for him to smoke. First, I must explain that I try not to hide anything from the students; therefore I feel I win their respect. It is a problem for me to deal with such questions.

Some possible expectations could include any combination of the following:

1. I want my students to respect me as a person rather than just as a teacher.
2. I feel I should answer any question a student asks me.
3. I want to be the friend and confidant of the students.
4. I want to establish a student rapport based on openness and honesty.
5. I do not want to have to enforce rules for students. Instead I want them to understand the rules and choose to follow them.
6. I want my students to think I'm really in touch with their world.

Note how different teacher expectations would alter the approach to the problem reported above. A teacher might act differently if, for example, he wanted to gain the students' respect for him as a teacher than if he wanted their personal friendship.

To solve this problem it is important to consider the student's expectations also. These could possibly include:

1. Teachers should justify their behavior.
2. I expect my teachers to help me understand the adult world.
3. Because this teacher seems to like to think we're his friends, I want to see if I can upset him because I don't like teachers who try to be too close.
4. I want the teacher to see how stupid the rule is and help us fight to establish a student smoking lounge.

The expectations this questioning pupil holds affect the eventual problem solution. It is important as a teacher to learn to identify pupil expectations and to consider them in the problem-solving process.

How can teachers identify pupil expectations?

There are a number of methods available for studying people's attitudes and expectations. Among them are questionnaires; interviews; examination of such personal documents as essays, diaries, and letters; ratings by other persons; and projective tests.

ACTIVITY
To try to discover how your pupils think a teacher should perform, use one of the techniques suggested for studying attitudes. A simple device is an open-ended statement which students complete anonymously. You can develop items that will provide the desired information, such as:

I expect my teacher to _____
I learn most when my teacher _____
I wish my teacher would _____
I enjoy class when my teacher _____
I dislike class when my teacher _____

How do teacher expectations affect pupils?

It is important that you as a teacher do not underestimate the impact your expectations have on students. Within every classroom there is a high consensus among the teacher and pupils about the relative abilities of class members. These opinions are not always accurate pictures of pupils' real abilities but they can influence future behavior. People are continually engaged in forming a self-concept and in developing patterns of behavior that are appropriate to this self-concept. The pupil we expect to be rude may also be viewed in a similar way by his classmates. Because of the self-fulfilling prophecy, because he is meeting and internalizing expectations, he is more likely to be rude than the pupil we expect to be courteous.

How can examining expectations lead to problem solutions?

A possible way to solve pupil affiliation problems is to examine and change inappropriate expectations. As a result of examining expectations, also, the teacher may decide not to value the original goal, and thus resolve the problem. In the previous vignette the teacher could decide that he does not expect his students to understand and accept his actions. Rather than feeling so concerned about explaining the justice or injustice of smoking in the teachers' lounge he might have just said, "It may not make sense to you, but I guess that's just one of the privileges that goes with my job—I can pollute my lungs if I want to." The situation remains the same, but by changing the expectations, the problem nature of the interaction is reduced.

By examining the expectations of the people involved, judging them to be realistic/unrealistic and worth/not worth striving to meet, then we can answer the question: Do I value this goal?

TEACHER-TEACHER EXPECTATIONS

What expectations do teachers hold for each other? This same expectation examination and decision about valuing the goal must take place when we deal with affiliation problems involving other teachers. This is complicated because there is not a consensus definition for "good teacher." What results is that each teacher applies his or her own personal criteria to measure colleagues and these expectations can differ greatly. Because there is a lack of objective criteria to judge performances, teachers are highly vulnerable to guesses about how others evaluate them.

What influence do staff norms and organization have?

Within any teaching staff there are norms and groups. It is helpful to understand this informal staff organization when trying to understand teachers' relationships with each other. There are a number of bases for staff groups, including subject area, sex, attitudes, seniority or age, and common interests and activities. Most teachers belong to several overlapping groups. Different groups have differing degrees of prestige and authority. Entrance into the "power clique" in a school is gained by having a recognized competence in an activity that is highly valued by the principal and/or the established power group. Often reputation is established by performance of students on public exams (especially highly publicized exams!) or in athletic or musical competition. The power structure differs in every school.

To become a member of a group involves identifying group expectations and then trying to meet them. Another viable alternative is not to conform and not to belong to these groups. Classroom performance need not be affected by relationships with other teachers.

ACTIVITY
One technique for identifying teacher expectations is to examine some of the behaviors that contribute to affiliation problems and then to reword those behaviors as expectations. For example, Do I gossip about other teachers? would be rewritten as the expectation that teachers should not gossip about their colleagues. The items on the following self-evaluation questionnaire (Cruickshank, 1967) represent some of the more common mistakes made which can disturb relationships with other teachers. Each item requires a yes or no response. As you answer, think about whether each mistake statement reflects an expectation you hold for your colleagues.

1. Do I criticize or report fellow teachers to the principal?
2. Am I inconsiderate of pupils?
3. Am I inconsiderate of my colleagues?
4. Do I gossip about other teachers?
5. Do I interfere in another teacher's work?
6. Do I complain constantly about students?
7. Do I complain constantly about school conditions?
8. Do I complain constantly about school duties?
9. Do I engage in petty arguments?
10. Am I intolerant of others?
11. Do I criticize the former teacher's achievement with children?

12. Am I unsympathetic with other teachers' problems?
13. Am I jealous of other teachers' success?
14. Do I expect special privileges?
15. Am I *constantly* talking shop?
16. Do I take out personal feelings on children?
17. Do I criticize or gossip about children in front of others?
18. Do I belittle my co-workers?
19. Do I belittle my supervisors?
20. Am I sarcastic with my pupils?
21. Do I fail to settle complaints in a professional manner?
22. Am I "cliquish" with other teachers in the building?
23. Do I go to the principal with petty problems?
24. Do I spread rumors?
25. Do I borrow materials and not return them?
26. Do I borrow without asking?
27. Am I unable to take criticism or suggestions?
28. Do I discipline other teachers' pupils without informing them?
29. Do I snoop?
30. Do I dwell on personal troubles?

If you want to know what your staff values or what they think of your teaching ideas, you might try to organize a small discussion group. The task could be to try to define the "ideal teacher" or more specifically "the ideal subject or grade level teacher." Before embarking on such a task you need to consider how discussion groups fit within the school staff norms. In some situations such an activity could alienate teachers rather than form the basis for improved relationships.

How does the teachers' lounge affect affiliation?

The location for a great deal of teacher affiliation activity is the teachers' lounge. Following extensive observation of teachers' rooms, Hargreaves (1972) identified five general values or norms.

1. *Autonomy* (principally classroom) *of teachers.* Most teachers prefer to go their own way, within obvious limits; in order to defend this right, they have to be willing to allow all other teachers to go their own way too.
2. *Loyalty to staff group.*

3. *Mediocrity norm.* This seems to prohibit too great an enthusiasm and too great an effort (don't arrive too early, work too hard, supervise too many activities...). When teachers do contravene this norm they find themselves teased by their colleagues and are laughingly accused of seeking promotion.
4. *Cynicism.* Teachers are not expected by their colleagues to be enthralled by the job of teaching or rapturous about pupils. It is more normative to grumble in the staffroom—about the principal, the pupils, the facility.
5. *A degree of anti-intellectualism* (p. 435).

Teachers who do not enter the informal life are viewed by their colleagues as "odd."

ACTIVITY
The next time you are in the lounge, try to identify examples of Hargreaves' categories. If you do not personally agree with these expectations and yet find that they exist in your school, what difference will it make as you try to establish positive affiliation with your fellow teachers?

How do new teachers become part of the staff?

Teachers do hold expectations for their colleagues, and many teachers are concerned about how others view them. The staff organization is very complex and primarily informal so that the rules and expectations are not publicly defined but instead need to be discovered. This discovery is difficult—especially for the newcomer to the staff.

A teacher's experiences in her first position contribute to a firmly developed view of herself as a teacher. Yet any new teacher enters a school in which relationships are fairly well ordered. As a newcomer, she finds herself at the bottom of the order, an outsider in relation to the school and its culture.

It is interesting to think about whether these hidden expectations always need to be self-discovered or if they can be shared. It is important to help all teachers deal with both the formal and informal staff expectations. Possibly new teacher orientation could assist in this area.

How do teacher needs relate to expectations?

It is also important to remember that teachers are all individuals with very different needs, and that those needs affect expectations. A new teacher as a young adult generally is occupied with selecting a mate, learning to live with a marriage partner, starting a family, rearing children, managing a home, getting started in a profession, taking on active civic responsibility, and finding a congenial social group. In contrast the teacher in midlife, having accomplished these tasks to some extent, is confronted with a different array of needs such as achieving adult civic and social responsibility, establishing and maintaining an economic standard of living, assisting teenage children to become responsible and happy adults, developing adult leisure-time activities, relating oneself to one's spouse as a person, accepting and adjusting to psychological changes of middle age, and adjusting to aging parents. The differing needs of these two groups could naturally lead to different expectations for professional experiences. Needs of individuals cannot be stereotyped by merely describing age groups but it is critical to remember that personal needs alter profession expectations and affect interactions with others. Recognizing this requires being sensitive to others and trying to understand other points of view.

What expectations might be present as teachers face problems in their relationships with each other?

Let us now apply some of these ideas about teacher expectations to an actual teacher-reported affiliation problem.

> I wish to have the students and staff in my school respond to and respect my development of a new drama program. To have it viewed as appropriate educationally and professionally and to support it are the goals I have set for myself and the drama program.

The teacher describes both staff and pupil affiliation as being his goal. For our purposes here, only the staff expectations will be described.

A partial list of expectations this teacher might have for colleagues could include any or several of the following:

1. I want my colleagues to become actively involved in our drama program by helping with productions.
2. I want teachers in the staff room to ask about our program and be interested in it.
3. I want teachers to support me by attending our productions and talking up the program with students and the community.
4. I want my colleagues who are involved in the teacher organization to try to get our program included for supplemental teacher contracts.
5. I want teachers to let my students come in their homerooms for advertising events and for selling tickets.
6. I want teachers to understand that a drama production is a learning experience and not just playing and want them to make it possible for students to earn credits for drama.

The problem solutions will be dictated in part by the teacher's expectations for his staff.

Now think about what the other teachers might expect of this person establishing a drama program. Such a list could include:

1. I wish this teacher would stop making such a fuss about the drama program. Pretty soon the principal might expect all of us to spend extra time in activities.
2. Teachers should realize that what students need is more of the basics. They already have too many extracurricular distractions.
3. A teacher should be able to do his projects without interfering with me. I don't want any extra announcements or paperwork in homeroom.
4. The drama program sounds good. Maybe I could get involved and also get some of the recognition.
5. Students seem really excited about this program. By supporting it I can both help and improve my relationship with them.
6. I would really like to know the drama teacher socially. Maybe this is the way!

What can examining expectations accomplish?
Again, identifying the expectations held by all the involved people does not eliminate teacher affiliation problems. It does enable a person to understand the situation more fully and then to determine if he still values that goal. Problems can be eliminated without altering the situation by changing expectations and devaluing goal(s). If the teacher above decided that staff support was not realistic or crucial to the program, then the lack of support would no longer be a problem. If he decides that the affiliation goal is of value, then he would continue following the steps in the problem-solving process.

TEACHER-ADMINISTRATOR EXPECTATIONS

Why do administrative expectations matter?
The third area of affiliation problems in schools is a teacher's relationship with her administrators. Again, the expectations held by all involved persons affect the eventual problem resolution.

The teacher-administrator relationship is one in which the administrator does have some control and power. Many principals view themselves as the policy makers of the school and view the teachers as executives whose task it is to make that policy operational. A real affiliation problem can arise when a principal holds this view and a teacher does not agree with a policy.

Teachers are dependent on their administrators in three main areas: (1) for internal promotion to positions such as department chairman; (2) for references; (3) for various favors such as duty assignments and supplies. Ignoring the importance of this relationship can adversely affect a teacher's success.

Teachers seem to feel that the ideals principals hold for them are very different from either their own ideal or real teaching behavior. Teachers tend to view principals inaccurately, often seeing them as being less liberal because they are the authority figures who need to raise objections and to remind people about requirements and regulations (Rasmussen, 1962).

How do principals define effective teaching?

How administrators define effective teaching varies among individuals. Part of an administrator's role is to make comparisons among teachers. Brown (1966), in studying the ways administrators discriminated between the most effective and the least effective teachers, found that principals looked at teaching methodology, attitude toward job, interpersonal relationships within the school, and personal attributes. Principals want teachers to do a good job in the classroom and show a positive attitude toward the institution. Continuing confusion exists because there is no clear description of good teaching.

How can teachers identify administrator expectations?

Many teachers express concern because administrators seem to make important judgments on a limited number of observations or contacts or on secondhand information such as parent complaints. This infrequent contact tends to obscure true administrator expectations and to create distrust. (See Chapter 7, dealing with parent relationships, for a more complete discussion of the problems of infrequent contact.) Inviting administrators to the classroom, discussing ideas about teaching with them, and generally increasing contact with the school administration can help teachers identify the expectations their administrators hold for them.

ACTIVITY
To understand more clearly a principal's definition of effective teaching, ask your principal to engage in the activity of discriminating between effective and ineffective teachers.

1. He should think of any three teachers he has ever worked with whom he classifies as effective and three he considers ineffective. You should not know their identity.

2. He then describes the teaching and classroom behavior of each person.
3. Look at the descriptors for the effective and ineffective people. Items that discriminate between groups would be key to his definition of an effective teacher. For example, if telling a lot of jokes was part of the description of all three effective teachers and not using humor was part of the description of ineffective teachers, then using humor would be one of his criteria for effective teachers.

How can leadership style affect expectations?

Administrators are in leadership roles. Basically there are two contrasting styles of leadership: *task-oriented* people, who derive major need satisfaction from the successful completion of the task; and *relationship-oriented* people, who drive basic need satisfaction from successful interpersonal interactions. A task-oriented person might expect reports to be completed, students to demonstrate progress, honors to be won at the Science Fair, or special bulletin boards to be displayed. A relationship-oriented leader would place higher value on the camaraderie that existed among the staff or on having a warm relationship with students. Most people exhibit both sets of leadership characteristics but tend to place a higher value on one.

Teachers are also in positions of leadership both in the classroom and on the school staff (e.g., department head or committee chairperson). Therefore, a teacher's leadership style influences her expectations in both leading and following situations.

What expectations might exist in a teacher-administrator affiliation problem?

Let us examine expectations in relation to an actual teacher-reported problem.

> I work with my principal closely but I can never talk with him about anything but business. I feel uncomfortable dealing with good or bad

feelings, books, ideas, personal events, ... anything but school. This seems to be a problem he has with other people too.

The teacher's expectations could easily include any combination of the following:

1. I want to know my principal as more than a robot-professional.
2. I want my principal to view me as more than a professional.
3. When I work closely with someone, I want to be able to share feelings as well as task-related ideas.
4. I can deal only with "whole people" and always feel there is something mysterious about working with just one part of someone's life in isolation.
5. If my principal valued me, he would be interested in other things about me—my feelings, my interests....

A partial listing of what the principal might expect of the teacher could include any combination of the following:

1. I want my staff members to keep a professional distance.
2. Becoming involved in the personal lives of staff members interferes with the professional relationship. I expect my staff to keep them separated.
3. I want my staff members to be task-oriented and not to spend their time socializing and discussing unrelated topics.
4. I would like to know my staff members better but they might reject me if they knew I had a retarded son (or any personal situation).
5. I would like to know my staff members better but my superiors discourage fraternizing.
6. I want to know as little as possible about my staff members so that my evaluations will be objective and based on actual performance.

Again the expectations which the principal and teacher actually hold affect understanding of the problem and finding of workable solutions. If the teacher decided to devalue the original goal and to change her expectations for this relationship, then the situation would remain the same but its problem nature would be reduced.

PART II: UNDERSTANDING INTERACTION

Not all affiliation problems can be eliminated by just examining the expectations and devaluing the original goal. Many times a teacher will decide. "I do value this goal" and will then need to continue using the problem-solving process to identify ways to develop a better relationship. An understanding of some of the principles of human interaction can enhance the development of creative solutions.

Teachers who are concerned about improving affiliation need to understand the interactions in which they are involved in order to develop feasible solutions and make desired changes. Teachers interactions are varied and complex. Teachers interact with individuals and groups in both formal settings, such as the class lesson, a staff meeting, or planned conference, and informal settings such as a conversation in the hall or a discussion over lunch. They also assume various roles, acting as leader, equal, and follower. Interactions are further affected by both verbal and nonverbal communications.

This section will examine some of the principles that govern social interaction, will explore techniques for identifying social relationships, and will discuss the impact of nonverbal communication. Because so much of interaction occurs in groups, special attention will be given to the dynamics of this setting. The key to this entire section, however, lies with the application of this knowledge.

SOCIAL INTERACTION

What are the principles of social interaction?
The exchange of meanings between people—social interaction— is governed by rules which solve problems and make social interaction easier and more predictable. Some universal rules are:

1. People interacting turn toward one another to coordinate the auditory and visual information.
2. People take turns to speak.

3. Questions lead to answers.
4. Encounters have greetings at the beginning and farewells at the end, and not elsewhere.

Notice how people feel if these rules aren't obeyed. Examples of breaking these rules are the teacher in the lounge who leaves without completing the conversation or indicating some form of farewell, or the pupil who does not look at the teacher while listening. Not following these universal rules interferes with satisfactory interaction and, if repeated even infrequently, it can create affiliation problems.

In interactions it is important for people to be rewarding to one another. This principle is closely related to meeting other people's expectations. If one relationship is not sufficiently rewarding for a person, he or she will seek the company of others. The people who are viewed as most rewarding become both popular and influential.

What enhances or detracts from social competence?

There are things people do that either enhance or detract from their social competence. Social competence is enhanced by:

> Sensitivity to others (ability to recognize and interpret nonverbal behavior accurately).
> Communication skills.
> Rewarding others.
> Poise and confidence.

Social competence is diminished by:

> Failing to communicate clearly.
> Quarrelling and annoying people.
> Being unable to influence and persuade.
> Being unable to deal with the opposite sex, children, particular social classes, or other groups.
> Finding many personalities difficult to deal with; suffering frequently from embarrassment or social anxiety.

A list such as this provides a focus for looking at an affiliation problem and seeing if any of these components contribute to it. Trying to be realistic about how a person is perceived by others is difficult, but it is often the beginning point for understanding problems and finding solutions.

NONVERBAL COMMUNICATION

Nonverbal communication is behavior that conveys meaning without words. It includes facial expressions, posture, gestures, movement, vocal tone and inflections, arrangement of space and objects, and it involves the use of body, space, and time. Nonverbal signals are often more important than verbal communication for establishing the basic relationships in a group.

There are three main types of nonverbal communications (NVC).

1. NVC which *communicates interpersonal attitudes and emotions,* such as a hug, a smile, an eye roll, or a yawn.
2. NVC which *supports and complements verbal communication,* such as a friendly greeting coupled with a warm handshake.
3. NVC which *replaces speech,* such as a stare or a frown to indicate displeasure.

Why is it significant?
Research has shown that nonverbal signals have a far greater effect than verbal messages in communicating inferiority and superiority. Reaction to these nonverbal signals is partly innate and often outside of awareness. Some elements of this communication include:

1. Bodily contact—indicates level of friendship and intimacy.
2. Bodily proximity—changes in closeness signal beginnings and ends of encounters; also, people sit closer to those they like.
3. Bodily orientation—*cooperating pairs* sit side by side; *competing or*

hostile pairs sit facing; *discussion or conversation* occurs at a 90-degree angle.
4. Bodily posture—indicates whether the person is tense or relaxed. The person of highest status sits least formally.
5. Gestures.
6. Head nods—act as reinforcers to encourage others to talk more.
7. Facial expressions—communicate emotions and attitudes.
8. Eye movements.
9. Appearance of clothes, face, hair, etc.
10. Emotional tone of speech—this is often a more reliable indicator of emotions than facial expressions, since it is not as well controlled as other forms of nonverbal communication for most people.

Nonverbal signals vary within different cultures. For example, in some cultures (Puerto Rican and some groups of blacks) lowering the eyes is a sign of respect for authority. To middle-class whites this same motion indicates one is dishonest or has something to hide. Touching and standing close to other people also have cultural significance, and misinterpreting such behavior can cause serious misunderstandings.

How can nonverbal signals be recognized?

Since nonverbal communication is so significant, it is important to be aware of the signals we may be sending. An excellent technique for doing this is to videotape any group session and then view this tape without sound. Notice what messages are received without words. Do the words and actions agree or are they in conflict? Also pay close attention to the responses of the other group members.

What functions does eye contact serve?

Eye contact, which is one form of nonverbal communication, serves a number of functions. One of the most important is to gather feedback about people's reactions. Eye contact is also used as a signal for attending to and interacting with others. Sometimes just looking at a person cues him to take his turn. People tend to judge disinterest by failure to look up. How might the principal feel if a teacher graded papers all through the next staff meeting? Social relationships are established and recognized through eye contact.

Eye contact is one of the factors that establishes the level of intimacy between people. This level of closeness is a balance between physical distance, eye contact, intimacy of the topic, and the amount of smiling. When one of these elements is out of balance for a person, she changes the other elements to try to restore the balance. If someone stands too close, she may try to restore a comfortable balance by looking away. If someone is too far away, she may strive to establish direct eye contact. A conflict can result when two people disagree on a comfortable distance. Both people misunderstand. The person preferring closeness interprets distance as rejecting friendship. The other person interprets closeness as being pushy.

Often eye contact is not carefully considered when one is arranging a group and yet it may be one of the elements that contributes to affiliation problems. In interactions you should try to make sure that good eye contact with all people is possible. Sommer (in Breed and Colaiuta, 1974) found that a student's visual contact with the teacher increased interaction and that such eye contact was related to comprehension.

How does a room arrangement affect affiliation? One element of nonverbal communication over which a teacher has control is the arrangement of the furniture and equipment in the classroom. This influences the types of interactions that can occur and affects the way people feel about the entire situation.

Most teachers spend almost three quarters of their time in front of the classroom. In extensive classroom research, Adams and Biddle (1970) identified an "action zone" in classrooms which extended from the front of the room directly up the center line, diminishing in intensity the further away it was from the front. These researchers found that almost three quarters of the classroom interactions occurred within that area.

Discovering patterns of interaction can help explain the

98 *HELP RELATED TO YOUR PROBLEMS*

FIGURE 5-1. (Adams and Biddle, 1970, p. 50.)
THE "ACTION" ZONE

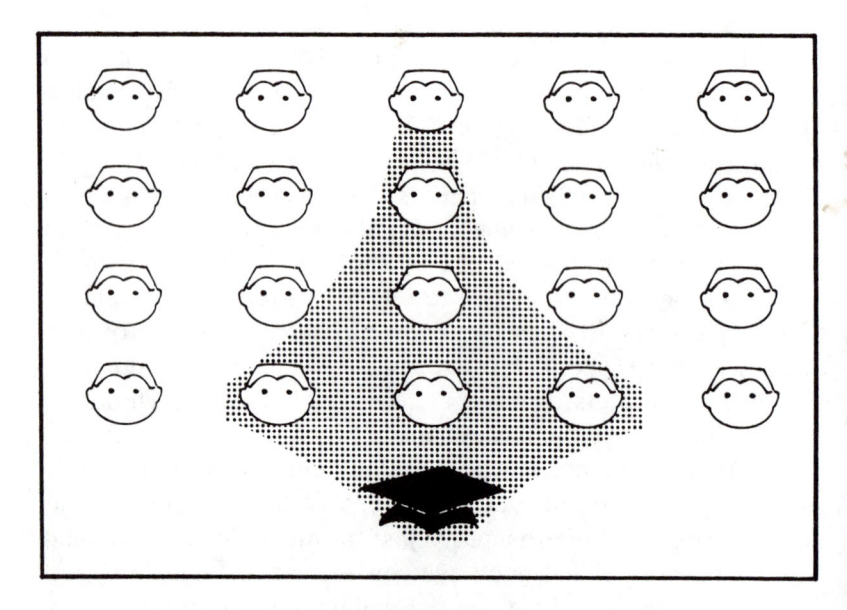

FRONT

lack of affiliation with certain people and can provide possible solutions. For example, if a teacher wanted to establish a better relationship with a new student who sat in the rear left-hand corner of the room and that teacher had identified his "action zone" as being in the front and toward the right-hand side of the room he might infer that the lack of interaction was the reason for the poor relationship. Solutions could include moving the student's desk or varying the pattern of interaction.

Room arrangement can contribute to interaction in several other ways. Distance between people helps establish the level of intimacy. Also the position of people partially defines the nature of the relationship. As we have seen, competing pairs sit across from one another, cooperating pairs sit side by side, and discussion or conversation occurs at a 90-degree angle.

When considering any affiliation problems, avoid relying on generalizations or single factors as explanations of behavior. The use of space is certainly one factor in this complex puzzle that should not be overlooked.

ACTIVITY
To consider your classroom arrangement and its relationship to interaction, make a scale model of the room, including the fixed points such as doors, windows, blackboards, and cupboards. Have cardboard scale pieces of all the movable furniture and equipment so that you can experiment with alternatives in miniature. Think about the following questions.

1. Does this instructional activity require interaction? If so, how much and between whom?
2. How does the room arrangement help facilitate this interaction?
3. If it does not, what arrangement would be more effective?
4. How can I make the rearrangement most efficiently and effectively?

Different activities have different goals and are best served by different types and degrees of interaction. It seems logical that the spatial arrangement should also be tailored to meet the goals of specific activities.

Let's review this and the preceding section. Social interaction occurs in many settings and is governed by rules. Breaking these rules or not using appropriate communication and interaction skills interferes with relationships and contributes to affiliation problems. Nonverbal communication conveys many messages, and cues such as eye contact, body posture, and physical distance reveal valuable information. Teachers must become more sensitive to all forms of communication and more perceptive about their own behavior and its effects on others.

GROUP INTERACTION

In the school setting social interaction takes place most often in groups which have specific characteristics and rules.

How are groups organized?
Each kind of group within a school (i.e., classrooms, teachers' lounge, committee meeting, lunch time bridge group) and each specific group (i.e., Ms. Brown's class, the lounge at Seaview Junior High, the Athletic Council at Hartley High School) have a unique way of doing things. All groups have a goal(s), participants, leadership, and relationships to other groups. The school is a work- or task-oriented setting and it includes many groups and subgroups.

In the classroom both the goal of learning and group membership are mandatory. Control and leadership of the classroom group are legally and traditionally given to the teacher, and pupils normally have no formal control in selecting teachers. The mandatory quality of group membership, goals, and leadership is also evident when one considers the school as a single group. Teachers are assigned to classrooms; schools or districts set broad educational goals; and the principal is the designated leader. Both the classroom and the school are just single links in a sequence of overlapping groups (neighborhoods, families, gangs, teams, clubs . . .).

Jean Grambs (1952) outlined basic assumptions about group activities which are still valid today. When thinking about interactions within the classroom and school and when applying theory to modify interactions and to improve affiliation, it is important to remember that basically "no class becomes a genuine group except for short periods of time when it has successfully accomplished a class goal through the efforts of the subgroups in it." One must identify, recognize, and consider these subgroups instead of always dealing with the class or faculty as a single unit.

What principles govern groups?
A group is a group because people outside the group and people inside the group perceive it to be one.

ACTIVITY
Make a list of all the subgroups you think exist within your classroom and list the members in each subgroup. Ask the students to do the same activity and then notice differing perceptions of existing groups and group membership.

A group is also defined by the patterned interaction of its members. A principle of this interaction is that when two or more people form a group they must work out a pattern of behavior which is more or less satisfying to all. They must agree on the following (Argyle and Lee, 1972):

1. Amount of speech.
2. Tempo of speech.
3. Dominance.
4. Intimacy.
5. Cooperation and competition.
6. Emotional tone.
7. Task, topic, and procedure.

People normally do not sit down and discuss these items. The agreements occur by trial and error, and group members are often unaware that such patterns have been established. Much of this process is carried out through nonverbal communication.

ACTIVITY
Take the list of subgroups within your classroom and answer the following questions related to the seven areas mentioned above.
1. What patterns exist for each of these areas?
2. How were these patterns developed?
3. What leadership role have I played in this process?
4. How do these patterns of behavior affect my relationship with various students?
5. Might changing some of these help me to achieve a more satisfactory level of affiliation?

These same questions can be applied to any group or subgroup in which you are involved.

Another principle is that all groups have norms or share ways of acting or thinking. People conform to such norms because of fear of rejection (anticipation of negative feedback), as a result of social pressure (feedback received from the environment such as rewards and punishments), or through a belief that the majority knows best (part of the internal structure upon which feedback is judged). The more powerful members of a group are allowed to talk more and their suggestions are taken more seriously.

There are probably classroom norms dealing with student behavior and participation. Answering too many questions or helping the teacher may carry with it the peer tag of "teacher's pet." Be aware of the norms within the student group. Not understanding them and violating them can contribute to teacher-pupil affiliation problems.

A principle which specifically applies to educational groups is that motivation for learning is based on attitudes which to a large extent are shaped by psychological processes within the group. This means that success in achieving educational goals depends in part on the extent to which group norms permit or encourage members to become involved in the educational process.

Hilda Taba (1951) was a leader in introducing teachers to group methods. She stated that "productivity of groups . . . (is governed by) . . . the feelings group members have about each other and . . . the skills they have to carry their jobs forward." In the classroom setting this productivity could include completing assignments, participating in discussions, or mastering a variety of skills. The role teachers play in helping students deal with both feelings and skills is part of the complex process of group interaction.

What leadership roles exist in groups?

There are usually two leaders in a group: the task leader and the social leader. The task leader keeps the group engaged in work and must often apply pressure which can irritate people and hurt group unity. The social leader provides considerate treatment for individuals and helps keep work groups unified and satisfied.

A teacher may try to be both the task leader and the social leader in the classroom. These roles are not always compatible and can contribute to affiliation problems.

Various students may assume some of the leadership in the classroom group or subgroups. If students in such roles share the teacher-accepted classroom norms, this can help the smooth functioning of the group. At times, however, students with different norms assume leadership. Their subgroups can create problems. For example, class clowns encourage others to follow an example that is counterproductive to the general classroom goal of learning and yet some students choose to follow such leadership and be members of this subgroup.

In general, within task- or work-oriented groups such as the classroom or staff meeting, there is an alternation between communications (interactions) dealing with the task and communications dealing with emotional or social reactions among members. The work-related interactions tend to create or increase tensions whereas the social/emotional communications tend to reduce tensions and achieve harmony.

Failure to achieve this balance might be what causes teachers to leave a staff meeting feeling, "We didn't get anything done!" or leave a principal's conference with the feeling: "She doesn't care about me as a person; she only wants to see lesson plans." The task and social leaders play key roles in being sensitive to group needs and establishing a satisfactory balance.

What is a cohesive group?

Another way of describing groups is to examine their degree of cohesiveness. In a cohesive group the members like each other and are attracted to the group. In cohesive groups there is more conformity than in other groups and more cooperation to accomplish group tasks. The members enjoy belonging to the group and spend more time with it. There are a number of conditions which make groups cohesive:

1. A harmonious set of personalities.
2. Members with similar attitudes, interests, and backgrounds.
3. Frequent interaction.
4. Rewarding experiences in the group.
5. A skillful leader who can resolve conflicts and deal with different members.
6. The absence of aggressive, schizoid, and other disturbing personalities.
7. A task that requires cooperative activity for its completion.

In larger groups there is less cohesiveness and subgroups are likely to appear.

Cohesiveness has certain negative features. Very cohesive groups develop strong "in-group" feelings. The group members feel warmly toward the other members and value them highly, but they feel hostile toward or undervalue those outside the group. Members of a very cohesive group may enjoy each others' company so much that they spend most of their time in social activity and get little else done.

Think about this description of cohesive groups. Identify such groups within your staff or classroom. What degree of cohesiveness do you think is best in these situations?

The way students feel about the classroom group and about themselves within that group affects academic performance. Schmuck (in Yee, 1971) described classrooms according to liking structure. He used the term *diffuse liking structure* to describe a room in which preferences were evenly distributed, and he contrasted this with a *central liking structure,* in which a few people receive most of the preferences. The most positive emotional climates exist for students within classrooms that have evenly distributed liking relations. This notion helps to explain both teacher and pupil feelings regarding affiliation.

How can relationships within a group be identified?

Recognizing the importance of the underlying relationships present in any group is not enough. Accurately identifying these relations is also necessary. Just observing a group yields some information, but experience has shown that perceptions are often inaccurate or incomplete.

One very effective technique for discovering the relationships that exist within a group is to construct a sociogram, which is a diagrammatic way of using information about the social relationships in a group. This is done by asking each group member to list a specific number of people in the group with whom he would most like and least like to do something. The purpose of the sociogram determines the focusing question. For example, the task could be:

1. If you were working on a committee, what three (or four) people would you like to work with the most (the least)?
2. If you could sit anywhere, by what three people would you want to sit? Not want to sit?
3. When you go to the outdoor school for a week, what three people would you want to share a cabin with? Not have in your cabin?

This information can then be translated into a diagram with arrows indicating the directions of the feelings. (Figures 5-2, 5-3)

A sociogram reveals four typical structures involving popular group members.

1. The star—most popular.
2. The reciprocal or mutual pair.
3. Chain structures.
4. The triangle or "clique," in which each member chooses and is chosen by other members.

A sociogram also reveals isolated (the rejectee, the neglectee, or the isolate) members. Figure 5-3 represents some of the choices of six members of the class when asked to indicate whom they

FIGURE 5-2. This is how one person's choices would appear. Joan indicated that she would like to work or sit with Rick, Jean and Allen. She would not like to work with Sam, Patty, and Julie.

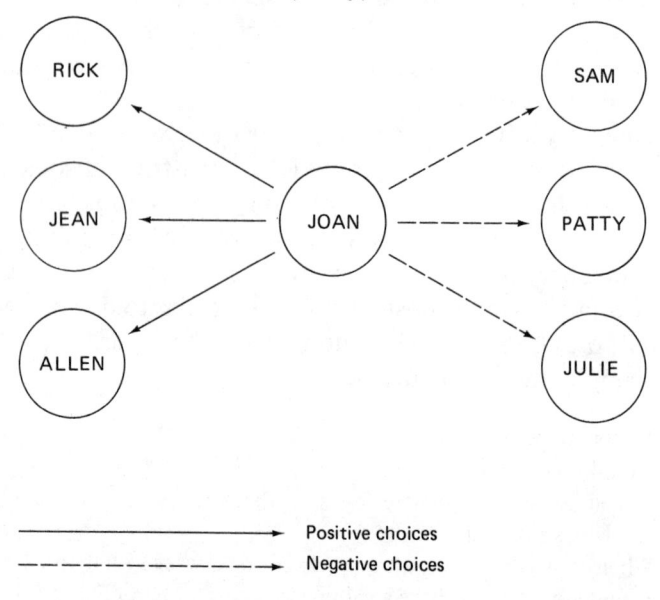

——————————→ Positive choices
— — — — — — — —→ Negative choices

would like to work with on a committee project. In this example Bill appears as the star because four people wanted to work with him. Bill, Joe, and Jack are a clique or triangle because each of them chose and was chosen by the other two. Frank appears as an isolate because no one indicated any feelings about him, and he made no choices himself. Paul is a neglectee because no one chose him, even though he made choices. Sam is the rejectee because the people he wanted to work with did not want to work with him.

Some of the advantages of using a sociogram are that it shows a pattern of social relationships, gives people's judgments, and shows the extent of the relationships between subgroups. Some disadvantages are that sociograms tend to give a black-and-white picture rather than revealing the grays and that

FIGURE 5-3.

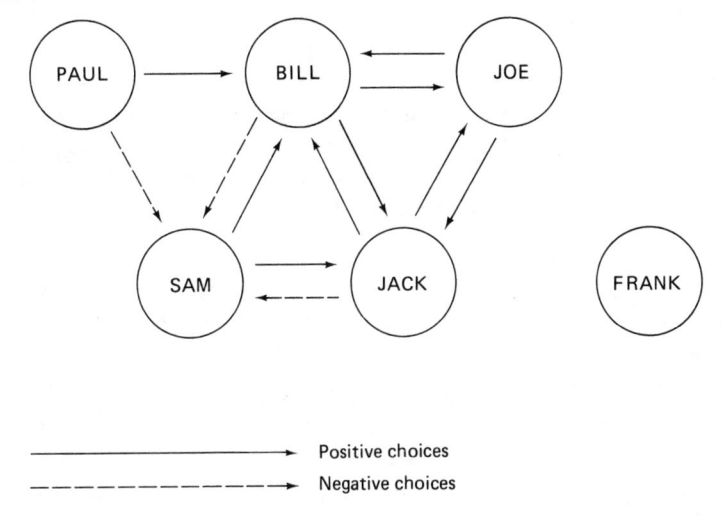

```
───────────────▶  Positive choices
─ ─ ─ ─ ─ ─ ─ ─▶  Negative choices
```

teachers sometimes object to having their students make negative choices.

Use of the information obtained from sociograms has a number of implications for teachers.

1. The delegation of responsibility: often-chosen students have already won the confidence of their classmates and can be given responsibility positions.
2. Helping the isolated student: these students can be identified and can be paired to work with well-integrated students who have not rejected them. It must be remembered that not all pupils who are isolates are maladjusted or even need help.
3. The reorganization of the class: groups can be formed which are based on the pupils' choices. This releases strong motivational pulls because the group situation satisfies the pupil's social needs such as security.

ACTIVITY

Use a sociogram to gain greater understanding of the interaction in your classroom. It is extremely important in using this technique that the

choices pupils make are kept confidential. You could use the information in a sociogram to determine if cliques exist in your classroom or to establish committees for the PTA program. What are some other ways you might use this information? Your focus for the choices will relate to its application. For example, if you plan to organize groups to produce short plays you would ask: What people would you like most (least) to produce a play with? Remember that students will want to understand who will see this information and how it will be used.

Let us now briefly review this section. Groups have certain structural features such as goals, membership, and leadership. Every group has a specific pattern of behavior and is norm governed. Task-oriented groups require two types of leadership—task and social—which can be in conflict with each other. Often two people assume these leadership roles. The emotional tone of the group and the affiliation felt by the people involved are affected by group cohesiveness and the patterns of positive relationships within the group. Sociograms are a very helpful tool when used to understand the relationships that exist within a group.

SUMMARY

Affiliation problems, those which involve relationships with pupils, fellow teachers, and administrators, are troublesome to many teachers. It is important to seek solutions to these problems because the quality of interactions and the degree of affiliation with others greatly affect feelings of personal and professional satisfaction.

When dealing with an affiliation problem, people must examine the expectations held by all the people involved. Not meeting expectations of self or others leads to conflict and frustration. Sometimes problems can be eliminated by devaluing the original goal. At other times examining expectations reinforces the goal and its value.

The research about interaction provides helpful information for developing problem solutions. Gaining understanding of a situation does not automatically eliminate problems, but such principles as the nature of the group process, the dynamics of social interactions, and the impact of verbal and nonberbal communication can be applied to specific situations and used as the basis for generating appropriate solutions.

Problems do not usually "self-destruct." They must be identified and examined. People must develop solutions and then implement and evaluate them. This is a continual process and it is more effective when accurate information is used.

Affiliation is a critical and complex issue for teachers. Valuable information can be learned by studying the research in such fields as communication, social psychology, sociology, and psychology. There are no simple explanations for human behavior or simple solutions for establishing better affiliation.

RELATED READINGS

Adams, R.S., and B. Biddle. *Realities of Teaching: Exploration with Video Tape.* New York: Holt, Rinehart & Winston, 1970.

Argyle, M., and J. Dean. "Eye Contact, Distance and Affiliation." *Sociometry,* 28 (1965), 289-304.

Argyle, Michael, and Victor Lee. *Social Relations.* Walton Hall, Stratford, England: The Open University Press, 1972.

Bates, R.J. "Classroom Location, Learning and Status." *New Zealand Journal of Educational Studies,* 8, 2 (1974), 142-53.

Bourne, Geoffrey Howard. *The Ape People.* New York: Putnam's, 1971.

Breed, G., and N. Colaiuta. "Looking, Blinking and Sitting: Nonverbal Dynamics in the Classroom." *Journal of Communications,* 24, 2 (1974), 75-81.

Brown, A.F. "How Administrators View Teachers." *Canadian Education and Research Digest,* 6, 1 (1966), 34-52.

Cruickshank, Donald R. "Teacher v. Teacher." *Clearing House,* January 1967, pp. 305-306.

Galloway, Charles. *Silent Language in the Classroom.* Bloomington, Ind.: Phi Delta Kappa Educational Foundations, 1976.

Grambs, J. *Group Processes in Intergroup Education.* New York: National Conference of Christians and Jews, 1952. in Lindgren, H.C. *Educational Psychology in the Classroom.* New York: John Wiley & Sons, Inc., 1972, p. 301.

Hahn, Emily. *On the Side of the Apes.* New York: Thomas Y. Crowell, 1971.

Hargreaves, D.H. "Staffroom Relationships." *New Society,* March 2, 1972, pp. 434-37.

———. *Social Relations in a Secondary School.* Boston: Routledge and Kegan Paul, 1967.

Holland, J. *Making Vocational Choices: A Theory of Careers.* Englewood Cliffs, N.J.: Prentice-Hall, 1973.

Maslow, Abraham. *Toward a Psychology of Being,* 2nd ed. New York: Van Nostrand Reinhold, 1968.

Rasmussen, G.R. "Perceived Value Discrepancies of Teachers and Principals: A Threat to Creative Thinking." *Bulletin of the National Association of Secondary School Principals,* 45, 272 (1962), 1-12.

Strum, Shirley C. "Life with the 'Pumphouse Gang.'" *National Geographic,* May 1975, pp. 672-91.

Super, Donald E. *Work Values Inventory,* p. 47. Boston: Houghton Mifflin, 1970.

Taba, Hilda. "Generalizing, Summarizing, and Developing Group Methods." Paper read at Conference on Group Processes, San Francisco State College, June 1951. in Lindgren, H.C. *Educational Psychology in the Classroom.* New York: John Wiley & Sons, 1972, p. 307.

Taylor, P.H. "Children's Evaluations of the Characteristics of a Good Teacher." *British Journal of Educational Psychology,* 32 (1962), 258-66.

Yee, A.M. (ed.). *Social Interaction in Educational Settings.* Englewood Cliffs, N.J.: Prentice-Hall, 1971.

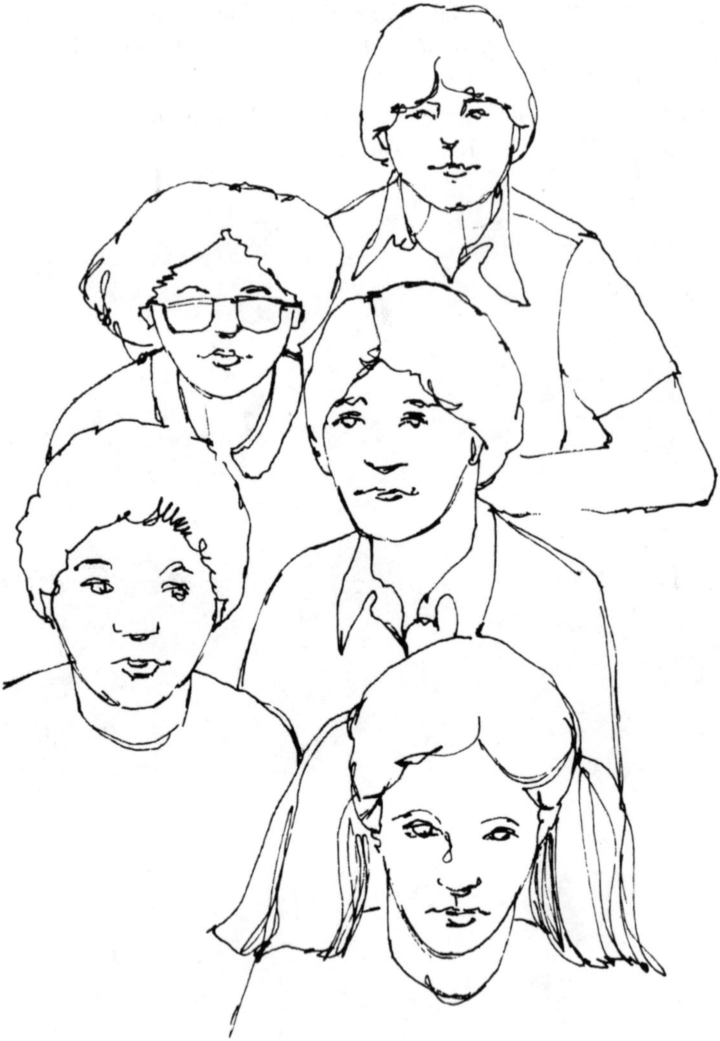

chapter 6

control
CHARLES NOVAK

Chapter 6 Outcomes: *After reading Chapter 6 you should be able to:*
—*explain why control is an important area of teacher concern,*
—*explain the relationship between good instruction and effective control,*
—*explain the importance of pursuing appropriate and important control-related goals,*
—*explain the importance of identifying obstacles that block achievement of control-related goals,*
—*describe techniques for managing behavior in positive ways,*
—*describe techniques for using punishment appropriately and sparingly,*
—*describe techniques for teaching students to manage their own behavior, and*
—*apply management principles to make control less of a problem.*

What is control? Why is it a problem for teachers?

Abraham Maslow (1968), an eminent psychologist, asserts that the need for an environment that is orderly, stable, and secure is one of the most basic needs of mankind. Before individuals can feel free to satisfy what Maslow calls higher-level needs for affiliation, esteem, or self-actualization, they must feel physically and psychologically "safe"—in other words, they must feel that their environment is under control. Consequently, each of us seeks to control our environment. We want to shape both the persons and things in it so we can feel secure.

Teachers, like other individuals, strive to control their environments, especially in their classrooms. Administrators and communities expect teachers to exert control. Public criticism of schools frequently includes statements such as, "If only teachers controlled their classes the way teachers used to, students would learn what they are supposed to learn." The public generally perceives the school to be a place where students must be controlled and learn self-control. So, teachers struggle daily to maintain orderly, stable, and secure classroom environments.

When teachers speak of problems of control, they refer generally to difficulties in establishing and maintaining an orderly classroom or, to be more specific, difficulties in getting students to be relatively quiet, orderly, and courteous. They also expect students to display honesty and to show respect for others and their property.

When students don't behave appropriately, teachers often feel their goals are being thwarted. For example, inappropriate behavior presents an obstacle to the goal of promoting achievement. Teachers who spend a great deal of time and energy dealing with misbehavior will have little time, energy, or patience left for teaching.

Thus control exists as an area of teacher concern because (1) all individuals, teachers included, are naturally inclined to try to create orderly, stable, and secure environments, (2) administrators and communities demand that students be controlled and learn self-control, and (3) failure to establish and maintain an orderly classroom interferes with student achievement and teacher satisfaction.

What kinds of control problems do teachers have?
Consider the following incident that was reported by a classroom teacher:

> The same boy who has been causing all the trouble in my one class was "off-and-running" again today. He had the girl behind him combing his long hair. His explanation, even though I didn't ask for it, was that she was combing out the tangles. Later in the period he threw a paper wad across two rows to a boy diagonal to him. And he was talking to the boys and girls around him. I think that the time has come for the school authorities to be called in, and I'm sure that the situation can be cleared up.

Most veteran teachers probably would not consider this incident an indicator of a serious control problem, but certainly they would agree that it is typical of the kinds of student antics that plague teachers. Other kinds of control problems frequently cited by teachers were listed in the Teacher Problems Checklist in Chapter 2. Some of the control-related problems included:

Maintaining order, quiet, or control.
Responding appropriately to improper behavior such as obscenities.
Soliciting appropriate student behavior.
Controlling aggressive student behavior.
Getting students to use their leisure time well.
Teaching self-discipline.

These statements and the teaching incident that was cited provide some examples of problems with control. You probably have in mind some teaching incidents that you would consider control problems and that have been bothersome to you. Take a moment to identify a few such incidents. As you read the remainder of the chapter, try to apply what you read to the problems you have identified.

How can control be made less of a problem?

Control can be made less of a problem only when teachers are willing to become less controlling or are willing to acquire the attitudes, knowledge, and skills necessary to achieve effective control. Some of the most critical of these attitudes, knowledge, and skills are presented as Five Principles. These Five Principles are:

1. *Pursue goals that are appropriate and important.*
2. *Analyze factors that affect problem situations.*
3. *Use positive techniques for managing behavior.*
4. *Use punishment appropriately and sparingly.*
5. *Teach students to manage their own behavior.*

These Five Principles and the knowledge pertinent to each represent key elements for establishing and maintaining appropriate student behavior. The principles reflect an orientation toward classroom management that is positive, systematic, and sensitive.

One caveat is in order, however. It is important to remember that effective control is not a substitute for appropriate, effective instruction. Focusing efforts on making students behave when instruction is inappropriate is shortsighted and professionally unethical. Research on teacher effectiveness reveals that teachers who neglect instructional preparation or who are obsessed with trying to control behavior tend to end up having more control problems than teachers who are well prepared and who succeed in helping students achieve academically (Brophy and Evertson, 1976). Reducing problems by improving instruction should be a first consideration of teachers. If you haven't done so already, you may want to turn to Chapter 8 at this time and preview the information related to promoting student success. Providing good instruction is critical for making control less of a problem.

FIVE PRINCIPLES THAT CAN MAKE CONTROL LESS OF A PROBLEM

Principle 1: Pursue goals that are appropriate and important. Exercising control, like any aspect of teaching, requires good judgment, and good judgment involves pursuing goals that are appropriate and important. In Step 4 of the problem-solving process (discussed in Chapter 3) you were instructed to value the goals you have selected, that is, to consider whether the goals being pursued are, indeed, appropriate and important.

To avoid being too controlling, modify goal expectations. Many teachers feel compelled to react to inappropriate behavior regardless of the significance of the behavior. Teachers cannot and should not attempt to control every instance of inappropriate behavior. It is impossible to do and only results in teachers' being perceived as overly dominant, petty, and inflexible. As you read the following teaching incident, value the teacher's goals.

> This was the day of the football game to decide whether we won the conference championship outright or tied for it. All of the students were keyed up for the game. It was very difficult to get students to concentrate and be quiet.

How much would you value the goal for students to concentrate and be quiet in this situation? If you consider the goal to be highly important, you should be aware that efforts to achieve student attentiveness will likely require stronger measures than usual and that such efforts tend to promote student resentment. Sometimes teachers make control more of a problem by being too controlling.

One way to be less controlling is to modify goals that

are of marginal importance. For instance, football games to decide conference championships do not occur frequently. They do not pose a continued threat to goal achievement. Rather than exerting a high level of control in an attempt to achieve a goal that is being only temporarily obstructed, teachers might be wiser to consider modifying their goal expectations for this particular day. Instead of requiring complete attention for an entire class period a teacher might offer students ten minutes of discussion time at the end of the class period contingent on a reasonable level of attentiveness during the planned lesson. Such a negotiated solution would likely result in higher productivity and a more positive classroom atmosphere than if the teacher had attempted to achieve her goals at the expense of student goals. Modifying goal expectations can make control less of a problem by allowing a teacher to be less controlling.

Discard goals that interfere with more important goals. In some cases, teachers may find that a goal they are pursuing is interfering with rather than facilitating the achievement of more important goals. Consider the following teaching incident. Is getting students to be quiet the most important goal to pursue?

> I have a problem with my tenth grade English class. I expect the students to come into the room and be quiet when the bell rings. There are a few boys who I have to talk to every day. Their responses are usually something like, "Okay, buddy!" which gets the whole class laughing and really gets to me. I've sent the boys to the office on several occasions but that hasn't worked, and I've kept the whole class for detention, which made the whole class mad at me and made teaching even more difficult. I've lowered the boys' grades and have threatened to call in their parents. I don't know what to do to get them quiet when the bell rings.

Having students become quiet when the bell rings is an appropriate goal, but could it in reality be interfering with the goal of getting students involved in the lesson? Sometimes teachers have difficulty achieving really important goals because they get sidetracked hassling students on behaviors that will likely be resolved anyway once the more important goals are achieved. Sometimes the best antidote for behaviors such as talking and inattentiveness is to launch enthusiastically into the task at hand. Less effort is spent in getting students to be quiet, and more time is available for promoting student interest and involvement—a much more positive focus.

An excellent example of a classroom study in which a teacher acquired improvement in behavior by focusing attention on important behaviors was conducted by Ayllon and Roberts (1974). Instead of focusing attention on the disruptive behavior of students in the fifth grade class, the teacher provided special reinforcement for higher levels of correct responses on academic assignments. Not only did the academic performance of the students improve, but the frequency of their disruptive behavior decreased from a mean of about 45 percent to only 5 percent. The teacher succeeded in acquiring improved student behavior by focusing on ways to improve their academic achievement. The primary goal was shifted from getting students to behave to getting them to achieve.

In summary, it is a measure of good judgment when teachers can avoid being too controlling. This can be accomplished by modifying or discarding goals that are inappropriate and of little importance. Good control begins with the pursuit of appropriate and important goals.

ACTIVITY

1. Describe an example of a control problem you have experienced that probably could have been avoided or minimized if you had changed your goals. What goals would have been more appropriate to pursue?
2. Describe a situation in which a problem likely could have been avoided or minimized if you had negotiated goal expectations

with students. What behavior would you have been willing to accept? What would you have offered in return?

Principle 2: Analyze factors that affect problem situations. Problems can more readily be resolved when teachers analyze problem situations and identify obstacles obstructing goal achievement. It may be helpful to look again at the problem-solving process (Chapter 3) and especially at Step 5, which involves identifying obstacles blocking goal achievement.

Identifying obstacles that block goal achievement is made easier when teachers focus their analysis on (1) the task and expectations for the student, and (2) events that happen before and after the problem occurs.

First, analyze the task and expectations for the students. Analyzing the appropriateness of the task and expectations causes teachers to ask themselves, "Is there anything that I am doing or expecting students to do that is an obstacle to the goals I seek? Were expectations for task involvement and behavior clearly understood? Do students have the ability to perform the task and expected behavior satisfactorily? Can the task be presented more effectively? When the problem is even partly caused by inappropriate expectations and/or ineffective instruction, teachers should direct their efforts first at what they, as teachers, can change before focusing their efforts on changing students. (Again, you are referred to Chapter 8, Student Success, which provides information directed at maximizing student learning). Analyzing the task and expectations to determine their appropriateness should be the first step in analyzing factors that may be contributing to problems.

Analyze events that precede and follow the problem behavior. In addition to analyzing the appropriateness of the task and expectations, teachers will find it useful to identify and analyze events that happen before and after the problem occurs. Teasing by other students, distractions in the hallway, or a new seating arrangement are examples of events that may serve to trigger undesired behavior. Making changes in such events is one way to reduce the probability of the undesired behavior recurring. Events that follow a problem behavior should be analyzed also. Peer laughter, ineffective punishment, and success in delaying working on the lesson assigned are examples of events that may be following and reinforcing undesired behavior. Identification and analysis of events that contribute to a problem require an awareness on the part of the teacher that the behavior of students can be influenced in many different ways. It is the teacher's task to determine these influences so they can be more readily controlled.

A recent article on the management of profanity (Bloom, 1977) provides a good illustration of the importance of analyzing problem situations. Bloom notes that individuals use profanity for a number of different reasons. It may be used to express anger or frustration, to gain attention, to produce embarrassment, or simply as a form of peer-accepted communication. Though teachers probably could stop most occurrences of profanity, at least temporarily, with high-power techniques, the profanity would likely occur again if important factors affecting its use were not considered.

For instance, if a student swears because he is venting frustration over a fifth unsuccessful attempt to solve a critical problem, some teacher supportiveness and understanding seem justified. On the other hand, if a student swears merely to get attention, the attention-seeking student needs to be ignored or possibly punished. In each of these cases, it is helpful to identify the factors affecting the use of the profanity. You can pretty well guess what might result if the frustrated student were punished and no consideration were given to modifying the assignment to promote successful achievement. It should not be surprising if the student were to fly off the handle again under the pressure of continued failure and frustration.

Similarly, teachers who fail to identify circumstances when profanity is being used to get attention may employ techniques that produce undesirable results. Whereas supportive help would be effective in reducing frustration and profanity with the first student, supportiveness with the attention-seeking student would most certainly encourage the use of profanity.

In summary, teachers need to know about the circumstances of the problem in order to select and employ effective techniques to resolve it. They need first to consider the appropriateness of the task and expectations for students. This will help eliminate problem behavior that is due to inappropriate expectations and/or poor teaching. Teachers also need to identify and analyze the events that precede and follow problem behavior in order to be able to select techniques that are least likely to trigger unwanted behavior or to reinforce such behavior. Analysis of problem situations can make control less of a problem for teachers.

ACTIVITY
1. Describe a situation in which your efforts to resolve a problem were unsuccessful because you did not have adequate knowledge of the circumstances involved.
2. Conduct a situational analysis for a control problem that you have experienced. Identify and analyze factors that relate to (1) the appropriateness of the task and expectations for the student or students involved, and (2) the influence of events that preceded and followed the problem. Which factors would you attempt to modify first? Why?

Principle 3: Use positive techniques for managing behavior. Students who are told only what not to do may never learn how teachers expect them to behave. Getting students to behave appropriately is a *constructive* approach, involving teaching and rewarding *desirable* behavior. If students haven't learned to behave appropriately, new patterns of behavior must be taught. If students aren't motivated to behave appropriately, more appropriate consequences for desirable behavior must be arranged.

Catch students being good and reward their behavior. Teachers want to be positive and reward desirable behavior.

Sometimes, however, desirable behavior is not noticed as teachers become consumed in their teaching or become sidetracked by relatively unimportant classroom events. It seems that the only time that many teachers attend to student behavior is when the behavior demands their attention because of its inappropriateness. Desirable behavior is often taken for granted. Teachers come to expect that it will and should occur whether or not it is adequately rewarded.

Rewarding desirable behavior is the foundation, though, for achieving and maintaining good classroom control. Students learn to come to class on time, pay attention to teachers, work quietly, and exhibit a host of other behaviors when these behaviors result in desirable consequences. By rewarding desirable behavior teachers demonstrate that the behavior is valued. Teachers are saying, "I care enough about your behavior to give you recognition for it."

It is not enough, however, just to wait for desirable behavior to happen. Teachers have a responsibility for making it happen by looking for good behavior to reward. In short, teachers need to catch students being *good* and reward this behavior. This is a positive and constructive approach that improves the classroom atmosphere and induces students to respond more positively in return.

Make reinforcement available only for desirable behavior. Sometimes good intentions produce undesirable results when teachers are not aware of which behaviors they are actually reinforcing. Consider the plight of the teacher in the following example, and ask yourself whether reinforcement has really "failed."

> Mickey still cannot take an out-of-book achievement test alone. I had hoped by this time of the year she could concentrate and work alone. It took me so much time to continually encourage her. It really isn't fair that Mickey always gets so much individual attention simply because of the threat of one of her temper tantrums.

The teacher would like to get Mickey to take an out-of-book achievement test alone, and to accomplish this the teacher has provided Mickey with quite a bit of encouragement and individual attention. The result, however, seems to be no improvement in working alone and no reduction in temper tantrums or threat of them. But before you conclude that reinforcement has failed, take a second look at when the rewards (encouragement and individual attention) were provided. The rewards were provided when Mickey threatened to throw one of her temper tantrums. Reinforcement did not fail! It succeeded! Unfortunately, it succeeded in strengthening the wrong behavior.

Reinforcement can work to the teacher's advantage if it is used when *desirable* behavior is being demonstrated. It must not be given during or as a response to behavior that is undesirable. Teachers must be alert to the student behaviors they are reinforcing.

Ignore attention-seeking behavior and reinforce alternative desirable behavior. Teachers do need to take action when inappropriate behavior occurs, but sometimes the best action is withholding or removing the reinforcement that is maintaining the behavior. As in the incident involving Mickey, teacher attention often serves to encourage temper tantrums, whining, or other attention-seeking behaviors. When it is the teacher's attention that is reinforcing the inappropriate behavior, teachers must make a concerted effort to ignore that behavior and find some other desirable behavior to reinforce.

One of the best illustrations of this principle is reported in a study by Madsen, Becker, Thomas, Koser, and Plager (1968). In this study, observers recorded the number of occasions that students were out of their seats and the number of "Sit down" commands given by the teacher. Results clearly demonstrated that the use of the command "Sit down" led to an *increase* of students' being out of their seats rather than to a decrease. Teacher attention was reinforcing the inappropriate behavior. However, when teachers were instructed to ignore students who were out of their seats and reinforce students who were seated, the amount of out-of-seat behavior decreased.

Ignoring attention-seeking behavior is difficult to do. The behavior seems to demand attention. Three things can be done to maximize success when dealing with attention-seeking behavior. First, make sure that you are consistent in your efforts to ignore the behavior. Students will expect you to "give in" and provide the reinforcement (attention) that you had provided when they behaved inappropriately before. Their behavior will probably get worse before it gets better. During this time, especially, you must ignore the behavior consistently so students will realize that only appropriate behavior will result in reinforcement.

The second thing that can be done to make ignoring more effective is to supplement it with reinforcement for desirable behavior. In other words, direct your attention to something the student or other students are doing that is desired. Combining reinforcement with ignoring is important because students realize they don't have to behave inappropriately to get the teacher's attention.

A third thing that can be done to make ignoring easier to accomplish is to involve class members in ignoring misbehavior. Some of the most difficult control problems are those in which inappropriate behavior is being reinforced by students. This is especially true at the junior and senior high levels when peers usually exert much stronger influence than teachers. Teachers can use peer pressure as a resource rather than fight it. At a very simple level this may involve an appeal for cooperation. For example, teachers might comment that students can be a big help in keeping another student from failing if they stop providing attention to the student's misbehavior. Cooperation from students might be made a little more worthwhile by providing some kind of incentive such as earning time at the end of the lesson to tell jokes, read riddles, or play a short game when inappropriate behavior is ignored. The time length for the class to earn reinforcement should be short at first, to assure that even small improvement in peer ignoring is amply rewarded.

Of course not all behaviors can or should be ignored. Behaviors that can result in injury, destruction of property, or hurt feelings should not be ignored even if they are being used to gain teacher attention. These behaviors need to be dealt with quickly and firmly. Ignoring attention-seeking behavior and reinforcing alternative desirable behaviors are positive and effective techniques best suited for promoting long-range, durable changes in behavior.

ACTIVITY
1. Describe a situation in which your attention to misbehavior served to maintain or encourage that behavior. What desirable behavior(s) could you have switched your attention to?
2. Think of an undesirable student behavior that is being reinforced by students in the class. Describe how you could get the class to pay less attention to it. What could you make available to the class to make their cooperation worth while? How will you structure the situation so that even a small effort in student cooperation will be rewarded?

Make sure that rewards for desirable behavior are indeed rewarding. Sometimes teachers aren't aware of the reinforcing (or punishing) value of the consequences they use. As a result, efforts to improve behavior sometimes fail. For example, a student approached a teacher to announce that he had just completed the assigned seat-work papers. The student was probably proud of the fact that he was first in the class to finish. When presented with the papers, the teacher praised the student for finishing his work and then proceeded to assign him additional work. The student might have enjoyed the teacher's praise, but by the look on his face it was unlikely that he considered the additional work much of a reward. It would not be surprising to find him working a little more slowly the next day. Additional work may be rewarding to some students and stimulate them to be more productive, but it may have the opposite effect on other students and encourage them to produce less.

Reinforcement will work only when the rewards that are provided are truly rewarding. Grades and teacher praise may be valued by some students and not by others. If teachers assume they always know what is rewarding without evaluating the effects of the rewards, reinforcement will be limited in its effectiveness.

How can a teacher know whether a particular reward will be rewarding to a certain student or group of students? Perhaps the best way is to involve students in selecting the rewards. Ask students what they would like to do when they finish their work. Observe what students do when they have some free time. Do they sit and talk? Do they bring a radio or engage in a game of some kind? Make a list of the things that may be possible reinforcers and then have students select those they would like to have made available. If the rewards work in producing a desired change in behavior, continue them. If they don't work, try new ones. The ultimate test of whether a reward is indeed rewarding is its ability to produce desired behavior.

Teachers have a variety of rewards that can be made available to students; they may be tangible, activity, social, or intrinsic. *Tangible* rewards include coloring books, small games, pencils, combs, cosmetics, records, raisins, puzzles, and other "things" that can be given. Such rewards may be especially effective for students who are young and/or come from homes where such items may not be readily available. The use of tangible rewards is especially important for students who do not respond to other forms of reinforcement.

Sometimes tokens are used to reward students. Tokens may consist of slips of paper, poker chips, straws, smile face cutouts, or checkmarks. These serve as a record-keeping system to show the amount of reward earned by certain students or the entire class. Tokens are convenient in that they can be given with little or no interruption of instruction. Since students are told the tokens may be exchanged for specific rewards at a later time, the tokens take on the reinforcing value of the actual reward.

A token system is flexible in that the amount and frequency of reinforcement can be easily adjusted. As students engage more regularly in the desired behavior, tokens can be given less frequently. Also, the exchange value of the tokens can be adjusted to require more work or higher levels of wanted behavior for the same amount of reinforcement.

A second kind of reward is *activity* rewards. These include games or activities that students enjoy. They may be activities that are just for fun or may incorporate some aspect of learning. Students of all ages enjoy a short game such as Hangman or a chance to solve riddles or tell jokes at the end of a period of work. Such activity rewards take only a few minutes yet they make school work much more enjoyable.

Many teachers make their instructional schedules work to their advantage by planning the sequence of instruction so that highly desired activities immediately follow the more tedious and/or less interesting ones. Students have something desirable to look forward to which serves as an incentive to complete the less enjoyable assignments. The key to the effective use of activity rewards (as well as any reward) is to provide them only *after* the desired behavior or task has been performed. If rewards are offered before the behavior is demonstrated there is less incentive to perform the wanted behavior.

A third kind of reward is *social* rewards such as a pat on the shoulder, praise, a smile or wink, and so forth. Social rewards can be very effective for changing behavior. Care must be taken, however, that these rewards are not misused. When recognition is given in a perfunctory manner or in a manner that results in embarrassment to the student, the recognition loses its rewarding value. Inappropriately delivered recognition may even cause students to reduce desirable behavior in order to avoid recognition and possible embarrassment. Rewards must be given sincerely and in a manner that will make them appreciated.

The fourth kind of reward is *intrinsic* rewards. When a task is engaged in that produces pleasure because of the nature of the task itself, it is said to be intrinsically reinforcing. For example, reading is intrinsically reinforcing to people who enjoy reading. Likewise, academic achievement is intrinsically rewarding when it results in feelings of mastery and success. Since success is often such a potent reinforcer, teachers should find ways to help students experience success for desirable behavior. Sometimes improvement in behavior is so gradual that students fail to feel successful even when they are succeeding. A simple and effective technique for helping students recognize and thus experience success is to have them keep progress charts of their behavior. On these progress charts they can record, for example, the number of homework assignments turned in on time, the number of times they were on time to class, or the number of class periods in which they did not have to be reminded to stop talking.

An advantage of progress charts is that they provide a visual picture of progress over time. Even if progress is only slowly being achieved, a visual inspection of the chart will provide a measure of satisfaction that behavior is indeed changing for the better. Unless a record of progress is kept, students as well as teachers may fail to recognize success when it is demonstrated, and thus potent intrinsic reinforcement is lost.

ACTIVITY
1. If you were to ask your students to list examples of tangible, activity, and social rewards they would like to have made available, what do you think they would list? Which of these would you be willing to offer?
2. Describe how you would introduce the use of progress charts with a student or an entire class. What would the progress chart look like? How would progress be recorded on the chart?

Accept small amounts of progress. Teachers need to be realistic and accept the fact that durable changes in behavior will take time to achieve. Students who have made it a habit to "forget" to do their homework, for example, will be difficult to change. Inappropriate behaviors have paid off for them in the past, and it will take time for them to learn that the behaviors will no longer be rewarded. Teachers will be less frustrated in their attempts to change behavior when only small amounts of change are required and expected. *Think small.* Remember the key is to have students feel good about change. Expecting small amounts of change provides greater opportunities for success and fewer possibilities for frustration and failure.

Use reinforcement consistently to develop behavior but only intermittently to maintain it. As has been said before, consistency is a good teacher. Consistency in reinforcing behavior helps students understand more quickly which behaviors are desired and which are not. Consistent reinforcement is especially needed when new behaviors are being formed. Consistency is also important when desired behavior has to compete with inappropriate behavior that is strongly reinforced. Students will give up their "old ways" only when it is evident that new behaviors will be equally or more rewarding. The more consistent the rewards, the more quickly the students are likely to associate the cause-and-effect relationships and engage in the behaviors teachers want to see.

However, once a behavior has been learned, only occasional reinforcement is needed to assure that it will continue to be performed. Provide just enough reinforcement to let students know the behavior is still valued. Then, gradually, reduce the frequency of reinforcement so students become less dependent on it. If the desired behavior starts to become erratic and/or decrease, provide increased reinforcement until the behavior stabilizes. Then resume gradual withdrawal of the reinforcement.

One other important point. Students have good and bad

days, and a wise teacher will adjust the amount of reinforcement accordingly. When students are having a bad day, this is the time to *increase* reinforcement for desirable behavior. Typically, teachers tend to bear down harder when student behavior is less than is expected. But think for a moment how you feel when you are having a bad day and someone starts finding fault with you. You probably feel worse and somewhat antagonistic. Students react the same way. Though it's easy to become fixed on inappropriate behavior, you should make a special effort to find *appropriate* things that students do and to give *more* reinforcement for these behaviors.

ACTIVITY
Think of a control problem that occurs fairly frequently. Does the problem continue because the desirable behavior has not been reinforced consistently? Was the amount of reinforcement reduced too quickly?

Model or have someone else model the behavior you want. Another positive technique for managing behavior is modeling. Much of human behavior is learned by observing others. Our selection of clothes and hairstyles, our language and eating habits, our mannerisms, and numerous other behaviors are influenced by observing other people. As Bandura (1977) states, "The capacity to learn by observation enables people to acquire large, integrated patterns of behavior without having to form them gradually by tedious trial and error." In short, observing others is an efficient way to learn new behavior.

Students are most likely to observe and imitate individuals perceived as prestigious and successful. Since teachers are often viewed as prestigious, especially by younger students, it is important that teachers be models of the kind of behavior they expect to see in students. By observing how teachers act, students can learn to behave calmly and analytically when solving problems, or they can learn to react aggressively and impulsively. How do you react to problems? Teacher influence as a model of behavior cannot be taken lightly.

Of course teachers are not the only individuals whose behavior influences students. Students acquire new behavior by observing other students, especially students who are highly esteemed because of leadership status, athletic ability, or other such factors. Since appropriate as well as inappropriate behavior may be learned by imitation, it is important for teachers to find ways to strongly reward desirable behavior of students who are likely to be imitated.

ACTIVITY
1. Which students in your class are highly esteemed by other students? Describe how you capitalize on the positive impact of esteemed students. Can you use their influence to better advantage? If so, how?
2. Evaluate the impact that your behavior has on students. What kind of behavior do you display that you hope students will imitate? What kind of behavior do students observe you use that you wish they didn't?

Modify tasks and use "active listening" to defuse frustration-related behavior. Sometimes control problems erupt when students become frustrated and vent their frustrations in ways that teachers find inappropriate. The use of profanity or obscenities is an example. A typical reaction to such behavior is for teachers to scold the offending student and to issue a warning not to let the remarks be heard again. If the reprimand is strong enough it may succeed in suppressing the student's behavior, but punishment does little to reduce the frustration that triggered the remarks. Teachers need to be concerned about removing the source of frustration if the problem behavior is to be effectively controlled.

Teachers can do two things to defuse and perhaps even resolve frustration-related problems. First, it would be wise to take some action to modify the task or expectations that may be causing the frustration. Second, teachers can communicate with the student in a supportive rather than an accusatory or threatening manner. A teacher might say something like,

"Tom, you sound upset about something." This lets Tom know that the teacher is not going to start out by scolding him. He knows his feelings are being recognized. The teacher's statement prompts the student to clarify the problem, thus giving the teacher more information to make better decisions.

The process of restating or feeding back what the student is saying or appears to be feeling is what Gordon (1974) terms "active listening." The purpose of active listening is to acquire accurate information about the real source of the student's concern. As the teacher restates, or feeds back, what he or she perceives is bothering the student, the student has an opportunity to clarify the problem. Active listening serves to defuse frustration because the teacher can respond more accurately to the student's real concern, and the student is reassured that the teacher understands the reason underlying the frustration.

Active listening is not likely to be an effective technique for students who are misbehaving to get the teacher's attention, however. Attention-seeking behavior would only be encouraged by such teacher supportiveness. (Remember the incident of Mickey, whose temper tantrums were reinforced by teacher attention?) Teachers might expect some continuance of the unwanted behavior when active listening is employed, but if the supportive comments seem to be prolonging the misbehavior, then teachers should adopt more direct, and probably stronger, techniques for reducing the problem. Active listening is most likely to be successful when the inappropriate behavior is truly frustration related and the student is willing to respond to supportive attempts to reduce the frustration.

Use group discussions to generate solutions to problems. Teachers want students to be problem solvers, and one technique that is useful for teaching and practicing problem solving is the Classroom Meeting described by Glasser (1969). The Classroom Meeting provides a forum in which problems are raised either by the teacher or by class members. The meeting has a nonevaluative focus to promote open thinking about problems and their solution. The teacher serves as a facilitator to assure that comments are kept positive and the discussion is directed toward analyzing the problem and generating possible solutions. All participants in the meeting may ask questions about the problem and express what they think might be possible solutions. The decision of what to do about the problem, however, is left to the individual or individuals who own the problem.

It takes time for problem-solving discussions to produce results. The process cannot be rushed without compromising the commitment that students can learn to assume responsibility for solving problems and need to be given the opportunity to do so. Adequate time should be set aside for problem solving. Problem-solving discussions require an atmosphere of trust, and it is, therefore, important that teachers not engage in the process unless students can be supportive of one another. In order to be prepared to participate in a positive and constructive manner, students need to acquire skill in critically analyzing problems and in suggesting and evaluating solutions that may be adopted. The focus must be on what can be done to resolve a problem rather than who is at fault.

Some teachers find it helpful to follow a step-by-step problem-solving process such as the one suggested in Chapter 3. In such a process the problem is identified, goals are valued, factors influencing the situation are analyzed, solutions are thought of and selected, and plans are made to implement and evaluate the effectiveness of the chosen solutions.

Problem-solving discussions can be a very effective means for reducing control problems and for teaching students how to be problem solvers. Teachers must be willing, however, to spend the time that is needed to engage in thoughtful problem solving and to prepare students to engage constructively in analyzing and finding solutions to problems.

Teach proactively to prevent problems from occurring or getting worse. A series of classroom studies conducted by Kounin (1970) and his colleagues provides important information concerning the prevention of undesirable behavior. Kounin found that the way teachers acted before problems had a chance to occur or get worse seemed to be more important than what teachers did in response to the problem. In other words, "proactive" teaching—teaching in a way that makes problems less likely to occur—is extremely important for achieving and maintaining good classroom control.

Kounin identified eight teacher behaviors that were significantly related to effective classroom control. Two of the behaviors were termed *withitness* and *overlappingness*. Withitness refers to the ability of teachers to know what is going on in the classroom and to react to initiators of the deviant behavior and not to onlookers or students drawn into the problem. Teachers who demonstrate withitness react quickly to keep problems from spreading and getting worse.

Closely associated with this ability is the ability to handle more than one situation at the same time. Kounin referred to this as overlappingness. For example, teachers who have reading groups or who are engaged in individual instruction must, at the same time, be able to handle disruptions involving other members of the class. Control is less of a problem for teachers who are able to resolve disruptions while maintaining work involvement among other students in the class.

Two other teacher behaviors that appear to relate to classroom management are *smoothness* and *momentum*. Students have less opportunity to engage in inappropriate behavior when teachers maintain a smooth, uninterrupted flow of academic events. Conversely, teachers invite control problems when they lose momentum by straying off the subject, interrupting students who have begun working, or jumping back and forth from one activity to another. In addition, spending too much time on minor points invites boredom and tempts students to engage in more "interesting" behavior.

Group alerting and *accountability* were also found to be related to effective classroom management. It seems that fewer problems arise when teachers maintain a high level of student involvement. Alerting students that an important question is about to be asked and asking frequent questions helps keep students alert and involved. Having students hold up and show their answers or recite answers in unison, and similar techniques help students feel accountable for attending carefully to the lesson.

Finally, teachers who are able to build *challenge arousal* and *variety* into their instruction have a better chance of reducing control problems. Challenging statements such as "This problem is a real brain jogger" frequently can be used to stimulate enthusiasm and interest. Variety in the kinds of tasks assigned, in levels of student responsibility required, and in patterns of presentation also promote interest and reduce the inclination for students to engage in unwanted behavior.

ACTIVITY
Read the following incident and think about the eight teacher behaviors that Kounin identified as relating to control.

> My students are working on research papers this month and today we spent the period in the library. I try to give each student individual help while in the libary and I become involved in what I'm doing. During the library period four students slipped back to the classroom and started pitching pennies. The principal caught them and took them to his office for punishment. The incident really embarrassed me.
>
> Which of the eight behaviors listed by Kounin do you think the teacher lacked? What specific recommendations would you make to this teacher? Which of Kounin's behaviors do you need to work on?

In summary, teachers have available a variety of positive management techniques for achieving and maintaining effective control. Positive management techniques are those that cause teachers to focus on desirable behavior and to teach in ways that make problems less likely to occur. Teachers who use positive management techniques try to catch students being good and reward their behavior. The focus is on what students are doing that is appropriate. In strengthening desirable behavior, teachers will likely use a combination of tangible, activity, social, and intrinsic rewards. The key to effective reinforcement is selecting rewards that are desired and structuring their use to have the maximum effect. Rewards must be made available only for desirable behavior and must be presented in a systematic manner so students learn which behaviors are wanted.

Positive management techniques often produce more durable changes in behavior than is accomplished with punishment. Durable changes, however, are not attained instantly. Teachers must be willing to give positive techniques a chance to work. Teachers and students will be less frustrated when gradual changes in behavior are expected.

Providing rewards for desirable behavior is not the only way to achieve desirable behavior. Teachers also need to know how to engage students in problem solving using techniques such as Glasser's Classroom Meeting. Students can and need to learn problem solving. Teachers should also be able to respond effectively to frustration-related behavior. Techniques such as Gordon's active listening provide teachers with a means for being supportive and for acquiring clues for reducing the source of the frustration. Finally, positive management involves prevention. Teachers will have fewer problems to deal with when they provide appropriate and interesting instruction, maintain student involvement, and respond quickly, accurately, and sensitively to behavior problems that arise.

Positive management techniques provide teachers with highly constructive and effective measures for strengthening desirable behavior and reducing behavior that is unwanted. Because of their effectiveness and likelihood for avoiding adverse side effects, positive management techniques should be first-choice techniques for managing behavior.

Principle 4: Use punishment appropriately and sparingly. It is not always possible to prevent unwanted behavior from occurring or to control it with positive management techniques.

Students will get into fights, call each other names, refuse to do assignments, goof off, interrupt instruction, and engage in many other unwanted behaviors in spite of teachers' efforts to focus on desirable behavior. When punishment is used, however, techniques should be employed that are least likely to produce adverse side effects. In other words, punishment must be effective but it must not be overly aversive. How much punishment to use and how to use it are very important questions for teachers to consider.

Use as little punishment as possible but enough to be effective. Teachers do not do themselves or their students any favor by meting out punishment that doesn't work. Using punishment that is too mild to have the desired effect only serves to prolong the unwanted behavior. Students become hardened to its use, causing teachers to become frustrated and turn to stronger and more aversive measures. When punishment is deemed necessary, it should be administered in an amount sufficient to stop or reduce the behavior quickly.

On the other hand, using punishment that is too strong can also cause problems. Strong punishment is more likely to cause student resentment and alienation. In some cases, its use may lead to more open or higher levels of belligerence. At the minimum, strong punishment creates tension in the learning environment and makes it more difficult for students and teachers to interact thoughtfully in the learning activities.

There are two things that a teacher needs to keep in mind when determining the amount of punishment to use. First, consider what is known about the individual(s)' past responses to punishment. How much and what kind of punishment seemed to work? Whereas a teacher's frown may be a devastasting punishment to a student who craves the teacher's attention, another student may respond to such a technique with a chuckle of amusement. Punishment, like reinforcement, will vary in its effects among individuals. Knowing what has worked and what has not worked in the past provides important clues as to the amount and kind of punishment that is likely to be effective again.

Second, consider the conditions that may be causing the behavior to continue. If the unwanted behavior is being maintained by strong reinforcement, then strong punishment will probably be needed to change the behavior. If the behavior is to be changed, the cost of engaging in the behavior must be more than the benefit.

Selecting the right amount of punishment depends, then, on the individual being punished and the conditions that are maintaining the unwanted behavior. There are dangers in using too much or too little punishment. Teachers must try to use as little punishment as possible but enough to be effective.

Make punishment informative. If punishment is to have an optimal effect in changing behavior, it has to be more than just an unpleasant consequence for behaving inappropriately. Students must know what behaviors are being punished and what alternative behaviors are wanted. A statement such as "John, your talking is keeping other students from doing good work" is more informative than "John, stop it!" Hearing the first statement, John does not have to guess that his talking is the problem. Punishment is made even more constructive when students are told what behaviors are desired. Does John know, for example, what to do when he can't work a problem, is unable to find resource materials, or is bothered by another student? Many times teachers erroneously assume that students know or can figure out the appropriate alternative behaviors. It is important to inform students which behaviors are inappropriate and which are wanted.

Administer punishment soon after the misbehavior occurs. Punishing an inappropriate behavior soon after it occurs helps to minimize any reward that may be produced by the behavior. Remember that students usually behave the way they do because they find it rewarding to do so. For instance, the class clown enjoys the attention that he gets from other students and the teacher. It makes sense, then, that if punishment is to be used to stop the clowning, it should be used before the student has achieved enough satisfaction to make the clowning worth the consequences. The more satisfaction that a behavior produces the more punishment will be needed to stop the behavior. Punishing a behavior soon after it occurs makes it easier to change the behavior with the least amount of punishment.

Be consistent in the use of punishment. Students will stop using unwanted behavior more quickly once they realize punishment will predictably follow. Inconsistent use of punishment encourages students to gamble that they will escape being punished. Teachers who are inconsistent in punishing a certain behavior will likely be plagued with that behavior until they are consistent.

Remove or withhold privileges as a punishment rather than inflict verbal or physical hurt. While punishment is meant to be unpleasant, there are some techniques that are especially aversive and should not be used for any reason. Humiliating, intimidating, and striking students are forms of punishment that should be avoided. These strong measures often result in high levels of resentment and hurt. Their ultimate costs in student alienation from teachers and the school are too high to justify their use.

Fortunately, there are less aversive and more effective punishment techniques that can be used. Two of them, time out and response cost, are of special merit because they reduce unwanted behavior by removing or withholding privileges rather than inflicting something unpleasant.

Time out is a technique in which an individual is removed from a rewarding situation. Sending a student to work in a corner of the room or to the principal's office are examples. It is important, of course, that wherever the student is sent there are no opportunities to be rewarded for the inappropriate behavior. If it was attention that the student was seeking, the student should be situated so that other students can no longer respond to his antics. If the attention-seeking student is sent to the office, the secretary or principal should be informed of the problem behavior so the student will not receive reinforcement for that behavior in the office.

For this to be effective, the duration of time out should be relatively short. Long periods of isolation tend to increase resentment and cause students to fall behind in their work. Return students to the regular activities soon after they display appropriate behavior or after a specified amount of time has elapsed. When a student is returned, be sure to find some appropriate behavior to reinforce to let the student know what kind of behavior can result in positive consequences and to let him know that you are willing to make good things happen when desirable behavior is demonstrated.

It is usually a good idea to hold students accountable for work assigned while they are in time out so they realize it is not a "vacation" from their assigned tasks. Students may be requested to complete the missed work on their own time or at home. It would probably not be a good idea, though, to request this work to be done during a fun time since the student has already been punished for the misbehavior. Additional exclusion would prevent the student from engaging in social interactions in which desirable behavior can be practiced and reinforced.

The other form of punishment that is positive in nature is response cost. The technique is very simple: when a student engages in misbehavior, a cost is charged for that behavior. For example, a teacher may announce that two minutes of free activity time will be deducted for every thirty seconds of instructional time wasted while students settle down. The more serious the misbehavior, the greater the cost. Since students can't be charged for something they don't have, however, response cost is only effective when rewards and privileges are available.

An advantage of response cost is that students often

perceive it as a logical and sensible consequence for misbehavior. Misbehavior has its costs. Though it is a mild form of punishment, it is often very effective in reducing inappropriate behavior.

Combine positive reinforcement with punishment. Perhaps the most important thing that teachers can do to make use of punishment more effective is to supplement it with positive reinforcement. Combining reinforcement with punishment makes punishment less aversive and less necessary. The effectiveness of combining these techniques is well illustrated in a study involving stealing reported by Switzer, Deal, and Bailey (1977).

Teachers in three second-grade classes had tried lecturing as a means for reducing stealing of items such as money, Magic Markers, erasers, felt tip pens, and gum. Lecturing, however, failed to produce any improvement. Teachers were then instructed to use a combination of reinforcement and punishment. Students could earn ten minutes of free time when no items were missing from the room. If it was noticed that items were missing, students were given an opportunity to avoid punishment by returning the items while the teacher left the room for a short time. Failure to return the missing items resulted in punishment of having students remain quiet during snack time. The reinforcement-punishment combination was highly effective in almost eliminating stealing.

Combining reinforcement with punishment is effective probably because the emphasis is on promoting desirable behavior rather than on punishing inappropriate behavior. It is clear from the techniques used in the study that the main concern was getting students to not steal and to return items that were stolen, both desirable behaviors. The focus on desirable behavior allowed teachers to use low-power, positive-oriented techniques. Punishment was *not* the sole alternative open to students. They could also receive reinforcement by not stealing or by returning stolen items. Combining reinforcement with punishment will likely produce less student resentment and be far more effective than punishment used alone.

In summary, most teachers want to be more positive and use less punishment in managing behavior. They know punishment is not constructive and that it makes teaching less enjoyable and less productive. Teachers continue to rely on punishment, though, for three reasons. First, punishment often succeeds in rapidly stopping or reducing unwanted behavior. Though the effects may be only temporary, teachers see punishment work and are more likely to use it again. A second reason why teachers continue to use punishment is that they rarely notice the side effects that result. Side effects may be long delayed or may be associated with other events, so that teachers are often unaware that the reactions are the result of punishment. Finally, teachers continue to use punishment because they have never learned what else they can do to manage unwanted behavior.

You are no longer in the position of *having* to use strong or frequent punishment to manage behavior. You are aware of how to use punishment appropriately so only small amounts of it are necessary to produce desired behavior. Appropriate use of punishment includes using punishment that works, using only as much as is needed, and informing students what behavior is being punished and what would be considered acceptable. The appropriate use of punishment also includes administering punishment soon after the misbehavior occurs and doing so consistently so students associate the consequences with their behavior. Finally, techniques should be employed that are least likely to produce adverse side effects. Time out and response cost are two techniques that reduce misbehavior by removing or withholding privileges rather than by inflicting verbal or physical hurt. Combining reinforcement with punishment is another way to make punishment less aversive. When teachers use punishment appropriately, they will also find they are using it effectively and less often.

ACTIVITY

Think of a situation in which you used some form of punishment. Analyze the appropriateness of its use by answering the following questions:

	YES	NO
1. Was the punishment effective in stopping the unwanted behavior?	___	___
2. Were serious side effects avoided?	___	___
3. Was it clear to students what behavior was punished and what would be acceptable?	___	___
4. Was the punishment administered soon after the unwanted behavior occurred?	___	___
5. Have repeated occurrences of the behavior been punished consistently?	___	___
6. Did the punishment consist of removing or withholding privileges rather than inflicting hurtful consequences?	___	___
7. Was reinforcement for desirable behavior included with the use of punishment?	___	___

Describe any changes that could be made to make the use of the punishment more appropriate and effective.

Principle 5: Teach students to manage their own behavior.

Teachers are expected not only to exert control but to teach students to use self-control. Self-control is a commonly shared goal among teachers, school administrators, parents, and the community. When people speak of self-control they are usually referring to students' behaving appropriately in the absence of external control and taking responsibility for managing their own behavior. Both of these are worthy goals which can and should be taught.

Teach cause-and-effect relationships. Students acquire self-control by learning to predict the consequences of their behavior. The more quickly students learn to predict which behaviors tend to result in pleasant consequences and which in unpleasant ones, the more quickly they will learn to control their behavior to acquire or avoid these consequences.

Teachers can do a number of things to help students learn the probable effects of behavior. First, teachers can be consistent in rewarding and punishing particular behaviors, so that students can associate behaviors with their respective consequences. Second, teachers can draw attention to rewarded and punished behaviors. Students do not have to experience cause-and-effect relationships to learn from them. Observing others receiving rewards or punishments or hearing about what happens as a consequence of behavior is a frequent and much less painful way to learn.

A third thing that teachers can do to help students understand cause-and-effect relationships is to make sure that consequences of behavior are clear and effective. Obviously, students won't learn the desired cause and effect if the effect is unclear or unimportant to them. Analyze the effectiveness of rewards and punishments you use, and if they aren't producing the behavior you want, try different consequences.

Teach students to recognize when desirable behavior is required. Just as parents teach children that receiving a gift is a cue for the child to say "Thank you," so too can teachers help students recognize and respond to cues for desired behavior. Students can be taught that calling on a student to speak is a cue for other students to lower their hands until the student has finished talking. Giving directions is a cue to listen. Clowning around by a student is a cue to ignore the student and continue working.

An interesting study by Levine (1973) demonstrated that students do look for and use cues to determine how and when to behave. As a matter of fact, Levine concluded that what teachers perceive as self-control may often be little more than alert student attention to cues on how and when to behave in certain ways. Of the three kindergarten children observed in the study, two had been identified by the teacher as lacking self-control. The other child was rated as having self-control. However, in actual observation it was discovered that the self-controlled child demonstrated just as much misbehavior as the other two children but displayed it less when the teacher was facing him and more when the teacher was facing away! In addition, the self-controlled child glanced at the teacher twice as often as did the other children. Apparently, students do look for and profit from cues that signal when a particular behavior is likely to be punished or rewarded. It is the teacher's task to teach and draw attention to those cues that signal when appropriate behavior is required.

Teach students to evaluate their behavior. Learning self-control also requires skill in self-evaluation. Students cannot change their behavior unless they are aware that this behavior creates a problem. Teachers often try to make students aware of their problems with comments such as, "Bobby, sit down! Jenny, you forgot your pencil again today! Brad, I'm not going to warn you again. For the tenth time, stop talking!" Teachers often label these comments as informative feedback. Students probably consider the comments something quite different.

There is a better way for students to become aware of their behavior: let them monitor and evaluate it themselves. This is commonly referred to as *self-recording.* The easiest method of self-recording is to have students keep track of how often the problem behavior—or, taking a positive focus, the desired behavior—occurs. Name calling, completing assignments on time, asking to have directions repeated, and talking without permission are examples of positive and negative behaviors that students can monitor and record themselves.

Students can record the frequency of their behavior by placing tally marks on a sheet of paper or by placing checkmarks on a progress chart such as the example shown in Figure 6-1.

Progress charts are especially helpful because they provide a visual picture of how often a behavior has occurred and students can tell at a glance whether their behavior is becoming more or less of a problem. Teachers do not have to nag students to make them aware of lack of progress. Teachers thus have more time to help students decide *what to do* about their

FIGURE 6-1. From *ABC's for Teachers* by E. B. Rettig and T. L. Paulson. Copyright 1975 by Associates for Behavior Change.

ABC Behavior Record

Target Behavior No. 1: <u>Ann's complaints of other peers' behavior.</u>

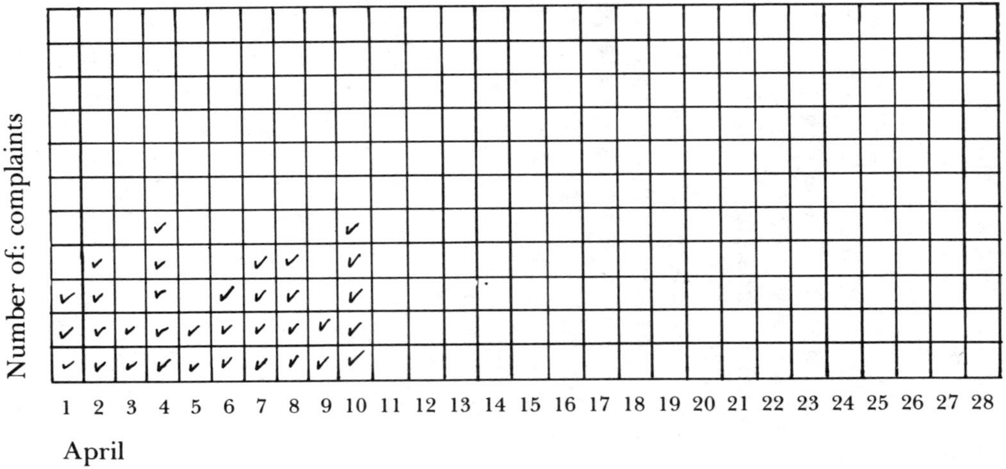

One check equals one occurrence of the behavior.

Number of: complaints

April 1 2 3 4 5 6 7 8 9 10 11 12 13 14 15 16 17 18 19 20 21 22 23 24 25 26 27 28

147

problems rather than trying to convince them they have a problem.

Accuracy in self-recording is important, of course, if the technique is going to be helpful in evaluating behavior. Sometimes students are tempted to be dishonest, either because they are eager to please the teacher or to acquire rewards that might be available for desirable behavior. Fortunately, dishonest self-recording is fairly easy to remedy. Accurate self-recording can be enhanced by providing bonus rewards when student recordings closely match those made by the teacher. Making self-recording a privilege entrusted to students who demonstrate accurate self-recording is another way to promote honesty and accuracy. Finally, students will realize that self-recording is only a means for evaluating change in behavior when rewards are provided only for actual improvement in behavior.

Teach students to problem-solve. Being aware of a problem is only a first step in self-management, however. Students need to learn, also, how to engage in a process for changing behaviors they wish to change. Students need to know how to analyze problem situations and to generate, select, and plan strategies to bring about the desired changes. In short, students need to learn to problem solve. The problem-solving process that was presented for resolving teaching problems in Chapter 3 involves the same steps students can be taught to use. The problem-solving steps can be introduced and practiced through the use of class discussion and role playing.

All of the problem-solving steps do not have to be taught at the same time. Each step in the process is a worthy element of learning even by itself. Teaching problem solving is similar to other forms of long-range teaching in which teachers work at the students' particular level of sophistication. As students mature and acquire new potential for solving more complex problems, additional instruction and opportunities to practice problem solving are provided.

In summary, teaching students self-control includes the

goals of having students behave appropriately in the absence of external control and having students assume greater responsibility for managing their own behavior. Self-control can be improved when students learn that behavior has predictable consequences and can be controlled to make good things happen. Self-control can be improved also when students learn to recognize and respond to cues that signal when and how to behave. Finally, students improve in self-control when they learn to evaluate their behavior and to engage in problem solving to achieve goals they have set for themselves.

ACTIVITY
1. Describe how you could employ the techniques discussed in the section on teaching cause-and-effect relationships to help students better predict consequences of their behavior.
2. Think of a behavior you would like a particular student to assume greater responsibility for controlling. Describe how you would introduce the use of self-recording to help the student evaluate the behavior. Describe how you would teach and involve the student in the problem-solving process described in Chapter 3.

SUMMARY AND CONCLUSION

Teachers strive to establish environments in which they and students can interact in an orderly manner. Teachers realize that school administrators, parents, and other community members expect students to be controlled and to learn self-control. Equally important, teachers believe that school experiences can be far more productive and enjoyable when students behave appropriately. Thus, achieving effective control is an important concern of teachers.

Five Principles were described in this chapter that can make control less of a concern for teachers. The Principles represent the attitudes, knowledge, and skills that appear to be most related to achieving and maintaining effective control.

The information presented can best be viewed as guidelines for decision making. There are no recipes or techniques specified to solve specific problems. As you have probably already concluded, the process for achieving and maintaining control is too complex for that. Control, just like teaching, involves a process in which knowledge must be applied in context-specific situations. It is believed that the following Five Principles provide teachers with the most useful knowledge for engaging in that process.

1. *Pursue goals that are appropriate and important.* One way to make control less of a problem is to make sure your goals are reasonable. Evaluate your goals and pursue only those that are important.
2. *Analyze factors that affect problem situations.* The more you know about the circumstances of a problem, the more likely you will select and employ effective techniques to resolve it. Take time to analyze conditions and events that may affect problem behavior.
3. *Use positive techniques for managing behavior.* Behavior management is basically a constructive process. Structure the learning environment to make desirable behavior likely to occur. Then, look for and reward desirable behavior.
4. *Use punishment appropriately and sparingly.* When punishment must be used, use as little as possible but enough to be effective. Its appropriate use will result in less need to use it again.
5. *Teach students to manage their own behavior.* Teach students how to achieve self-control. As they assume greater responsibility for their behavior, control will be less of a problem for you.

One point needs to be emphasized. Don't be too controlling. Seek reasonable control. It is a lot easier to achieve and less stressful on you and students as well.

RELATED READINGS

Ayllon, T., and M. Roberts. "Eliminating Discipline Problems by Strengthening Academic Performance." *Journal of Applied Behavior Analysis,* 7, (1974), 71-76.

Bandura, A. *Social Learning Theory.* Englewood Cliffs, N.J.: Prentice-Hall, 1977.

Bloom, R., "Therapeutic Management of Children's Profanity." *Behavioral Disorders,* 2, (1977), 105-11.

Brophy, J.E., and C.M. Evertson. *Learning from Teaching: A Developmental Perspective.* Boston: Allyn & Bacon, 1976.

Glasser, W. *Schools Without Failure.* New York: Harper & Row, Pub., 1969.

Gordon, T. *T.E.T.: Teacher Effectiveness Training.* New York: Peter H. Wyden, 1974.

Kounin, J.S. *Discipline and Group Management in Classrooms.* New York: Holt, Rinehart & Winston, 1970.

Levine, C.S. "Teacher Cues as Controllers of Classroom Behavior." In W.S. MacDonald and G. Tanabe (eds.), *Focus on Classroom Behavior: Readings and Research.* Springfield, Ill.: Charles C Thomas, 1973.

Madsen, C.H., Jr., W.C. Becker, D.R. Thomas, L. Koser, and E. Plager. "An Analysis of the Reinforcing Function of 'Sit Down' Commands." In R.K. Parker (ed.), *Readings in Educational Psychology.* Boston: Allyn & Bacon, 1968.

Maslow, A. *Toward a Psychology of Being.* Princeton, N.J.: Van Nostrand Reinhold, 1968.

Rettig, E.B., and T.L. Paulson. *ABC's for Teachers: An Inservice Training Program in Behavior Modification Skills.* Van Nuys, Calif.: Associates for Behavior Change, 1975.

Switzer, E.B., T.E. Deal, and J.S. Bailey. "The Reduction of Stealing in Second Graders Using a Group Contingency." *Journal of Applied Behavioral Analysis,* 10 (1977), 267-72.

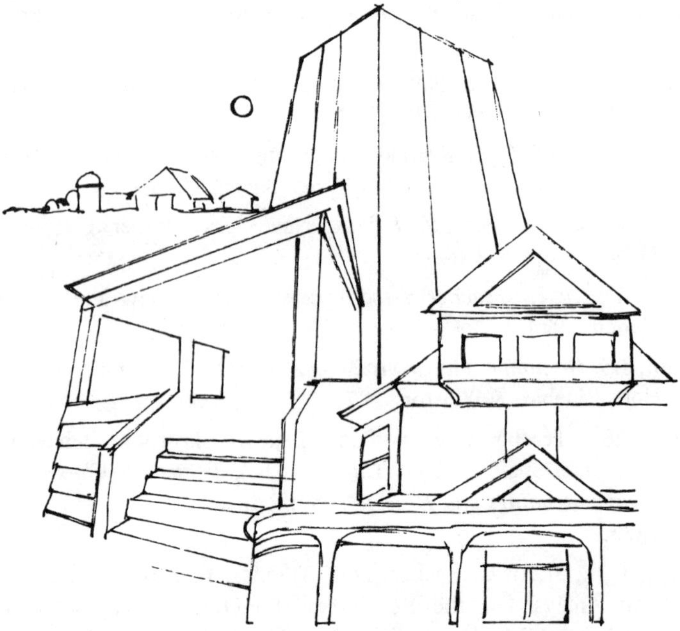

chapter 7

parent relationships and home and community conditions

GERALD MAGER

Chapter 7 Outcomes: *After reading Chapter 7 you should be able to:*

—*describe major teacher goals in the area of parent relationships and home conditions,*
—*list factors which cause problems in this area,*
—*list a variety of roles parents and teachers could play in the school community,*
—*state principles which should guide a teacher who wishes to improve parent relationships,*
—*state principles which should guide a teacher who wishes to work toward optimal home and community conditions,*
—*apply the principles to reported problem situations, and*
—*summarize general knowledge related to the area.*

TEACHERS, PARENTS, AND NEIGHBORHOODS

Most of a teacher's day is spent planning for and working with students. The daily contact with youngsters is a source of great satisfaction for many teachers, whether they work with five-year-olds in kindergarten or teach adolescents in secondary school. Teachers generally enjoy being with kids. Teachers are keenly aware, however, that they are not the only important adults in the lives of their students. Youngsters' parents of course play a major role in their development. And school is not the only setting in which the youngsters live and grow. The larger world of the home and community influences their learning as well.

PARENTS INFLUENCE STUDENTS IN MANY WAYS

Teachers recognize the role parents play in the lives of the students. A teacher is not likely to be heard saying, "What goes on at home has no bearing on what goes on in school." But a teacher might be heard saying, "These parents don't give a damn!" or, after a parent conference, "Now I understand why Johnny behaves the way he does!" giving testimony to their belief that parents do play an important role in the development of the child. More specifically, the kindergarten teacher knows how important parental care is to the development of certain basic skills in the preschool child. The middle school youngster who regularly tells stories about home life to the teacher is indirectly telling how important it is that the two worlds—home and school—not be entirely separate and not be in conflict. Teachers who work with adolescents know that home life can provide security and support for the student, but that it can also give rise to value conflicts and stress. In these and other contexts, teachers are reminded of the influence of the parents.

Teachers are also aware of the tradition in this country which gives parents the right and responsibility to play a major role in deciding how their children are to be schooled. Some parents exercise this responsibility by sending their children to private or parochial schools. Some parents join the parent-teacher association of their school or regularly attend school board meetings and thereby influence policy and practice. Some parents influence the conduct of schooling for their sons and daughters by talking directly with the teacher about classroom events. Some parents rely heavily on the judgment of school personnel and make decisions only when called on to do so.

Realizing that the responsibility for a youngster's education is shared with the parents, teachers are concerned that their relationships with parents be constructive. Parent relationships might be defined as the general rapport that grows out of all the contacts between the two parties. When this rapport is good, teachers feel encouraged. When rapport is strained or in doubt, teachers have a parent relationship problem. Then teachers worry.

NEIGHBORHOODS INFLUENCE STUDENTS IN MANY WAYS

A youngster's development is also influenced by the home and community conditions in which he or she is raised. In part these conditions are created by the parents; in part they are the product of the larger community. Home and community conditions might be defined as the economic, cultural, and familial characteristics that describe a particular setting; they may set the stage for a student's response to the school experience. For example, a closely knit ethnic neighborhood may set a different stage than one that is culturally diverse. Or, a student whose parents must cope with the constant threat of layoff might have different goals for schooling than one whose parents are financially secure. Teachers know that home and community conditions affect the student's school experience. When that influence enhances a student's schooling, teachers are pleased; when it does not, teachers once again have a problem.

TWO GOALS OF TEACHERS

Teachers hope that the influence of parents and home conditions is in a direction compatible with the efforts of the school. When it is not, teachers may have problems. Two general goals held by teachers—mutual support and optimal home and community conditions—may be thwarted.

The First Goal: Mutual Support

Teachers recognize the role parents play in the lives of the youngsters, and they hope that that role does not conflict with their own. Teachers desire what might be called a state of mutual support. That is, teachers want their values, attitudes, and practices to be in harmony with the values, attitudes, and practices of the parents—complementary in the education of the youngster. When teachers come into contact with parents, they want to be supportive, and to be supported in return. When they sense that mutual support does not exist or is in jeopardy, they become concerned.

> Carole Washington, an experience teacher at Montgomery Middle School, received a noontime phone call from a parent, Mr. Simmonds, who questioned the worth of an upcoming field trip to the riverfront. Carole feels strongly that the trip is worthwhile, and she feels she clearly explained her reasons to Mr. Simmonds. At 8:00 that night she is still reviewing the phone conversation, wondering what else she might have said and wondering why the parent had doubts to begin with. She senses Mr. Simmonds is not convinced of the value of the trip, and more important, is not fully supportive of her program. Though the immediate concern regarding the field trip was resolved, Carole is plagued by the thought that she has lost some support. She may carry that thought until she has evidence to the contrary.

Carole Washington may never get that evidence, because she may not have contact with Mr. Simmonds again during the school year. Though some parents and teachers maintain frequent and varied contacts, most teachers' contacts with parents are limited in time, in topics of discussion, and in frequency—perhaps only two or three times per year. Obviously, these limitations heighten the relative importance of each contact: each interaction must serve to reinforce the state of mutual support, or it is left in doubt. An incident which openly questions the support of the parent or teacher causes a great deal of concern because it represents a large portion of the total interactions. In their personal lives, a parent or teacher may bear with a strained relationship for days or even weeks if there is a history of good feelings and events to provide a context in which the strain seems not so great. There is hope that the future will provide real opportunities for renewed good feelings. Between a parent and a teacher such a history may not have been created; such a future may not be anticipated. Therefore, any strain that occurs is critical. Thus, each contact between parent and teacher is all the more important for establishing and maintaining mutual support.

Obstacles to Achieving Mutual Support. The teacher's goal of mutual support may be frustrated when differences surface in values, attitudes, or practices between the parent and teacher. An eighth grade physical education teacher describes a situation in which there seems to be a lack of support:

> I was talking to the class about all the fights they had been getting into. My problem came when they told me that their parents tell them to hit anyone who does something they don't like. I suddenly realized why there are so many fights and that it's the school's "no fighting" policy vs. the parents' "don't be a sissy" policy.

If this teacher's understanding of the parents' values is correct, then a sense of mutual support will be difficult to develop. The teacher seems not inclined to condone the "don't be a sissy" policy, and it may be difficult to change the values encouraged by the parents.

A high school mathematics teacher describes a situation in

which he feels he has not upheld his end of the mutual support "agreement":

> A youngster asked my advice on a problem with her parents. The student has been in trouble in school last year (one incident). Now that she's a senior, her parents won't allow her to live at a college, but rather she must commute. The college of her choice requires boarding. I advised her to go against her parents' wishes and to tell them she'll not go to college if they demand her to commute. I am now worried if I made the right decision.

This teacher feels that the parents are not acting in the best interest of their daughter. He disagreed with their decision and counseled the student to stonewall. In retrospect, he realizes that he may have put the girl in an even more awkward position and that certainly the parents have a right to express their values in such a matter. Though this teacher could not support their decision, he realizes he did not have to directly contradict it. In this instance, his open withdrawal of support has created a problem for him.

Another teacher describes a problem growing out of differences in values:

> I have a child who still can't read! He knows the sounds one day and not the next. There are problems at home and his mother says just to make sure he's happy here. He hated school last year. His attitude is great and he *is* happy—very! But I can't seem to get him to read.

Though the mother and the teacher would probably both like the child to be happy *and* to learn to read, their priorities are different. It can be reasoned that the two objectives are hardly mutually exclusive: learning to read and happiness in school more often go hand in hand. Nevertheless, the teacher feels a conflict and senses a lack of mutual support.

A second source of jeopardy for mutual support is the situation which calls into question the competence of the teacher. Teachers want to be competent in the eyes of the parents. They sense that without this recognition, they have little hope of gaining parental support. For the most part, parents trust the judgments and efforts of school personnel; directly and indirectly they say, "We have confidence in your professional abilities." In some instances, however, the teacher's competence may be suspect:

> This day was very good. But one thing was most frustrating on this day before vacation: a mother came to observe in the afternoon. The problem was me—I felt bad because she saw me reading a story and having sharing [taking time to share ideas]. It wasn't too exciting, and not much was going on.

In this case, the parent may have been very pleased with what she saw in the classroom. But the teacher, judging herself that the class was "not too exciting," feels the parent may now have reason to doubt her competence. The teacher is worried that she may lose some support from that parent.

In another situation, a teacher of high school history has severe doubts that his judgment would be trusted by the parents of his students. He expects little support from them in dealing with a classroom problem he must face:

> Several of the 37 students in the fifth period make slang references to sexual matters. If I took them to the office, their parents would be up here claiming that I had a dirty mind or their sweet children would never mean it that way. Of course, this disrupts my class and there are no measures that I can take to *effectively* remedy this.

Finally, misunderstanding of program, procedures, and events which occur in school can serve to raise doubts about the competence of the teachers. An eighth grade teacher who attempted to strengthen relations between herself and the parents found one instance where her efforts backfired.

> When report cards went out I wrote notes to several parents to try to improve understanding between parent and teacher and to try to

> help public relations in general. One parent answered with a very sarcastic note. Her son had been given a note stating that he had not made up any of his work that he had missed during an illness. He'd been told what he missed and reminded several times. The mother seemed to think she should have been given an itemized list of his work. This is impossible to do with 153 students.

This teacher feels that the mother is insensitive to the realities of being a teacher. Furthermore, since the teacher felt she was making an effort which would improve relations, she was particularly upset when the parent responded in the opposite way. Her competence in doubt, the teacher may feel she has lost the support of that parent.

The Second Goal: Optimal Home and Community Conditions

Teachers recognize that their students' development can be heavily influenced by their environment outside of school. Though they have less control over the conditions of the home and community in which the students live, teachers would like those conditions to enhance the students' intellectual, emotional, and social development. Conditions which seem to hamper this development are a source of concern for teachers.

> Jim Packer and Molly White have just finished rewinding the last reel of *Butch Cassidy and the Sundance Kid.* They sit and reflect on how successful the Saturday Night Film Series has been, how well it has been attended. As teachers at Greer High, they became aware that youngsters in this suburb had few if any places to carry on a social life in the community itself. Jim and Molly often heard students complain, "There's nothing to do around here!" Traveling ten miles or more to "find something to do" on a Saturday night was a common student practice. Word of "joy rides" and near-accidents filtered through the halls of the school each Monday. When several boys got into a fight at a crosstown hangout, Jim and Molly's concern gave rise to the idea of a film series in the school auditorium.
>
> After a great deal of planning and work beyond their regular duties as teachers, they were able to initiate a five-film program. The stu-

dents had responded with some enthusiasm, with greatest interest coming from those who had no "wheels." Now that the series is over, Jim and Molly consider how the idea could be continued and expanded next year. They are concerned that without the series, youngsters will once again be left with "nothing to do" or something worse. As teachers they would like to see those conditions which best promote the students' intellectual, emotional, and social development.

Obstacles to Achieving Optimal Home and Community Conditions. The chief obstacle to achieving optimal conditions is that teachers do not control many seemingly important conditions. Elements of the students' environment that are beyond the control of school personnel may be within the control of parents or community members. Teachers may or may not be able to influence that control. Some conditions are beyond the control of even the parents and community. Jim and Molly attempted to minimize the impact of an adverse condition—the lack of opportunities and places for students to gather socially in their own community—through the use of school facilities and a good deal of their own effort. Still they had little control over the environment, and once their program was completed, the condition prevailed.

An industrial education teacher has a problem when the conditions in the home seem to prevent a student from meeting his school responsibilities:

> Today a student came to my first hour class late for the ninth time in four weeks. I feel I have done all in my power to change his attitude toward this problem. The main problem is that most of his excuses are legitimate. The fact is that his lateness can be directly attributed to his parents: car wouldn't start, alarm didn't go off, his mother got breakfast late, he had to baby-sit 'til 2:00 last night, etc.

The teacher in this instance has little control over the circumstances that have made the student late to school many times. He feels that the parents do have control over those circumstances and could change them to eliminate the problem. However, communicating his concern to the parents and influencing their control may be difficult: they might become defensive and close off communication; they might not feel able to alter the "series of accidents"; they might not value school's requirement of arriving on time and suggest the teacher adapt. The range of possible responses to the teacher's concern makes the teacher unsure of how to proceed. Of course, the parents may agree with the teacher and make every effort to resolve the problem. Not knowing for sure that this would be their response, the teacher is faced with a problem.

A visiting teacher describes a situation which may be beyond the control of both teacher and parents:

> February 5th, Monday
>
> I visited the home of a new seventh grade student, coming from a rural elementary school. He is having a difficult time adjusting, is failing all subjects, and has begun to stay home because he says he cannot do the work. There are no standardized test scores on his transcript; therefore we do not know his ability level. The purpose of the visit was to get papers signed for psychological testing. My concern in this situation is with the home environment. I come in contact with many deprived families, but the hopelessness of this family is very frustrating. Both parents appear to be extremely retarded, as is another 16-year-old son, who has never been in school. The home was sparsely furnished but as straight and clean as an old house of this type can be. Neither of the parents could read or write and it was extremely difficult to get the information needed to complete the form.

This visiting teacher has great concern that the conditions of the home will hamper, if not preclude the best social, emotional, and intellectual development of the youngster. It is a problem not easily addressed, for the teacher has little hope of being able to alter these conditions. Again the teacher's goal of having optimal home conditions is unmet.

TEACHERS AND PARENTS IN THE SCHOOL COMMUNITY

Teachers come into contact with parents in many different ways and different settings. In each instance, teachers pursue their goals of mutual support and optimal home and community conditions. However, because the nature of these contacts varies from teacher to teacher, parent to parent, and school community to school community, pursuit of the goals takes many forms. What one person intends as goal-directed activity, another person may see as an unimportant use of time and energy. For example, a primary school teacher may encourage parents to carry out activities at home which augment school learning; some parents may respond enthusiastically while others do not see this as a condition important for student development. Parents of some middle school youngsters may request that homework be given regularly so that they may keep in touch with the students' progress; teachers may value the parents' interest but may not see homework as a means of developing mutual support. Each school community establishes its own ways of involving parents in the schools and teachers in the community. What might be highly valued in one setting might be less so in another.

PARENT ROLES AND TEACHER ROLES

Opportunities to foster mutual support and encourage good home and community conditions come in many forms. Traditional parent and teacher roles provide many such opportunities. But some opportunities have come about as a result of new roles for parents, roles which take the parents beyond the traditional roles of provider and protector. Other opportunities have been created because teachers have taken on additional roles outside of the classroom. The actions of both teachers and parents in these roles can foster goal achievement.

A catalog of roles that involve the parents in their child's education could be compiled. Parents are decision makers: they make decisions about public or private schooling, about tax supports, about curriculum materials, about permission for field trips, and a host of other matters. Parents are volunteers: they are field trip helpers, clerical workers, special event chaperones, and classroom aides. More recently, the parents' direct contribution to the education of the child has been recognized and fostered. In preschool and the primary grades, parents' tutelage is considered more and more important in the child's intellectual development. As the child grows older, parents act as sources of information and counsel. Career choice, moral development, and family traditions are three "subject areas" in which parents play major roles, even as the child grows into adolescence and young adulthood. Thus, parents are also teachers of a sort, and the teachers in school increasingly recognize their contribution. In these and other actions taken by parents, teachers can find evidence of progress toward the goals of mutual support and optimal home and community conditions.

But parents generally perceive their roles in the schooling process as limited. They often feel they have little power to affect what happens in schools. Teacher education programs seldom prepare teachers to work with parents. Teachers often don't know how to involve parents in ways that will enhance a student's schooling. Experience has shown that parents' understanding of the school and schooling process is a function of the teachers' efforts to educate and involve them. Any efforts to establish a new pattern of parent-teacher involvement in the school community will likely be more successful if accompanied by appropriate efforts to educate all participants for their new roles.

In many communities, programs have been started which redefine the kinds of involvement parents have in the school. These programs have given rise to new knowledge about what can be done, how it can be done, and what the effects are of having done it. Though each program is unique, some general patterns are developing. Particularly interesting are reports of programs which relate parent participation to greater student achievement. When teachers have taught parents how to teach their young children important readiness skills through simple home activities, the result is greater achievement in school. This greater achievement is sometimes evident even years later. When parents have been involved in the school program, for example through school-to-home and home-to-school communications, student achievement has been enhanced. There seems to be little doubt that certain kinds of parental involvement do correlate with greater learning, but these involvements require new role definitions on the parts of both teachers and parents. And, finally, there is some evidence to suggest that the hoped-for outcomes of such efforts may take longer than expected to emerge; changes in attitudes, changes in roles, changes in student performance, and the like are long-range outcomes and may require several years to develop fully.

A wholly different perspective on fostering mutual support is taken when the question is asked, "In what ways do teachers participate in the school community?" The most common description of a teacher's role places the teacher in the classroom as planner and director of activity and as student evaluator. Yet teachers have successfully assumed other educational roles which function outside the classroom. In other words, there are alternate settings in which teachers might foster goal achievement. Teachers have acted as community organizers, as adult educators, as community leaders, as volunteers in community projects, and as guests at community celebrations. All of these activities are legitimate undertakings which have, in some communities, broadened the teacher's role. Insofar as they provide for increased understanding and sharing of values, they are opportunities for strengthening mutual support and encouraging good home and community conditions.

ACTIVITY

Teachers spend about six hours each day in class, for about 180 school days per year. This presents each teacher with a highly coveted 1,080 student contact hours each year. (It does not begin to reflect the time spent on preparation or follow-up work that must be done at other times of the day and year.) If some of this time were given to parent contact instead of student contact, a strong impact might be made. Some programs of parent-teacher contact have correlated with desirable outcomes: noticeable increases in student achievement, more positive attitudes, and greater satisfaction.

List the kinds of parent-teacher contacts that could successfully be undertaken if twenty of the 1,080 hours were spent in contact with parents rather than their children: twenty hours spent teaching parents how to teach their children simple skills, how to supervise homework, how to cope with children; or twenty hours spent conducting small group discussions in the home or in school; or twenty hours spent producing a newsletter or a series of television spots about the school; or twenty hours spent with parents in the community to refurbish a playground, set up a youth club, or participate in adult education.

Choose one activity and list the intended outcomes of that undertaking. List the arguments in favor of the action and against the action. List the problems that could prevent reaching the intended outcomes.

Consider what dimensions could be added to the activity if more than one teacher were to commit twenty hours to it. What if the entire faculty were to do so? Take your considerations to your fellow teachers and the principal to get their reactions.

SCHOOL COMMUNITY NORMS

It has been noted that each school community establishes its own norms for parental involvement in the school and teacher involvement in the community. Within a school community, however, there is a range of tolerance away from the norms. If it is the norm that parents are free to visit the school anytime if they call ahead, a parent who just "drops in" once may be made perfectly welcome. But repeated violations of the norm might be met with coldness, rejection, or even hostility. Of course, many norms govern the behavior of each school community, and some are on the borderline between conscious and unconscious thought. Norms are most obvious when their limits of toleration have been violated. They are often expressed indirectly: "Mr. Bowman never sends notes explaining Julie's absences!" "Mrs. Brennan calls on parents all the time to help in the classroom, but she's never yet called on me." "Kay Phillips' dad had the nerve to tell me to spend more time in class reviewing homework! Who told him he was the teacher?!"

It is also true that norms for behavior change. What may be unacceptable one year may be an encouraged practice the next. Parents or teachers new to the school community, and as yet unfamiliar with the established norms, may behave differently, thus effecting a small change. Teachers sometimes undertake to change the norms; parents do too. But just as it is impossible to keep norms from changing, it is difficult to change them in exactly the way deemed desirable. Thus, norms for parent and teacher work in the school community vary considerably from one setting to another, and the norms themselves are constantly changing.

ACTIVITY
Ask the teachers in your school to describe the normal kinds of contact they have with parents during the course of the year. Also ask them to describe one problem they've had related to parent contacts. From this information, sift out the norms for parent-teacher interaction that exist among the teachers in your school community. Don't overgeneralize. Report your findings back to the teachers and invite comment.

WORKING TOWARD THE GOAL OF MUTUAL SUPPORT

The teacher's goal of mutual support between parent and teacher was earlier defined as a state in which the teacher feels that values, attitudes, and practices of parent and teacher are in harmony. A teacher wants to be supportive and to be supported in return.

A BASIC PRINCIPLE

In working toward the goal, a teacher can keep in mind this basic principle: Increased and continued interaction between parent and teacher holds the promise of stronger mutual support. For example, if a teacher starts a monthly newsletter to keep parents informed of classroom activities, and sustains the effort over time, the teacher's efforts are likely to be met by stronger support from the parents, if they value such a source of information. If the parents of a community undertake to invite teachers to community celebrations, and do so regularly, the teachers are likely to feel greater support both from the parents and for the parents, if the teachers value this type of inclusion in community affairs. Increased and continued interaction is characterized by stronger mutual support.

The converse of this principle is also true: Where teachers feel there is a state of strong mutual support, they are likely to seek ways to sustain interaction with the parents and perhaps increase it. For example, if teachers in a particular school feel that their values, attitudes, and practices are in close harmony with those of the parents, then the teachers are likely to encourage communication with parents. Depending on what the teachers and parents value as a good medium, this communication may take different forms: school visits, school community meetings, or perhaps parent conferences. Where there is a state of strong mutual support, interaction will be sustained.

The relationship between continued interaction and mutual support is not a cause-effect relationship. One does not cause the other to occur. Rather, when either one occurs, the other is likely also to be present. In a relationship not characterized by mutual support—for example, when two neighbors have had a difference of opinion on some important topic—interaction will likely decrease. The neighbors may allow a hedge between their properties to grow tall so they don't have to see or speak to each other. Teachers do the same thing. They avoid persons who are likely to challenge their values, attitudes, and practices, and they seek the company of persons who support them. This is typical human behavior. When teachers are "forced" by circumstances to interact with someone with whom they do not sense a mutual supportiveness, they will seek ways to minimize interaction: avoid phone calls, discourage conferencing, keep conversations brief and superficial, and adopt other such measures. Parents can also find ways to decrease unrewarding interaction. Conversely, when teachers find a parent who is very supportive and whom they can support as well, many opportunities for interaction are likely to be used and new ones may be found.

THE CONTEXT OF INTERACTION

The substance of the principle of interaction/support is augmented when a further consideration is made. Earlier it was stated that because direct contact between parents and teachers may actually occur only a few times each year, each contact assumes more importance in establishing and maintaining mutual support. If the number of interactions increase, however, a "context of interaction" develops. Consider this problem reported by an elementary school teacher:

> I was working with a group of volunteer mothers when the first grade came into the area for class. The kids organized themselves into the separate groups quickly, which was great. Unfortunately, the mothers were watching as the class which had been performing so beautifully dissolved into petty fighting and general "goofing off."

By itself the situation is embarrassing to the teacher. She is concerned that she and her colleagues will appear less than competent and may lose some parental support. In and of itself the occurrence is significant. However, placed in the context of other contacts which were positive, and of future contacts which could offset a poor impression, the single occurrence is not so important. In general, increased and continued interaction is accompanied by stronger mutual support.

Objections might be raised that only certain kinds of interactions will increase support whereas others might tend to decrease support. While this might be true for single interactions, continued interaction is more likely to be characterized by mutual support. Thus, if the teacher, because of her embarrassment, decided not to continue with the parent volunteer meetings—that is, to cut off further interactions—then the parents would have only the single, unimpressive contact on which to base their support. Similarly, if the teacher decided to continue the meetings and each one was marred by a similar occurrence, she might then want to call a halt to the meetings. Cutting off further interaction at a time of lowered support would provide little hope for improving the relationship. More interaction would be needed if improvements were to occur. Parents and teachers will find ways to decrease interaction if they do not derive the reward of mutual support from it. But mutual support will certainly not result from the termination of interaction.

Consider the following problem reported by a high school teacher. Judge whether the relationship, if it is to be characterized by mutual support, will lead to a continuation or to an end to interaction. If the teacher wants to increase the support he is receiving from this parent, should he continue to interact with him or end such interaction?

> My biggest problem was getting the Dad's Club President pinned down to some definite commitments regarding our school's annual fund-raising event. He gets nervous when approached for specifics, and I get nervous without firm commitments.

If three more meetings produced no satisfactory results, what would the teacher probably feel like doing? Would terminating contact with the parent at that point result in mutual support?

Thus, relationships characterized by mutual support will

likely have increased and continued interaction. Relationships in which interaction is sustained are likely to be characterized by mutual support.

ACTIVITY
Test the basic principle that increased and continued interaction between parents and teacher will be characterized by stronger mutual support.

Choose a parent with whom you feel no particularly strong relationship of support, or with whom you've had particular problems. Plan a program of increased and continued interaction over a period of three months. Select whatever channel of communication you feel is appropriate or choose several. Carry out your plan and record your impressions and feelings as it develops. Record the reactions of the parent. At the end of the three months, discuss with the parent what you had attempted to do and record the parent's point of view on what happened.

If several teachers undertake this investigation at the same time, each working with a different parent, at the end of the three months they can discuss the results together, comparing the different approaches they took and the outcomes they experienced.

INDICATORS OF MUTUAL SUPPORT

Mutual support has been defined many times in this chapter. It is a way of generally describing the kind of relationship teachers would like to have with parents. In the everyday language of teachers, support translates into comments like, "Mrs. Brock said she is very pleased with the progress Tommy is making this year," "Mr. Kaminisky backed me up on my way of dealing with Joey when he misbehaves," "Whenever I need an extra hand in the classroom or on a field trip, Brenda's mother is always right there," and "I've seldom had any problems with Mr. Schoen when I want to discuss Ellie's work." Of course, examples could also be chosen in which support is not evident: "Three times we've scheduled a conference, and three times Mr. Krause canceled," "Mrs. Lupes didn't seem to care when I told her what Daren had done to the library books," and "Mrs. Davies told every mother there about the day I lost my cool with the sixth period class!" This is everyday teacher talk about parental support, or lack thereof.

If support is to be mutual, then the parental values must also be considered. A teacher who is supportive might expect to hear these comments from parents: "Mr. Bentley, I'm glad you're working to help Lucy get some new friends from among her classmates," "Coleen comes home with some bit of homework every night, which I think is good," "Ed and I appreciate your sending notes home to keep us informed about Marty's work in Spanish, Sister Caroline." A seeming lack of teacher support for the parents' values is evident here: "Katy's teacher told the class that homes that don't get a daily newspaper are 'deprived.' I guess that's us!" "I asked Mr. Eriksen to watch over Tammy's algebra work, but he's never sent me word of how she's doing," and "We've encouraged Alice to keep her career plans open, but Mrs. Schmidt seems to encourage her only toward nursing." Each phrase gives evidence of some value, attitude, or practice in which the parent hopes to be supported by the teacher. When teachers are not supportive, mutual support is in jeopardy.

ACTIVITY
Choose a particularly disturbing parent-teacher contact you've had and describe it to a colleague. Set up a mock confrontation. Have your colleague assume your role, and you assume the role of the parent. Go through the role play, continually approaching the situation from the parent's viewpoint and maintaining the attitudes the parent might reasonably hold. After the role play, discuss with your colleagues how well you seemed to place yourself in the parent's role. Discuss any insights that might have come about from this counterattitudinal role play.

Teacher-Parent Expectations. Teachers must identify and examine what specific actions they will interpret as indicators of support from the parents. "What do I, as a teacher, expect parents to do? When and what kinds of actions will I take to be indications of support from the parent?" Chosen indicators of support may be stated as expectations. Consider the following problem again.

> When report cards went out I wrote notes to several parents to try to improve understanding between parent and teacher and to try to help public relations in general. One parent answered with a very sarcastic note. Her son had been given a note stating that he had not made up any of his work that he had missed during an illness. He'd been told what he missed and reminded several times. The mother seemed to think she should have been given an itemized list of his work. This is impossible to do with 153 students.

Though not all the information relevant to the problem is available, several of the teacher's expectations can be inferred. Several of the parent's expectations have also been inferred and listed.

Teacher's Expectations of the Parent	Parent's Expectations of the Teacher
That the parent would see the note as a means of improving relations with the home.	That the teacher would inform the parent if a student is not doing well academically.
That the parent would accept the note sent home as a clarification or justification for the student's (assumedly) poor grade.	That the teacher will give such information when it is appropriate for corrective measures to be undertaken.
That the parent would know and appreciate the fact that the teacher taught 153 students.	That the teacher is capable of handling absences routinely and without special attention from the parent.
That the parent would know about and accept as sufficient the intermediate steps that had been taken.	
That if the parent responded to the note, the response would be supportive of the teacher and/or reflect concern about the poor grade.	

Each of these expectations for behavior should be examined. Each, if it had been met by the other party, could have been taken as an indicator of support. For example, if the parent had acknowledged the note-writing effort of the teacher as a good way of improving relations, the teacher would have felt rewarded for the effort and a bit more supported by the parent. If the parent's response acknowledged the steps the teacher had taken to inform the student of missing work, the teacher would have felt somewhat more supported. If the teacher had indicated that absences are routinely handled but that this particular instance called for more than routine attention, the parent would have felt somewhat more supported and still have been prepared to address the problem.

These expectations should be examined further: Which ones are realistic? Which are probably not? Which are incompatible? Which are held to consistently, across many parent-teacher contacts and over time? Without trying to be judgmental, it seems appropriate to make several observations.

1. The teacher objected that to send notes home to 153 students' parents was impossible. Yet 153 of the students were not in need of such attention, and indeed the teacher did send notes home after all. Perhaps the expectation was not as unrealistic as the teacher thought.
2. The teacher's notes may have had a good effect. Receiving the report card with the poor grade without the note might have led to a harsher reaction from the parent. That is, even though a nonsupportive response was received, the response might have been even more negative without the teacher's note-writing efforts.
3. There is evidence of grounds for agreement. Both the teacher and the parent held the same expectation for the student—that he complete assigned work.
4. If the response note is the final interaction between this parent and teacher, it is not likely that their relationship will be characterized by mutual support.

Examine the following reported problem situation and sift out the teacher's and the parent's hidden expectations.

> A mother who has been most helpful and faithful failed to appear. She did not call and indicate she would not be with me. I had planned many activities for the children which required two adults. I had to alter the day's plans and did it successfully, but still I was annoyed that some valuable activities had to be excluded.

Which expectations are realistic? Which ones are incompatible? Which ones are held to consistently, across many parent-teacher contacts and over time?

Thus, when establishing and maintaining mutual support, teachers act to understand and, where possible, fulfill the expectations of the parent, as well as seeking to have their own expectations met. They look to have their values, attitudes, and practices confirmed by the action of the other.

ACTIVITY
Write a number of short, realistic parent-teacher problem situations. Distribute these to the parents of your students and ask them to respond to two questions: What should the teacher do in this circumstance? What should the parent do in this circumstance? Respond to these questions yourself before you review the parents' responses. Convert their responses to statements of teacher and parent expectations. Compare the compiled lists with your own statements. Mark contrasts and contradictions. Note consistencies. Remove names from the material and objectively report the results of the exercise to the parents of all your students. Invite reactions.

Role Negotiation. When important disagreements in expectations are made evident, parents and teachers may enter into role negotiation to resolve the differences. It works this way: Both parties explain exactly what their expectations are, why they hold such expectations, and why the other's expectations seem unacceptable. If, after these explanations, a real disagreement has been found, a compromise set of expectations is formed by negotiating: "I'll do this if you'll do that. . . ." Each party must abide by the agreement and can hold the other party responsible for his or her part as well.

Again consider the problem described by the teacher who sent home notes at report card time. Just as there are some real differences in expectations between this teacher and the parent, so too are there some grounds for agreement. Both seem to expect the student to do the assigned work; both seem willing to accept some responsibility in monitoring the student's progress; both probably want the student to do well, an achievement reflected by a report card grade; and both teacher and parent recognize that they need each other's cooperation in meeting that goal. Building on these areas of agreement, what agreement might be negotiated to ensure that they reach the goal? What indicators of support ("I'll do this. . . ,") can the teacher suggest to the parent in return for indicators of support from the parent ("if you do that. . .")?

WORKING TOWARD THE GOAL OF OPTIMAL HOME AND COMMUNITY CONDITIONS

Teachers set a goal of having, encouraging, or developing optimal home and community conditions, that is, environments that enhance the students' intellectual, emotional, and social development. Though they often have little direct control over the conditions, teachers feel strongly about the impact environment has on the students' school experience.

THREE PRINCIPLES

In working toward the goal of optimal home and community conditions, a teacher may be puzzled about which, if any, course of action to take. There are seldom easy solutions to the difficult problems of working with home and community conditions. However, a teacher faced with a problem may be guided by three principles in coming to understand the problem and in deciding from among alternative actions.

Principle One

The relationship between home and community conditions and a student's school experience is a complex one and is not easily defined. That is, it's hard to know what factors of the student's home and community life are influencing the student's school experience, and in what way. Simple cause-effect axioms are likely to obscure important factors. A teacher who firmly states, "This child could do 100 percent better in school if his parents just paid more attention to him," implies a strong relationship between school achievement and parental concern. Though there may indeed be a strong relationship in that particular case, there are probably other factors which need to be considered. If the teacher is to best understand the problem, it would be wise to steer away from such simplistic statements.

Principle Two

Of the many home conditions which affect student development, the nature of parent-child interaction may be the most important. Consider some of the different home conditions that could be an influence on the youngster. Housing, family income, and number of siblings are factors that are easy to cite; the amount of reading by family members, the general orientation to work, and cultural ties and traditions are somewhat more difficult to discover; the nature of parent-child interactions may be even more difficult for teachers to determine. Yet, the frequency and kind of contacts parents have with their children may be the most important of all home conditions influencing a student's development. Talking with each other about events in their lives, working together on family projects, going to places of common interest—these are activities which can be an important influence on the youngster. This is not to suggest that other factors are unimportant. Rather, it is to suggest that parents with different economic backgrounds may have equally rich interactions with their children; different cultural traditions may be equally useful in supporting a youngster's development; and merely having or not having books in the home is not the best measure of a youngster's intellectual stimulation.

Principle Three

If a teacher's effort to improve home and community conditions requires that parents or teachers take on a new role, then they must be educated to fill that role. People seldom do well or feel comfortable doing that which they've never done before. Parents and teachers both can learn new behaviors if these are clearly described and if opportunities to learn them are made available. If a teacher would like to open communication with parents through a regular newsletter, then the teacher may need to learn what topics are of most interest to parents, how to manage time to get the task done, and how to involve parents usefully in its production. If a teacher would like a particular parent to begin monitoring a child's homework, the parent may have to be taught how to do that effectively. If a teacher would like to have parents feel more comfortable in the school building and more involved in its operation, then the teacher may have to work with parents to achieve those objectives.

ACTIVITY

Study community conditions that might have an effect on student performances in your school. Include such information as family income, age and condition of housing, education levels of parents, and insitutions such as churches, libraries, and government agencies. Identify gathering places in the community, especially those frequented by the students. Do not attempt to form cause-and-effect relationships.

Display your information using visual and audio stimuli. Place the display where it will draw the attention of parents and other community members. Invite comment.

APPLYING THE PRINCIPLES

To see how the three principles might guide a teacher's response to a circumstance of less than optimal home conditions, consider the following problem reported by an elementary school teacher:

> A mother called today to talk about her son. It seems that he's been very upset since the death of his grandfather recently. I've not noticed any change but I promised to observe him for a week and tell her what I've seen. This problem has come up with other children before, and I find it very frustrating to deal with. If parents have not been open about their feelings and beliefs about death prior to having a death in the family, they might as well forget it. The attitude about death will have been set.

This teacher faces a difficult problem. He has limited control over the home conditions that gave rise to the problem, but because he is concerned about the child's development, he is cooperating with the mother to reach a solution. Applying the first principle, the teacher would be well advised not to oversimplify the problem; a child's attitude toward death is not formed only by parental actions. Strong attitudes develop over time and take into account a range of data. Television, news stories, comic books, and peers have probably influenced this boy's reaction to the death of his grandfather. Further, any amount of parental openness and effort to prepare a child might not have been adequate when the stark reality had to be faced. Thus the relationship between the home condition—parents not preparing a youngster to deal with a difficult situation—and the youngster's response—being upset—is probably not a simple cause-effect relationship.

The second princple also applies. The teacher recognizes that the interaction between parent and child is an important home condition. It can significantly affect a youngster's development. In this case, the interaction has not focused on an important life experience, and so the youngster is somewhat at a loss.

Finally, the teacher has stated that this problem is not new. Other children have also been shaken by a family death; this home condition—lack of preparation for a family death—is somewhat common. The third principle suggests that if the teacher were to embark on a program to change that home condition, he may be asking parents to take on a new, unfamiliar role. He may, for example, suggest that parents begin a series of discussions with their children on the topic of death. Parents may need help scaling information and concepts to a child's understanding. They may need to learn to listen carefully to a child's ideas and feelings. They may need to learn how to deal with childhood fears and fantasies. In other words, the parents may need to learn a new role and may need help in doing so. The teacher may be able to provide opportunities to learn.

Consider the following situation reported by a high school teacher.

> One of my freshman students has been a constant disruptive influence on my class. Her problem, I feel, stems from an extremely poor home life. Her father and mother are very strict with her. Her resentment toward authority causes her to rebel against any form of correction or discipline. Today her impertinence and total air of disrespect distracted me to the point that the class as a whole suffered.

Apply the three principles to this circumstance. Is the relationship between the home condition and the student's school experience likely to be simple cause-effect? What other factors are likely to be involved here? How important does the parent-child interaction seem to be in this problem situation? Would efforts on the teacher's part to modify the home conditions require a change of roles for the parents? What steps should the teacher undertake to promote the adoption of a new role?

KNOWLEDGE BEARING ON PARENT-TEACHER RELATIONSHIPS AND HOME AND COMMUNITY CONDITIONS

The first four sections of this chapter have attempted to provide a conceptual framework within which the problem area of parent-teacher relationships and home and community conditions may be understood. Real problems were reported and discussed so that the practical use of the conceptualization would be evident. Through our naming the goals, examining the bases of problems, exploring values and expectations, and stating several principles, the problem area itself, will have become better understood, and specific problems should be lessened. The conceptualization of these previous sections may itself be a problem-solving tool. In this section a more extensive toolbox will be opened. Knowledge tools will be laid out which may provide some further problem-solving capabilities.

Each of several areas of knowledge will now be presented as self-contained units, in order to make them more manageable. Though they are separated, the concepts are nevertheless related to each other in several ways.

INTERACTION

The important concept of interaction is discussed extensively in the chapter on affiliation. Interaction can be simply defined as the actions of two or more people, such that the behavior of one in some way affects the behavior of the other(s). A teacher who sends a note home with the student is interacting with the parent of that student. A parent who discusses school matters with his son, who in turn tells the teacher of the conversation, has, albeit indirectly, interacted with that teacher. But not all behavior is interaction. A teacher planning an upcoming unit of study is not interacting with parents. A mother and father who marvel at their child's reading progress but tell no one of their pleasure are not interacting with the teacher.

Several concepts and principles of interaction can be related to the problem of parent-teacher behavior.

First, *interaction potential* is the probability that interaction will take place. Several factors contribute to interaction potential. The potential is likely to be greater when people have a long-term acquaintance, or when people share a common fate. Interaction potential also increases when the relationship is rewarding to both parties—the more rewarding, the greater the potential.

The degree of interaction between two people may depend on several factors. *Propinquity,* or nearness to another person, influences the relationship. (People who are near to each other have more opportunity to interact.) If propinquity leads to an expectation of continued interaction, then a person will tend to accentuate the positive aspects of the relationship and downplay the negative, setting the stage for agreeable future interactions. As people who are near to each other come to know each other better, there is an increased predictability of behavior, making it possible to elicit positive, rewarding interactions. Propinquity leads to familiarity, which is normally more comfort-producing than the unfamiliar and unexpected.

Similarity influences the liking relationship between people. If two people perceive that they have similar values and attitudes, they tend to like each other. It is rewarding to a person when others agree with him or her and share values and attitudes.

Perceived *competence* affects the degree of liking between people, because persons perceived to be able, competent, and intelligent can provide a source of advice, information, and help. They are more rewarding persons to be with.

Finally, liking depends on being liked: *reciprocation.* Being liked can be a strong reward, and it sets the stage for offering help, at least more so than not being liked.

Through interaction with others, humans have learned how

to achieve goals that they could not achieve acting alone. *Goal achievement* is rewarding, and interaction, because it makes goal achievement possible, becomes an integral part of human behavior.

HOME CONDITIONS

Teachers believe there is a relationship between home and community conditions and a student's school performance. Often a teacher may be heard drawing a connection between a specific home or community condition and a specific student's school performance. For example, a teacher may say: "Kathy does well because her parents encourage her a great deal," or "It's no wonder these kids are always in trouble; they have no place to play but the streets!" Research supports the general notion that there is such a relationship, but the particulars of which conditions relate to which performances are still under study.

In general, there is a relationship between the family's socioeconomic status (SES) and the student's school performance. SES is often measured by variables such as father's or mother's occupation, level of family income, housing conditions, parents' educational achievement, and other demographic data. Students from low SES backgrounds tend to do less well academically than students from higher SES backgrounds. However, there is not a simple cause-effect relationship between SES and student achievement. Rather it is more likely that a complex of home and community conditions combine with school conditions to influence student achievement through a number of mediating variables: student motivation to achieve, student readiness to learn, student experiential background, student creative thinking ability, and so on.

Home conditions may be thought of as having two dimensions: material or physical elements, and the relationship between parent and child. Studies have shown that both of these dimensions can be related to student school performance.

For example, homes in which there is "intellectual stimulation," as might be indicated by the number of newspapers, the number of quality magazines, use of a library, or interest in classical music, correlate with student achievement in school more than homes in which there is no such stimulation. However, mere availability of such materials may not be as important as parent use of them. Parents' discussion of the news and ideas from reading materials, parent and child visits to museums and historical places, and parents' reading to their children are among the parental activities that seem to be related positively to student characteristics such as reading achievement and creative thinking ability. Again, though it is simplistic to identify cause-effect relationships, the evidence clearly points in that direction.

Parent-child interaction at levels ranging from kindergarten through secondary school has also been studied. It seems that parent-child interaction is important regardless of the SES of the home. Among other factors, parent approaches to discipline, parent awareness of a child's development, parent attitude toward the school, and child's perception of parent restrictiveness have been related to student characteristics such as withdrawing (socially and/or academically) in school, high or low use of intellectual ability, and creative thinking.

The effects of parent-child interaction and all home conditions are likely to be differential; that is, the effects vary from child to child, home to home, and school to school. For example, high parental restrictiveness may produce different results if the child is a boy rather than a girl, young rather than old, high SES rather than low SES, or attending a highly structured school rather than a less structured one.

PARENT EDUCATION

One of the new roles teachers play is that of parent educator. Recent years have seen an increase in the number and types of programs designed to assist parents in the job of raising and educating their children. These have not necessarily come about because the job of parenting is considered more difficult now than in the past, though some people would argue that it is indeed more difficult today. The programs have resulted from a recognition that many parents do have problems and that *all* parents can derive satisfaction, reassurance, and insight from contact with other parents and professionals in the field of child development. Parenting is no longer assumed to be a set of innate skills that come with adulthood and are activated by the birth of an infant. Being a parent is recognized as a complex and important responsibility which affects schooling, the culture, and the society as a whole.

The growing interest in parenting has led to a variety of programs, materials, and publications that address the subject. National organizations with local chapters have been formed which help parents cope with aggressive children, help parents adapt to children's handicaps, help parents with the problems of raising twins and triplets, and help parents with many other needs. Single parents, expectant parents, and whole families can receive help. The National Institute of Mental Health has prepared a publication entitled *Parents Are People, Too,* which outlines a number of the programs and lists the organizations which sponsor them. Many books, magazines, news articles, and newsletters are available which can assist in parent education. The federal government publishes and distributes a range of materials which parents may find useful.

Increasingly, local school systems are involving themselves in parent education efforts. The Ninth Annual Gallup Poll of the Public's Attitude Toward the Public Schools (1977) evidences that parents, by an overwhelming majority, support the idea of parent education in and through the public schools. In that poll, a number of topics were ranked by parents according to their interests. Local surveys may produce different results. In all, it cannot be denied that a new and significant type of parent-teacher interaction is developing in the form of parent education.

ACTIVITY
Conduct a survey of parents to answer such general questions as:

> What do the parents know about the class and the school?
> What kinds of parent-teacher contacts are most beneficial?
> What kinds of information about students are most desired?
> What kinds of parent education programs are most desired by the community?

Make the survey simple to administer, simple to respond to, and simple to summarize. Items must be clearly stated if they are to generate useful responses.

List the implications that the results of the survey have for your behavior as a teacher or for the conduct of the school.

HOME-SCHOOL COMMUNICATIONS

It is not only important that home-school communications take place, but *how* that communication occurs may well have a bearing on its value. For years, a variety of channels of communication have been used ranging from report cards, to school visits, to newsletters, to home visits. Each method of communication has its advantages, and it would seem that no single channel is adequate. Parents desire all types of information from the teacher, though some information is considered more important. Some practitioners have emphasized the need to communicate *with* parents as well as *to* parents if communication is to be effective.

Written communication is used frequently. It has the advantage of leading to greater parent recall of information. However, a lack of clarity of a written message may interfere with understanding. Words which are ambiguous, are technical, or evoke unfavorable emotional reactions should be avoided. The report card is a form of written communication which calls for clear, complete communication of meaning. Even so, the content and format of report cards vary considerably.

Oral communication with the parents, either in face-to-face meetings or via the telephone, also can be successful at producing desired outcomes. The telephone may be used efficiently and frequently, and may relieve the parent of some anxieties of face-to-face meetings. A planned program of home and school visits may also be very successful in generating understanding and support from the parents. The intent of all communications should be specified, and steps should be taken so that after the contact both parties feel satisfied with the experience.

FACE-TO-FACE INTERACTION

Perhaps no channel of communication is more potentially productive than a face-to-face meeting, such as a parent conference or home visit. Unfortunatley, these types of contacts also have the potential for producing great anxiety, and therefore they are used with reservation and sometimes avoided altogther.

Teachers are seldom prepared in teacher education programs to conduct either parent conferences or home visits. Each of these activities requires thoughtful preparation and a good measure of interpersonal skill. The time it takes to prepare for, conduct, and follow up on such meetings is often time taken away from the more immediate classroom concerns. Face-to-face interactions place mutual support on the line; either it will be reinforced or some uncomfortable doubts will be raised. Parent conferences and home visits are not easy, yet teachers who have successfully engaged in either almost inevitably report a feeling of accomplishment and satisfaction. They view the effort as worthwhile.

Parents are also often uncomfortable when faced with the prospect of a conference or visit. They are not sure what to expect and what is expected of them. Such a meeting may place an extra task into an already crowded daily schedule, and for a parent who has several teachers to meet, a series of meetings may be difficult to schedule. Parents may be unsure of the purposes for such a meeting. Going to the school or opening the home to a visitor may both be uncomfortable experiences for the parent to initiate. Yet, parents are generally interested in receiving information about their children, in having someone who will listen to their concerns, and in getting the personal attention evidenced by such an act. Face-to-face interaction may be difficult, but it can also be highly rewarding to both.

Most of the knowledge available about parent conferencing and home visitation has been generated from practitioners' experiences. Teachers, principals, counselors, and school community agents have written about their efforts, practices that have worked for them, and pitfalls to be avoided. Several sources of recommendations about parent contacts are available; school systems sometimes have their own guidelines. In the fields of counseling and personnel work, some efforts have been made to study the skills of dyadic or person-to-person interaction, and they may be helpful to the educator in parent conferencing. The following guidelines are suggested by practitioners who are regularly involved in successful face-to-face interactions.

The items apply to both parent conferencing and home visits.

1. *Allow sufficient time.* Allow sufficient time before the meeting to shift mental and physical gears from preceding activities. Allow time during the meeting to explore each area of concern of all the parties involved. Allow sufficient time between two meetings so that neither parent feels infringed upon. Avoid interruptions.
2. *State the purpose of the meeting.* At least in general terms, state the purpose of the meeting. Making such a statement at the time the meeting is scheduled may relieve anxiety and create a mental set for the nature of the meeting. Stating the purpose at the time of the meeting is reassuring, and it may serve to focus the discussion which follows. It is advisable to invite the parents to state any purposes or concerns they have. Introduce any extra participants and state clearly the purposes for which they are present.
3. *Manage the meeting.* Assure the relative comfort of each participant. Then begin the meeting. During the meeting, attend to the concerns and comments of each participant. Keep the discussion moving

ahead. Clarify misunderstandings. At reasonable points, summarize the discussion. Identify common understandings and disagreements. Seek resolutions. Then end the conference. Do not be domineering or insensitive to where a discussion is going, but avoid the rambling conversation in which no party is quite sure about when to speak or what particular concerns are appropriate for discussion. Take the initiative to direct the discussion in order to head off arguments or unproductive lines of thought. Even if the parent has requested the meeting and it is likely that they will do most of the talking, you have reason to manage the flow of the discussion. End the conference when your sensitivity to the discussion and to the participants indicates that it is appropriate to close.

4. *Be honest and open.* The best interests of all parties are served by an honest and open discussion. When there is a problem, it is sometimes difficult to share information. However, to supress information may lead to personal frustration and may also deprive the very people who could work toward a solution the means they need to do so. Use tact. Present information in such a way that it opens the way for constructive comment and reaction. Show the participants that you trust them to use the information as a place from which to begin discussion, and not as an indictment.

5. *Be specific.* Whatever the topic of discussion, a few specific, appropriate examples will help to clarify and define it. Examples of the student's work and anecdotes from classroom observation make a point. Even general impressions which a party may want to share or explore in a meeting will be well served by a concrete example or two. Avoid generalizations which cannot be supported by substantial and appropriate examples.

6. *Ensure that all parties participate.* Though one party may be the chief contributor to the discussion, other parties should be encouraged to express their sentiments. Silence cannot be assumed to represent either support or disagreement. Invite all parties to speak openly and honestly, and honor their contribution with attentive listening and reaction.

7. *Listen carefully.* Do more than hear what other parties have to say. Listen carefully and place yourself in their frames of reference. Attempt to see things as they see them. Restate what you've heard to confirm your understanding.

8. *Recognize your impact.* Remember that anything you say may be

taken very seriously. Recognize how what you say may be heard by the parents. Don't assume that they are using the same perspectives you are.

9. *Avoid technical language.* Examine your own vocabulary and consider how many lay people would correctly understand you. Avoid technical language and jargon. Clearly explain those terms that must be used. Do this not from a sense of superiority, but with a desire to be understood.

10. *Be sensitive to the nonverbal.* All parties in a discussion will communicate nonverbally. Be sensitive to the nonverbal messages that are being exchanged. Reflect on what you are telling the other parties through your use of time, space, eye contact, voice, gestures, and the like. Be open to what they are telling you. Nonverbal messages should be congruent with verbal messages; if there seems to be discrepancy, note it to the other parties. Explore to identify the accurate message.

11. *Present the positive and the negative.* Nearly every situation has both aspects to it. Present both the positive and negative aspects to provide a realistic picture of the discussion topic. One side may clearly dominate; if that represents reality, as you see it, be content that the picture is complete.

12. *Avoid comparisons.* In the sharing of information, reference points are sometimes sought by which judgments might be made. Other students, unrelated personal experiences, and unsubstantiated generalizations about "the way things are supposed to be" are commonly used reference points. Avoid comparisons. Judging a student's performance against such "standards" as these is unsound practice. People and the contexts in which they perform are different enough that comparisons are indefensible. Though you may be urged to make comparisons in the name of greater understanding, only a degree of misunderstanding can result.

13. *Judge performances, not people.* Professionals make judgments based on sound evidence. Because people may be ego-involved in topics of discussion, it is important that a distinction be made between people and performances. Judge performances, not people. A particular performance may be judged poor, but the performer remains unjudged and deserving of respectful consideration by others.

14. *Define expectations.* People may perceive their roles and responsibilities differently than other people perceive them; they hold different

expectations for each other. Define expectations. Whether dealing with a specific concern or a more general policy, state what you can be expected to do and ask others to do the same. If stated expectations differ, work toward a resolution.
15. *Set a course of action.* When the meeting has been called to discuss a problem or when a problem has surfaced during a meeting, discuss what must be done to move toward resolution of the problem. Set a course of action. To end the meeting with the problem unresolved and no plan set for dealing with it discourages the participants. Even a plan that seems less than optimal will be better than none.
16. *Open channels of communication.* The end of a meeting should not be the end of communication between parties. Open channels of communication. Set procedures by which messages can be exchanged. Phone numbers, times for calling, notes and letters, future meeting dates: each measure assures participants that future interactions are welcome. Honor messages received with a quick and appropriate response.
17. *Mark success.* At the end of each meeting, participants should feel that they have accomplished something, that they have been successful. Mark success. End the meeting on a positive note and point out the advances that have been made as a result of the meeting. Success breeds success. Future interactions are more likely if participants feel accomplished in the current one.
18. *Involve the student.* Meetings are often held with everyone but the subject of discussion. Involve the student. Increasingly, students are welcomed into the meetings between parents and teachers. This avoids miscommunications and sometimes allows for more immediate exchange of information. Problems may be resolved more readily. Some practitioners suggest student involvement starting in third grade. If the student cannot be directly involved, before the meeting explain to the student why it will be held and what will likely be discussed. After the meeting, review what actually happened. Respect the self-interest displayed by the student by supplying requested information.

One meeting, whether a parent conference or a home visit, is but one meeting. Limited effects can be expected from limited interaction. Increased and continued interaction, face-to-face or mediated, can be expected to accomplish more. Remember that increased and continued interaction is characterized by mutual support.

The norms of a particular school community may not encourage parent conferences or home visits. Scheduled conferences may be forgotten, ignored, or avoided. Home visits may be canceled. To change the norms of a school community is difficult; it may not be possible. Such face-to-face interactions as conferences and visits must be shown to be clearly beneficial and rewarding to the participants if such a norm is to be established and maintained.

ACTIVITY
Simulate a number of parent conferences to give yourself practice using the guidelines suggested in this section. Try to make the simulation as realistic as possible, so that the practice is on target. Invite a fellow teacher to act as the parent, then discuss with your colleague "how the conference went."

If a group of teachers wish to conduct the simulation together, the fishbowl technique may be used. The two actors—parent and teacher—conduct the conference in the middle of a circle of observers. After the conference is complete, each observer reports impressions and makes suggestions to the actors. Discussion follows.

Invite a parent(s) you trust to help you practice. Explain what you are trying to accomplish and set up several work sessions with the parent. Encourage candor in discussing each session.

If possible, audio or videotape the sessions so that you may hear and see for yourself how you conducted the conference and yourself.

REVIEW AND RESOLVE

Teachers commit themselves to the best intellectual, social, and emotional development possible for their students. But teachers recognize that much of this development is influenced by students' out-of-school experiences—with parents, and in the neighborhood. When the students' development seems to be enhanced by such experiences, teachers feel reassured that they are not fighting an uphill battle. But when parental and neighborhood influence seems to counter the teacher's efforts, the teacher becomes concerned. The teacher has a problem.

TEACHERS, PARENTS, AND NEIGHBORHOODS

The first section of this chapter offered many such problems reported by teachers. The problems were put into perspective by considering two goals generally held by teachers. The first teacher goal is establishing mutual support: teachers would like to be able to support the values, attitudes, and practices of the parent, and be supported in return. Value and attitude differences between teachers and parents sometimes frustrate reaching this goal. At other times, misunderstanding of policies and practices may raise doubts of teacher competence; when competence is questioned, mutual support is an unlikely result.

The second goal held by teachers is having, encouraging, or developing optimal home and community conditions. Teachers would like the economic, cultural, and familial characteristics which comprise a student's home and community setting to enhance that student's development. Because teachers often have little control over these conditions, they have problems reaching their goal.

TEACHERS AND PARENTS IN THE SCHOOL COMMUNITY

The roles parents and teachers play in the school community were discussed in the next section of the chapter. Parents and teachers come into contact with each other in many different ways and in different settings. Each contact is an opportunity for teachers to see evidence of progress toward their goals of mutual support and optimal home and community conditions. New roles for both parents and teachers are creating opportunities for more and different kinds of contacts. There are many different ways in which teachers see progress toward a goal or problem in goal achievement. Each of the roles is governed by school community norms. Norms offer general guidelines as to when and how teachers and parents should interact, and what the nature of that interaction should be. The norms change over time. With each there is a range of tolerance for behavior.

WORKING TOWARD THE GOAL OF MUTUAL SUPPORT

The goal of mutual support is accomplished when a teacher feels comfortable that his or her own values, attitudes, and practices are in harmony with the parents' values, attitudes, and practices. A general principle can guide a teacher's efforts toward this goal: increased and continued interaction between teacher and parent will be characterized by mutual support. This is not a cause-effect axiom, but intends to describe two factors that go hand in hand: where one occurs, the other is likely to occur as well. Where one is not present, the other is unlikely too.

Single interactions between parents and teachers carry a heavy weight: they must confirm or leave in doubt the hoped-for state of mutual support. Increased numbers of interactions share this weight, and a single contact looms less important. A context of interaction develops with increased and continued parent-teacher contact. In that context mutual support is a more stable quality.

Mutual support is a general goal. Teachers talk about mutual support or lack of it using everyday language. Teachers must examine when and what kinds of parental actions they will take as indicators of support. They must examine whether they are able and willing to be supportive of parents, and what kinds of actions they take to show their support to the parents. Chosen indicators of support can be stated as expectations. Teachers should study their own and parents' expectations to identify commonalities and conflicts. Mutual support is more likely to follow from understanding and communication than from misunderstanding and avoidance.

WORKING TOWARD THE GOAL OF OPTIMAL HOME AND COMMUNITY CONDITIONS

Teachers set the goal of having, encouraging, or developing optimal home and community conditions for their students. They feel assured that they are progressing toward the goal when they find evidence that the students' school experience is enhanced by out-of-school conditions.

Three principles can guide a teacher's work toward the goal of optimal home and community conditions. First, the relationship between the conditions and the observed student response is complex. Simple axioms obscure much of the reality. Second, parent-child interaction is a very important part of the home conditions. It may be more important than physical or material elements of the home environment. Third, plans to improve home and community conditions may require a new role of parents and/or teachers. People expected to function in those new roles should be given the chance to learn how to do so. These three principles should guide a teacher's approach to problems of home and community conditions.

KNOWLEDGE BEARING ON PARENT-TEACHER RELATIONSHIPS AND HOME AND COMMUNITY CONDITIONS

The next section of this chapter presented knowledge drawn from two sources, which applies to the problem areas. The first source was theory and research findings—knowledge generated systematically. It was drawn from the fields of sociology, psychology, social psychology, and communications, as well as education. The second source was educational practice—

knowledge generated over time from the experiences of successful teachers, administrators, counselors, and other professionals.

For convenience and manageability, the section was divided into five topic areas: Interaction, Home Conditions, Parent Education, Home-School Communications, and Face-to-Face Interaction. These topics all build on each other. More useful knowledge about parent relationships and home and community conditions will continue to be added as research and practice move forward.

AND FROM HERE, WHERE?

This chapter has attempted to present a conceptualization —a way of thinking about the problems teachers have with parent relationships and home and community conditions. Even at present, the problems, the roles for parents and teachers, their expectations of schooling and of each other, and the settings in which all this occurs vary so much as to make a single conceptualization difficult to mastermind. Nevertheless, there is some promise in that the ideas presented here—the goals, concepts, principles, and knowledge—can be applied to real life. The ideas make sense in the real world of the school community. It is hoped that the ideas will prove useful to the concerned teacher.

RELATED READINGS

Barletta, C., R. Boger, L. Lezotte, and B. Hull. (eds.). *Planning and Implementing Parent/Community Involvement into the Instructional Delivery System.* Lansing, Mich.: Midwest Teacher Corps Network, 1978.

Coleman, J.S. (ed.). *Parents, Teachers, and Children: Prospects for Choice in American Education.* San Francisco: Institute for Contemporary Studies, 1977.

Conference Time for Teachers and Parents. Washington, D.C.: National School Public Relations Association, 1970.

Gordon, I.J. (guest ed.). "Parents Are Teachers." *Theory Into Practice,* 9 (June 1972) 3.

Gordon, I.J., and G.E. Greenwood (guest eds.). "Home-school relations." *Theory Into Practice,* 16 (February 1977), 1.

Ivey, A.E. *Microcounseling: Innovations in Interviewing Training.* Springfield, Ill.: Charles C Thomas, 1971.

Lightfoot, S.L. *World Apart: Relationships Between Families and Schools.* New York: Basic Books, Inc., Publishers, 1978.

McGeeney, P. *Parents Are Welcome.* London: Longmans, 1969.

Miller, G.W. *Educational Opportunity and the Home.* London: Longmans, 1971.

Parents Are People, Too . . . National Institute of Mental Health, for Department of Health, Education and Welfare. DHEW Publication No. (ADM) 75-48. 1975.

Ryan, C. *The Open Partnership: Equality in Running the Schools.* New York: McGraw-Hill, 1976.

chapter 8

student success

JOHN HOLTON

Chapter 8 Outcomes: *After reading Chapter 8 you should be able to:*
—describe the nature of the problem area called student success,
—list obstacles to student success,
—discuss teacher behaviors which seem to promote student success:
  —clarity,
  —enthusiasm,
  —variability,
  —giving pupils an opportunity to learn criterion material,
  —businesslike behavior,
—discuss what is known about motivation and human needs, and
—discuss the nature of the helping relationship.

Teachers face a double-barreled difficulty. Not only must they possess certain knowledge, skills, and attitudes which are valued by their community, but they must also be able to transmit this knowledge, skill, and attitude to their students. A successful teacher, then, is one who knows something and can help a student come to know it too. Student success and teacher success are inseparable.

It might be further suggested that teachers feel responsible for the learning of their students. Thus for a teacher to get satisfaction from his job, he must feel that he has helped his pupils to be successful both academically and personally. Since teaching has never been a highly paid profession, we might suggest that many teachers find the challenge of promoting student success as one of the *principal* rewards of such a job. Thus, while barriers to the reaching of goals in other jobs may only interfere with one's ability to earn a living, interference with the student success goals of teachers may cause very deep personal pain since goals are so intimately tied to the nature of the teacher-person.

Our discussion of teacher-student success has ignored several important problems. We have been talking about "success" as if it were a term whose meaning was clear to all who use it. While we may refer to such and such a classroom as being "successful," we find it very difficult to define that success in terms of the factors involved in it. Even common sense seems to fail at such times. There are teachers, for example, who seem to do none of the things that common sense would tell us are important to being an effective teacher, but who are generally recognized by colleagues, students, and administrators as being excellent teachers. The great American philosopher and psychologist William James gave the impression of extreme disorganization. "He found it impossible to make a long, sustained, orderly, authoritative speech and to unfold, stage by stage, argument by argument, proof by irresistible proof, a philosophical theory." His students related that he would often stray from his subject. Yet his students also found him "stimulating . . . irresistibly charming" and most effective as a teacher (Highet, 1950).

At the other extreme, we might look at the well-organized and prepared teacher drawn by Charles Dickens in his novel *Hard Times*. This teacher

> had been put through an immense variety of paces, and had answered volumes of head-breaking questions. Orthography, etymology, syntax and prosody, biography, astronomy, geography, and general cosmography, the sciences of compound proportion, algebra, land-surveying and levelling, vocal music, and drawing from models, were all at the end of his ten chilled fingers. He had worked his stony way into Her Majesty's most Honourable Privy Council's Schedule B, and had taken the bloom off the higher branches of mathematics and physical science, French, German, Latin, and Greek. He knew all about all the Water Sheds of all the world (whatever they are), and all the histories of all the peoples, and all the names of all the rivers and mountains, and all the productions, manners and customs of all the countries, and all their boundaries and bearings on the two and thirty points of the compass.

Dickens ends his portrait (which has, despite its exaggeration, correspondences among acquaintances of ours) with the damning observation: "Ah, rather overdone, . . . if he had only learnt a little less, how infinitely better he might have taught much more!"

FIVE BARRIERS TO STUDENT SUCCESS

Student success is easier to talk about than to bring about. There are at least five barriers confronting the teacher.

1. The difficulty of finding a definition for "success."
2. The limitations of our knowledge about teaching and learning.
3. The barrier caused by the nature of human nature.
4. The barrier caused by the nature of schools.
5. The Sum of the Parts Problem.

DEFINITION OF "SUCCESS"

While it is quite easy to talk about success in teaching, it is much less easy to agree what that success is. We use the word success in a variety of ways in classroom contexts. Examinations of three different meanings of success might show the great range of possible meanings success has in classrooms. It will also demonstrate that some of the meanings contradict other meanings.

During her day of teaching her sixth grade class, Marcie Bowles might see success in her first period as being related to how well her pupils learn the words on the weekly spelling lists. In spelling, success means successful imitation. But on Friday afternoons, when Marcie's class goes to art, success usually is not related to imitation but rather to the freedom with which the children create forms and colors on paper. A successful art class might be seen in terms of creativity and freedom. Freedom and creativity have little or nothing to do with successful spelling. A creatively spelled word is wrong.

When Marcie teaches arithmetic during the hour before the morning recess, she has yet another meaning for success. This week her pupils are working on word problems. Marcie would not feel very successful (or that her pupils were successful) if the pupils simply memorized each story problem and could reproduce it on the weekly tests Marcie gives. In this case, success has to do with the ability of a pupil to learn how to analyze and attack story problems. In this case, success is neither imitation nor creativity. Rather it is tied to the development of a logical turn of the mind.

Marcie sees success in yet another way as she watches her young charges over the course of the year. She notes with pleasure how each year little fifth graders after a summer vacation enter her sixth grade class and grow and mature from September to June. By June Marcie can see more independence in her pupils. It is not the learning of facts or the development of new mental habits that defines this success. Marcie is here concerned with the personal growth of each child. Just the other day, Marcie was especially pleased by something that happened in class. She had been called from her room for a few moments. When she returned, the children were still intently working on their arithmetic workbooks. The fact that there hadn't been a teacher around to keep them working didn't matter. "Perhaps," Marcie thought with a pleasurable glow, "my pupils are growing beyond the stage where they need policing every moment."

Success might be termed a Humpty-Dumpty word. In *Through the Looking Glass,* Humpty Dumpty said, "When I use a word . . . it means just what I choose it to mean—neither more nor less." Just to say we want success solves no problems. We are still faced with choosing what sort of success it is that we want.

KNOWLEDGE ABOUT TEACHING

The state of knowledge about teaching and learning is also a barrier to teacher goals. Even when teachers are careful to define the sort of success that is to be sought, the knowledge of how best to teach something is often vague and general. Either such knowledge is difficult to apply to practical classroom situations, or it is simply not available in any form.

More than two thousand years ago a Roman teacher named Marcus Fabius Quintilianus wrote a book about teaching in which he gave the following advice about the qualities of a good teacher:

> Let him therefore adopt a parental attitude of his pupils, and regard himself as the representative of those who have committed their children to his charge. Let him be free of vice himself and refuse to tolerate it in others. Let him be strict but not austere, genial, but not too familiar: for austerity will make him unpopular, while

familiarity breeds contempt. Let his discourse continually turn on what is good and honorable; the more he admonishes the less he will have to punish. He most control his temper without ever shutting his eyes to faults requiring correction. . . . In correcting faults he must avoid sarcasm and above all abuse: for teachers whose rebukes seem to imply positive dislike discourage industry. (Butler, 1953)

While the above advice is intuitively appealing and reasonable, it does not gives us any specific information as to how we are to act when we are face to face with a classroom full of real children.

Even the very powerful twentieth-century tool of science, which has successfully been applied to many problems, has largely not been successfully applied to problems of teaching and learning. Much learning theory has its experimental origin in laboratories where researchers can carefully control all factors. Results of experiments in labs are difficult to apply to the very complex situation of the classroom. Instead of teaching one rat to run a maze, a teacher is confronted with thirty or more children who are to be taught very difficult things like reading, writing, and arithmetic (Jackson, 1968, p. 151).

Teachers tend therefore to rely on personal experience to solve problems. When something good happens during a lesson, teachers are grateful, cross their fingers, and hope that whatever it was that caused it will happen again. Young teachers tend to model their actions on those of older teachers (or teachers who seem successful) rather than on the advice they received in education classes. The wise teacher is perhaps the one who uses the best wisdom available—the statements from classic writers on education like Quintilian, the equally general statements about human behavior from science, as well as what one's experience and reason show—and tries to bring it to bear on the real classroom situations.

THE COMPLEXITY OF HUMAN NATURE

The character of human nature is also a barrier to reaching teacher goals in the domain of student success. If one calculated all the possible human characteristics and the resulting permutations (according to George Wells Beadle, the Nobel Laureate in Genetics), we would have the number of possible different human individuals being on the order of 2 raised to the 4 billionth power. (That is 2 X 2 X 2, 4 *billion* times. The magnitude of that number can be suggested if we realize that 2 to the 35th power is over 17 billion, or more than four times the present population of the whole earth!) "Individual differences" is no cliché.

When a doctor treats a patient, she is able to isolate and eliminate one by one the possible factors that caused the given problem. When she finds the specific factor that cannot be eliminated, modern medical science often gives her the means to treat and cure the ailment. A teacher is not working with diseases that have been explored by science. The teacher is trying to deal with human behavior about which knowledge is at best sketchy. Proven "treatments" are rare.

THE PROBLEMS OF SCHOOLS

The nature of schools is also a barrier to goals of student success. Perhaps if schools had as the sole pupose the teaching of a list of, say, twenty or thirty skills and attitudes, the goals of success might be more easily reached. But schools have many, many goals and not all of them are consistent with student learning.

It is a good journey when one knows where one is going. If we think of the goals of schools as being the places we want to get to, then most school "journeys" are not good since the goals tends to be ill-defined. Some people want schools to concentrate on the "basics" while others are intent on "developing the whole child," and still others see schools as a means for improving society. Teachers are caught in the middle.

THE SUM OF THE PARTS PROBLEM

A final hurdle that must be cleared on the way to student-teacher classroom success might be termed "The Sum of the Parts Problem." We try to speak about teaching by referring to the factors that compose the teaching acts. Teachers are trained to make lesson plans, to arouse interest in a lesson, to give examples, and to ask questions. But we have all had the experience of carefully attending to all of the factors and still having the lesson fail. Some days, however, the lesson will seemingly design itself. The day will take on a wonderful shape, we will go home feeling lighthearted and twenty years old—and not know the reason why.

Perhaps teaching is one of those things of which the "whole is greater than the sum of its parts." Even a careful analysis of the classroom experience that discovers each factor in that experience may well miss the essence of it.

The twentieth century has been the century of science. People who lived in the Egypt of the Pharaohs, the Greece of Homer, the Rome of the Caesars, or the England of the Georges all lived very much the same. Our lives are markedly different from theirs because of science. People in our century have seen the coming of the electric light, the airplane, and the landing of men on the moon. Even time and space, once the great constants of human life, have changed because of science. But science has yet to penetrate the mysterious ways of human behavior. One of the dark and mysterious corners as yet unilluminated by science is the x factor present in successful classrooms. While we sense the x, it has defied our attempts to weigh it, measure it, or catch it. It is like a rainbow whose end can never be reached. This x factor is what makes the successful classroom greater than the sum of its parts.

SUCCESS EXISTS

Nevertheless, classes are taught and students and teachers do feel successful. Teachers do things in classrooms (and out) that cause "good things" to happen. In short, it is possible to overstress the problems and the unknowns of teaching and learning. In some ways education is a natural human attribute. One of the things that divides humans from the rest of living creation is the human capacity (and need) for education. Within three or four hours after they are born, the African antelope, or gnu, is capable of doing all the things that adult gnus do. Human babies are incomplete at birth. We are entirely dependent upon adults, and our dependency lasts for nearly twenty years. What is more striking about humans is the fact that they must be educated into adulthood. Puppies become dogs simply by maturing. A baby would *not* grow *naturally* into a human being. All human cultures have recognized this fundamental fact of life and have provided a regular system of education to develop babies into responsible members of the community.

If education is a natural human trait, it is also a human art. By art we do *not* mean to imply that it is something merely spontaneous and beyond our capacity to think and learn about it. We would like to define art (and the art of teaching) as being the imaginative application of knowledge to human problems. Art is a demonstration of skill and knowledge. Michelangelo knew how to prepare paints, how to prepare a plaster surface, how to paint so that it would adhere, and how to protect the surface from the ravages of time. If his art had been nothing but spontaneous feeling, the Sistine Chapel would now have a ceiling in off-white. Teachers are artists in the same sense. They have great amounts of knowledge. They know when a group of children are hard at work: they can discern *that* sort of hum from the empty hum of a lot of bored pupils. Teachers know how to create tests, think up new examples, speak in front of an audience, sense when a child needs to be hugged and when he needs to be rebuked. While some of the knowledge and skill possessed by the teachers is of the intuitive variety, much more of it comes from the teacher's ability to observe the world of the classroom and then to learn from this observation. Over a period the teacher learns how early in the year smiling is permissible, how to pace a lesson, what "works" in teaching reading to sixth graders or history to high school juniors.

In addition to the observational knowledge that a teacher learns through experience, other knowledge is available to the teacher from the social and behavioral sciences. In the next sections of this chapter, knowledge about teaching and learning will be presented which teachers may find useful in going around, over, or under the obstacles to their goals of student success.

A CAUTION LABEL

Before we go on, we must add a caution label. The theory that we shall present is the product of science's investigation of human behavior. Knowing this theory will *not necessarily* help a teacher achieve the goals of the student success factor. There have been great and effective teachers who never took a course or read a book about educational psychology, just as there have been ineffectual teachers who know all there is to know about human psychology.

Teaching is an active use of knowledge. Theory will only be as useful as the imaginative and sensitive teacher can make it. Without the teacher to *apply* it, theory is merely a set of inert facts.

SEVEN IDEAS ABOUT TEACHERS WHO SEEM ABLE TO HELP STUDENTS BE SUCCESSFUL

The following ideas have been drawn from the research literature about teaching and learning. These general ideas seem to be associated with effective teachers, those teachers who help their students to be successful academically and personally.

1. Effective teachers are clear teachers.
2. Effective teachers are enthusiastic.
3. Effective teachers use a variety of teaching styles, materials, and so on to adjust the material covered to the learner.
4. Effective teachers provide their students with the best opportunity to learn the material covered in the course.
5. Effective teachers whose goals include a desire to have their students gain in achievement tend to be businesslike and work-oriented.
6. The effective teacher recognizes that pupil motivation is related to the personal needs of the pupil.
7. It is possible for teachers to go beyond information. Teachers can help the pupil-person to get the most out of school.

THE FIRST IDEA: EFFECTIVE TEACHERS ARE CLEAR TEACHERS

One teacher behavior that research has shown to be related consistently to student achievement is described by the term *clarity*. While research has not as yet been able to pin down the general notion of clarity, it does provide us with some hints as to how teachers might use the notion of clarity to reach their goals in the area of student success.

A common sense way to begin thinking about clarity in teaching might be to think very seriously about educational goals. If we want to be clear to others, we must ourselves understand what we wish to express. In planning a lesson, then, it is perhaps not enough to say, "I am going to teach about the causes of the Civil War." A clearer, more precise statement of purpose is needed. This purpose statement may come out of a series of questions that might be asked about the goals of the lesson:

1. Do I want my pupils to learn a set of *facts* about ___ ?, or
2. Do I want my pupils to understand certain *general principles about* ___ ?, or

3. Do I hope that learning ⎯⎯ will develop certain *mental habits* in my pupils?, or
4. Do I think that learning ⎯⎯ will help the *character* of my pupils?

A better statement about the lesson on the Civil War might be: "I want my pupils to know four causes of the Civil War (1, 2, 3, 4) so that they can relate each cause to an ambiguity in the federal Constitution."

Once you have your goals set out clearly, you can begin attending to the clear presentation of the material. In studying the notion of clarity, some investigators, Andrew Bush, Donald Cruickshank, Betty Myers, and John Kennedy at Ohio State University, have done extensive surveys of student perception of what a clear teacher is.

What Pupils Think Clear Teachers Do

1. Clear teachers provide for student understanding. They make an effort to find out what pupils know and do not know. Then they are careful to give explanations that the *pupils* understand at a pace appropriate to the topic and the pupils. These teachers are willing to take time with explanations. The explanations are such that the pupils know what the teacher expects of them. When the pupils ask questions, the teacher is willing to repeat answers. These teachers stress the difficult points and explain new words in easy to understand language. In short, the clear teacher tries to find out what pupils understand and then teaches that way.

2. Clear teachers explain with many sorts of examples. A math teacher, for example, works examples of problems for the class. In the working of examples, the teacher is careful to show *how* in an orderly, step-by-step manner. The clear teachers seem willing to show pupils all that the pupils need to know to complete the work successfully.

3. Clear teachers stick to the subject and are careful to

relate what is talked about to the topic at hand. In addition, these clear teachers relate the subject at hand to the real life of their pupils.

4. Clear teachers are verbally fluent. They use words carefully. Their sentences make sense. They also help their pupils with language. They are willing to repeat directions and to speak so that all students can hear what is being said. These teachers make language work for them. They speak expressively and use vivid, specific detail when explaining. An example: once a teacher told the writer about Thomas J. Jackson, the Civil War general. "Jackson had pale blue eyes," the teacher explained, "and he looked out at the world through them so fiercely that his men called him 'Old Blue Light.'" Such a description makes it hard not to remember General Jackson!

5. Clear teachers help students organize their work. It is known that teachers who are careful to provide clues as to the organization of the lesson, to indicate the main ideas in a reading passage, and to prepare pupils to meet unfamiliar words and concepts are teachers who see their students improve. Teachers do these things by, for example, using maps, diagrams, and outlines. The teacher might also make the pupils do an outline of the material. Pupils know that they are aware of the teacher's organizational patterns because the teacher gives frequent quizzes or tests.

SECOND IDEA: EFFECTIVE TEACHERS ARE ENTHUSIASTIC

Although *enthusiasm* is one of those words that is overused to the point where it is sometimes meaningless, it, like clarity, has been identified by researchers in teaching effectiveness as one of the handful of teacher behaviors that correlates with increases in student achievement. Originally the word "enthusiasm" comes from a combination of Greek words meaning "a god within." An enthusiastic person was seen to be someone who was quite literally inspired by a powerful force. Such inspiration was thought to give the person more power than the uninspired possessed. In the research on enthusiastic teaching, the word means "stimulating," "animated," "energetic," and "mobile." It has been found that all other things being equal, a teacher who presents materials with appropriate gestures, animation, and eye contact will have students who achieve better on tests than will the teacher who does not gesture, reads in a monotone, and generally behaves in an unenthusiastic manner.

The factor of teacher enthusiasm may well be related to another area of knowledge. Investigators into the mysteries of communication between people believe that while some of the information we impart to others is passed on by the words we use, a good part of it is passed on nonverbally. As one researcher put it, "The human being is a multidimensional creature who occasionally talks." Thus, human beings communicate in a whole range of ways. For example, we may hear a man use the words, "Good morning," but the actual goodness of the morning—at least as the man sees it—is communicated by the tone of voice, the gestures the man uses, and his facial expression. We may understand from these nonverbal signals that indeed it is not a good morning for the man. Nonverbal communications tend to be very potent, overriding verbal messages that contradict them. During the 1960's, when there was much talk about peace and love, the tenor of the times seemed more violent than peaceful. We might speculate that the violent tenor was related to the violent nature of the nonverbal communication that was signaled by those preaching peace verbally. In the same way, a teacher who truly enjoys reading and who reads extensively might well convey his enthusiasm to his students in nonverbal ways that will be more potent than all of his statements about how "reading is pleasant." Such a teacher might well not need to say that reading is worthwhile.

We might speculate—for there is no good evidence to support this except observational and personal evidence—that enthusiastic teaching has its origins in a passionate caring about the knowledge the teacher is conveying to the pupils. Passionate caring comes to us when we feel that whatever it is we care about—American history, French, basketball—is important in our lives. We know enough about it so that we can see how the knowledge is connected to our lives. A teacher who is interested in politics (enough, say, to run for a seat on the local school board) may teach her Civics or Problems of Democracy courses enthusiastically simply because she cares about the subject, and because she cares, she extends her knowledge of the subject constantly.

We will end this discussion of teacher enthusiasm by suggesting that it is an elusive quality. It would be very helpful if a formula for enthusiasm could be set forth, but such a formula does not seem likely to exist. Gilbert Highet notes that enthusiasm for teaching grows out of a mental attitude about the relationship between teachers and pupils.

> Young people hate grown-ups for many reasons. One of the reasons is that they feel grown-ups' minds are fixed and limited. Whenever they meet a man or woman who does not always say what they expect, who tells them novel stories about strange aspects of the world, who throws unexpected lights on what they sadly know as ordinary dull life, who seems completely alive, sensitive, energetic, and zestful as they themselves, they usually admire him or her. It is true that we cannot be fountains of energy and novelty throughout every day, but we ought, if we are teachers, to be so keen on our subjects that we can talk interestingly about unusual aspects of them to young people who would otherwise have been neutrally dull, or—worse—eager but disappointed. (Highet, 1950, p. 14)

THIRD IDEA:
EFFECTIVE TEACHERS USE A VARIETY OF TEACHING STYLES, MATERIALS, AND SO ON TO ADJUST THE MATERIAL COVERED TO THE LEARNER

Our society pays a good deal of attention to the individual. The rights of the individual are backed by the majesty of our law. Our literature is full of tales of the accomplishments of the rugged individualists who settled the West, made scientific discoveries and inventions, or performed heroic deeds in being true to their beliefs. There is perhaps not a school in the United States which does not pay tribute to "the individual child" in its Statement of Philosophy. Unfortunately, for all of the importance the individual has in our society, the day-to-day operation of schools seems to set barriers for teachers who wish to attend to the individual. Teachers interact with pupils at more than two hundred interactions each hour. Classes are seldom smaller than twenty-five, and in our cost-effective age, thirty pupils per class is perhaps closer to the national average. School systems buy textbooks and materials in wholesale lots so that it is likely that any given class in a system will be using the same series as any other class in the same grade level. In spite of school philosophies, circumstances make it very difficult for teachers to pay attention to individual differences in classrooms.

But teachers express the desire over and over again in surveys of teacher problems to "provide for individual differences" of pupils. Classroom teachers recognize that the importance of the individual is no mere slogan but a reality.

The question then is, what is known about individual differences that can be of help to the classroom teacher?

If we begin by turning to research in teacher effectiveness, it can be seen that along with the factors of clarity and enthusiasm, the factor called *variability* has been found to be one of the teacher behaviors that is positively related to student achievement. In the investigations of variability it has been found that teachers who use a variety of materials, approaches, and methods seem to be more effective than teachers who stick to a smaller range in the classroom. There should be little surprise at such a finding, given our feelings about the importance of the individual. If genuine and important differences exist between individuals, it might logically be concluded that individuals will differ in ways of learning. To recall an old joke, the classroom that uses only one method to teach pupils is like the hospital that treats all patients for a broken right leg.

It might be helpful to attempt to put individual differences into some sort of framework. Once upon a time, it was believed that children were merely small adults and should be so treated. If you have ever seen children's portraits from early America, you see that children (of wealthy families, that is) wore exactly the same clothes as their parents. In those days, a high compliment for a little boy was to be called, "My little man." In our own century, in contrast, investigators of human growth and development have come to the realization that human beings of all cultures pass through a series of developmental stages, and that they pass through these stages in the same order. Each stage gives the individual a different way of processing the information that comes to him through his senses. For example, according to Jean Piaget, the noted French-Swiss biologist and studier of children, very young children (to the age of about 2) believe only in objects that can be seen or touched. A child at this stage truly exemplifies the concept of "out of sight, out of mind." The next stage, according to Piaget, lasts from ages 2 to 7. (The child's chronological age is not necessarily an indication of the stage the child is in, however. One must examine the way the child handles her environment.) In this stage, children tend to explain events in ways that do not take into account all the possible causes, looking to the product or outcome rather than to the process which produced it, and they link events through a different logic than do adults. In one of Piaget's examples, a child who sees water poured from a short fat glass into a tall thin one will assert that there is now more water than before. Sometime between the ages of 7 and 11 the child begins to learn *compensation*: he sees that the tall thin glass holds the same amount of water as the short fat one; the tallness of the glass is compensated for by its thinness. The child also learns *reversibility*: he sees that the tall thin glass of water can be poured back into the short fat one with no loss. In a practical teaching situation, a child who is having difficulty understanding that 2 + 3 = 5 and that 5 = 2 + 3 might be suspected of simply not having matured enough to understand the process of reversibility.

The final conceptual stage is called *formal operations.* While Piaget himself suggested that children entered into this stage around age 11, current research indicates that it happens later. In *formal operations* a person comes to understand and use abstractions (things that exist as ideas rather than as touchable, smellable, tastable entities) and symbols. For example, formal operations make is possible for the mind to deal with conditions that are contrary to fact, e.g., "What if the South had won the Civil War?"

There are then differences among individuals based on developmental factors. A teacher ought to expect to find pupils who differ not only in height, weight, and hair color but also in the ways of dealing with information. A pupil who operates in Piaget's "concrete" stage will be helped by being provided with information that is low in abstraction and rich in sensation.

Another theorist of mental development, Jerome Bruner, suggests that there are three basic stages that describe the way humans deal with the information that comes through the senses. Bruner does not see the stages as being simply a function of maturity but believes that we operate in all three stages. A mature person uses each mode in combination with the others for a complete understanding. The stages are related to ability to deal with words and abstract concepts. Young children, who are less sophisticated in using words, tend to use the simpler ways of processing information.

In Bruner's scheme of things, the simplest mode is the *enactive mode*. This way of "thinking" is nonverbal and uses action or movement instead. A very young child, for example, does not contemplate objects; she is likely to put them in her mouth. She makes things real by touching or manipulating them.

In the next mode, the *iconic* (from the Greek word for "picture"), experience is dealt with largely by storing up pictures. A child's idea of Uncle Bill is his picture of Uncle Bill tossing him into the air. New experiences are matched against the "picture file." Some of the "darndest things" said by children have their origin in the limitation of this method of understanding. If a child is given a verbal idea (nonpictorial) he tries to understand it by finding a picture-idea he has had.

The third mode by which humans deal with information is linguistic and is tied to the development of ability to handle abstraction with language. Once words are mastered, it is possible to think about ideas that may have no concrete physical reality by using symbols of them. The *symbolic mode* enables one to contemplate an abstraction like "love" by viewing symbolic representation of a picture of two doves.

The wise teacher who takes Bruner's system into account might well attempt to provide the variety of children in a classroom with opportunities to receive information in as many modes as possible. A unit about the Civil War that is based on a text (symbolic mode) might be supplemented by many pictures (iconic mode) which in turn might be supplemented by a visit to the local historical society museum where actual artifacts might be seen and touched (enactive mode).

But the question of differences among individuals is not limited to a discussion of developmental differences, as important as they are. The classroom is a place of *interaction*. Children are not confronting the environment alone; they are confronting it both with classmates and with a teacher. Children at all stages of development, as well as their teachers, differ in the experiences that they have had.

It is a principle of behavioral science that what we perceive in our environment is determined to a large extent by our previous experience. A walk through the woods is a quite different experience for someone who has just completed a good course in botany. He is likely to see beech and maple trees that mark this forest as being a climax or mature forest. Before the botany course he noticed only that there were a lot of trees.

Perhaps the best strategy (or at least a good strategy) for teachers who are interested in the interactions in their classrooms would be to recognize the general principle, which *seems* to be true, that the effect of our actions is related both to the nature of the actions and to the personality of the one acted upon. One of the limitations of advice to teachers about "what to do on Monday" is that it often ignores the fact that actions are not simple things that are done to another person. The other person is very much a part of our actions. A teacher's smile (an action) may appear to one student as an expression of warmth while another student who has just gotten a failing grade from that teacher may see the smile as a kind of cruel sarcasm.

Research in teacher effectiveness is beginning to indicate that in this matter of interaction, teachers who help bring about academic gain with one group of children may operate differently than teachers who help bring about academic gain with other groups. For example, teachers of primary grade children from low socioeconomic backgrounds tend to:

> Devote more time to schoolwork and less on controlling misbehavior.
> Individualize assignments.
> Work with large groups more than with small groups.
> Ask more questions of a convergent (single-answer) nature.
> Be less critical and more supportive of pupils.
> Use a larger variety of control techniques (Chapter 6).
> Give pupils less freedom in choosing activities.

Give painstaking attention to student work.
Provide for immediate feedback of pupil work.
Be warm and convivial but very much "the boss."

Teachers of pupils from high socioeconomic backgrounds tend to:

Be very demanding and critical.
Ask more divergent questions.

In the upper elementary grades, the effective teacher tends to:

Talk a greater portion of the time.
Keep pupils working.
Be less permissive.
Ask easier questions.
Use less traditional materials.
Seem more traditional. (Brophy, 1976)

CAUTION: It should be remembered that the above information is based only on research done in elementary classrooms. The criterion for an "effective" teacher was "teachers whose students achieve on tests." Your criterion may be quite different.

*Also note that statements about "what is good for poor (low-socioeconomic) children" are **not** to be treated as being absolutely true. It can reasonably be argued that giving such children "less freedom in choosing activities" is simply another way to ensure that they will grow up unequipped to take advantage of a democratic society whose essence is intelligent choosing.*

Finally, to personalize any of the notions that have been

set down here, it is perhaps very important for the individual teacher to think carefully about himself and his ways of teaching.

What is valued in the classroom? Little structure, moderate structure, or high degree of structure? (Which pupils respond to what sorts of structure?) What sorts of knowlege are valued? Facts, concepts, or knowledge that tends to speculate about "what if" situations? What is the nature of work tasks? Is there a regular routine of homework and quizzes and tests? Are lectures given or is much of the work done in groups or individual projects?

The state of knowledge about teaching and learning makes the answers to these sorts of questions important because there is little evidence that one style of teaching is better than any other. In spite of current fashions that favor "individual discovery learning" over lectures, there is no good evidence suggesting that a teacher who lectures is less (or more) effective than a teacher who uses the project method and small task forces. The answers therefore ought not necessarily indicate that any one particular style of teaching dominates an individual classroom because it is the *right* method. Rather, the discussion of developmental psychology and pupil differences in experience suggests that a classroom that witnesses a *sensible* (orderly, predictable) *variety* or *range* of approaches may be exhibiting the best strategy.

A classroom survey might begin with teacher self-evaluation (as outlined two paragraphs above). Next, it might be profitable for the teacher to look at her pupils. What is the range of development and previous learning? How well does the range of teacher actions match the range of pupil development and experience? Is an opportunity provided for each pupil to take in information? Some pupils might enjoy and learn from good, highly structured lectures while others do better in open-ended discussions. Some pupils need to do a lot of manipulation of what is being studied; for example, some math pupils get fractions by seeing the well-known chalk pies drawn on the blackboard while others might need something more concrete like Cuisinaire rods to work with. Some pupils may listen well and therefore enjoy and learn from listening to tapes while others do better with films.

A class of pupils demands a variety of teaching methods, media, and levels of discourse. Billy needs a very stable routine in his day; Marie thrives on surprises, and routine bores her almost literally to tears. The burden is therefore on the teacher to be a sensitive observer of pupils. He must be flexible and adaptable, able to see the classroom and pupils as they are, not according to a set of preconceptions. In this connection, a worthwhile exercise might be to keep a daily journal about what happens in the classroom. Individual observations of pupil behavior may not tell very much about what is working or not working with that individual, but over a period of time a collection of observations may reveal patterns of behavior. While harsh criticism seems to be harmful in general, for example, there are probably individuals in any classroom who need some harsh criticism from time to time. Such journal entries may help the teacher come to understand his pupils.

We will conclude this section with a final warning. Once, during the early part of the space program, we were watching one of the Apollo shots to the moon. After the Apollo achieved earth orbit, the spacecraft was to separate from the third stage of the Saturn rocket that had boosted it into space. After separation, the Apollo was to dock with the Lunar Excursion Module (LEM) and then head for the moon. In its docking, the television cameras in the Apollo would turn toward the earth, Walter Cronkite told us. Very shortly, we were reminded, we would have a marvelous picture of the Western Hemisphere. We watched the television screen intently. Pretty soon a dark disk appeared on the screen. Mr. Cronkite, his voice now excited, began to point out the features of our world as seen from a distance of some five hundred miles up in space. Sure enough, we too could see the familiar outlines of North and South America. It looked almost as it did in the atlases we had seen. But then Mr. Cronkite's voice lost some of its enthusiasm. "No, wait," he said, "that wasn't the earth we were looking at; that was the third stage of the Saturn IVB rocket. Now here's earth!" We saw what we expected to see—even if it wasn't really there. It might be well in approaching our classrooms, to think about our human ability to see what we think we see. In deciding how to treat pupils, the generalizations ought to grow out of observations. Rather than saying, "This movie should really help the children understand oil exploration," we should approach the film in an experimental way. When our friend Billy puts his head down on his desk and closes his eyes during the showing of the film, we might try to think about what we know about Billy and think of other ways to teach that unique person.

FOURTH IDEA: EFFECTIVE TEACHERS PROVIDE THEIR STUDENTS WITH THE BEST OPPORTUNITY TO LEARN THE MATERIAL COVERED IN THE COURSE

The key word here is "opportunity." Schools are places where pupils come to get the knowledge, skills, and attitudes valued by their community. Being at school is not enough; the pupil must be given the opportunity to learn what she is to learn.

First, what is learning? A working definition of learning might be "a change in behavior acquired by experience or study (excluding changes brought about by physiological factors such as hunger, weariness, and so on)." This definition is broad and includes a wide range of possible learnings.

1. A child learns to flinch at a sudden loud noise. This would be what a psychologist calls a "conditioned response."
2. A high school pupil acquires the skill of pronouncing French like a native speaker.
3. A man learns a series of nonsense syllables heard in a song ("Marzedotes, and dozedotes, and littlelambzedivy").

4. A salesman recalls the meaning of a bulletin about changes in coffee prices.
5. A scientist comes to understand how he can measure the amount of gold in a crown without harming the crown. This understanding comes to him suddenly while taking a bath.

Because of such a wide range of possible learnings, perhaps teachers should be concerned with "what sort of learning" is meant in a specific context.

Benjamin Bloom and his colleagues created a Taxonomy of Educational Objectives that might help illustrate the variety of learning possible in school tasks.

A teacher may want pupils to acquire *knowledge*. According to Bloom, this knowledge has three possible ramifications. Pupils might be expected to gain "knowledge of specific facts"—the multiplication tables up to 10 × 10. In other contexts, pupils need "knowledge of ways and means of dealing with specifics." Finally knowledge includes "knowledge of the universals and abstractions of a field." Physics students learn about acceleration and the coefficient of friction.

But knowledge may not be enough. Basic knowledge can be built upon to create *comprehension*. A pupil with comprehension can translate knowledge into other terms—she can explain *friction* in her own words. The pupil who comprehends is able to interpret (tell what something means) and extrapolate (infer beyond known facts).

Comprehension too can be built upon. Pupils can *apply* knowledge and comprehension. Knowledge and comprehension of the metric system can become the ability to tell distances in kilometers.

Next comes *analysis*. To analyze means "to take things apart." Pupils can learn to analyze the elements of a whole, the relationship among kindred things, and the organizational principles that show how things fit together.

At the next level in the taxonomy, teachers may want pupils to *synthesize*—to put things together in new ways. A pupil may write an essay about the Civil War that uses the same elements but forms a "unique communication." A pupil may learn to make a new plan for solving a difficult story problem in mathematics. The same pupil may discover a new set of relationships in a set of facts.

Finally, a teacher might want pupils to be able to *evaluate*—to make judgments. One sort of judgment is based on the internal evidence. Pupils may judge the effectiveness of a persuasive speech given by a classmate based on skill of presentation. Another sort of judgment is made in terms of external standards. The effectiveness of the speech may be judged by how many times the speaker lost eye contact with the audience, the external criteria having been established beforehand by the teacher. (Bloom et al., 1956, pp. 201-7)

ACTIVITY
Take a lesson that you have taught recently. List your objectives in terms of Bloom's Taxonomy. Then indicate what activities you give your pupils that will help them reach the objectives:

Objectives:	*Activities:* (*Examples*)
Knowledge	a reading about the battles of the Civil War
knowledge of specifics	
Comprehension	
interpretation	
Application	
Analysis	
Synthesis	
Evaluation	a chance to grade each other's quizzes over the battles of the Civil War

Do all of your stated objectives have activities? Are some of your objectives just thoughts? Is there much difference between what you actually do and what you would like to do?

How do you go about deciding which objectives are chosen? This is a question which has no single best answer. It is, however, a question every teacher must attempt to deal with.

Once you have determined your educational objectives, you need to think of ways to provide your pupils with opportunities to meet those objectives. In the next pages, you will find some general principles of learning from the humanistic and behavioral sciences. It is hoped that this information will provide you with insight into ways you can provide your students with the best opportunity to learn.

Theory Related to Learning, Recall, and Skill Building

Research indicates that learning, recall of material learned, and the building of skills (skills we will define simply as the ability to do) can be conveniently divided into three stages.

Stage One: Cuing. Problems in learning often begin with the failure of the learner to understand what is to be learned. Pupils need to know the nature of the learning task. The teacher's first task, therefore, is to decide in as specific a manner as possible the nature of the learning task. "I am going to assign them a book report tomorrow," you say to yourself. You must go on to tell yourself what a "book report" is. Do you want a summary of the action in the book or do you want interpretation of the action? Do you want a report on a specific character or do you prefer to have the students tell about all of the important characters? In some simple situations, it might be adequate to state what the learning task is: "I want you to work the even-numbered problems on page 29 of the algebra text." In more complicated situations (as with the book report), it might be a wise strategy to provide pupils with a model of what they are to do. You could write a "model" book report and hand it out to all the students.

Stage Two: Attention. Pupils must pay attention to what is to be learned. Teachers help learners to notice and become aware of the material. What we pay attention to is related to three different factors: (1) our previous experience and learning—a physicist may listen to a lecture on quarks, but a bricklayer may not; (2) the nature of what is to be learned—the makers of television commercials have made a science of making what is to be learned attention getting; and (3) our needs, desires, wishes, and interests at the time.

1. What is the relationship between previous learning experience and attention to what is to be learned?

—We are more likely to see the parts of our environment that we anticipate, and we anticipate what we are familiar with. Implications: material presented ought to have some "fit" with a pupil's present knowledge. Imaginative effort on the part of the teacher to discover this fit may well pay off in student success. Teachers must be aware of the present knowledge and experience of pupils. Teachers, know your pupils!

2. What is the nature of attention-taking material?

- If there is a *difference* between material and its background, attention is likely to be paid to the material.

Attention is paid to $^{W}O_{R_{D_S}}$ in contrasting positions, colors, or type faces.

- Emotional words and pictures are attention takers. How many products use pictures of kittens, puppies, babies, and so forth to attract attention? Names too have emotional content. There is a company selling a series of children's books containing the names of specific children—when you order the book, you have a son, daughter, or other child's name put in the place where the hero's name goes. A teacher might take advantage of the emotional content of names by using pupil names in story problems in math, for instance.

- Things that are unusual or out of the ordinary are

attention taking. Humor, for example, is based on incongruity or inconsistency between what we expect and what actually happens. Having an historical character use modern slang might draw attention to an important point about the character.

- Complexity seems to draw attention to itself. Pupils may be drawn to examine a poem because it is complex in an interesting way. Can you read this poem?

> Infir taris,
> Inoak nonis,
> Inmudeelsis,
> In claynonis.
> Cana goateati vi?
> Cana mareetots?
>
> ANONYMOUS

- Ambiguity will draw attention. Students may find a picture with parts missing or a story that needs to be completed worth attending to.

In the initial attention stage, there is a difficulty. Researchers into the problems of memory suggest that humans have two types of memory, one short term and the other long term. An example of the short-term memory might be the looking up of a telephone number, dialing it, and then forgetting the number immediately. Pupil's first experience with material finds the material put into the short-term memory. It will therefore be quickly forgotten unless it is given a chance to be put into the long-term memory. Not only is the short-term memory short, it also seems to have a small capacity, able to contain only three or four items at a time. Therefore, the teacher should probably take into consideration some of the following principles relating to memory.

- Longer time on a task seems to allow new material to be better retained.
- Memory of material depends on how it is arranged or coded. It is probably easier to recall "Able was I ere I saw

Elba" than it is to recall "mbnc dsal out requ tyd" qxr bdq, which has the same number of words. Knowing that "Able was I . . . etc." is the same sentence when read backwards might also code it for better recall. A list of things like dogs, apes, opossums, echidnas, kangaroos, and platypuses might be coded into three groups (since three is about the capacity of the short-term memory) as follows:

Egg-laying Mammals	*Pouched Mammals*	*Placental Mammals*
Echidnas, Platypuses	Kangaroos, Opossums	Dogs, Apes

Other codings are the familiar *mnemonics* or memory aids like ROY G. BIV (the colors of the visible light spectrum in its proper order—red, orange, yellow, green, blue, indigo, violet). The use of place can also be effective. A list of things might be paired with the location (place) of familiar things in the classroom. The names of Columbus's ships might be paired with the sink (*Nina*), the aquarium (Pinta), and the teacher's desk (Santa Maria). Going from the sink to the aquarium to the desk, the teacher may be able to elicit the names of the ships.

- Things that resemble material to be learned tend to bump the new material out of the memory. During the short-term memory phase, therefore, distractors ought to be kept to a minimum until enough time has passed for the material to sink in.

How does material transfer into the long-term memory?

- New material seems to go into the permanent memory, better (and remember that memory here includes facts, data, skills, etc.) if the learner has an opportunity to deal with the material actively. Silent reading of material is more effective if it is accompanied by recitation, or even a physical activity such as mouthing the words. This implies that discovery learning situations should help learning. Care must be taken, however, to ensure that pupils discover correct things since active learning of misconceptions may be more effective than passive learning of wrong concepts!

Stage Three: Recall. There must be an opportunity to recall the material. Human beings need a chance to compare what they are putting into the mind with what is supposed to be put in. This comparison (feedback) gives the learner a chance to correct errors that have crept into the learning. Feedback may have another function. A principle of reward has it that an action which is appropriately rewarded is likely to be repeated. If a student works a math problem and discovers that he did it correctly, he is more likely to do the next problem. This principle is used in the design of teaching machines: a correct answer permits the pupil to go on to the next question; if the pupil gives an incorrect answer, the machine asks him to "Try Again." This sort of positive and constructive feedback helps learning.

Recall of material is made easier when selection of material to be recalled is limited. This implies that a test ought to help the pupil limit the material he considers to recall. Rather than ask students to write about "Colonial trade before the American Revolution," it might be more helpful to have a question that asks them to "discuss the relationship between the trading of molasses, rum, and slaves before the American Revolution."

Material is better recalled when associations have formed between the material and other things. Perhaps pupils who are able to remember a great deal about football teams (and seem to have no memory at all when it comes to school tasks) have the advantage of all the associations that football has in everyday American life—T-shirts with logos of teams, athletes plugging commerical products, and so on. A teacher of music might help his cause by wearing a Beethoven sweatshirt!

The human mind tends to organize experience into patterns. Individual items that do not fit into the pattern tend to be ignored. If the teacher helps pupils to organize material to be learned into patterns that demonstrate relationships (like causal ones)—for example, by using charts to show how each item fits—it might help pupils not only with initial learning of the material but also with recall of that information.

Organization of Materials for Learning

In addition to the stages discussed above, several other considerations must enter a teacher's planning to provide pupils with opportunity to learn.

First, it seems that for teaching a skill that includes a chain of actions—hitting a tennis ball backhand, writing a composition—the most efficient tactics for presenting the material depends on the nature of the skill. For example, hitting a good shot in tennis depends on smooth coordination of all the elements of the shot. It therefore appears that most efficient learning of the shot comes when it is taught as a whole. On the other hand, writing a composition depends upon a series of tasks—discovering a topic, designing a thesis, making an outline, writing, revising—that are more or less complete in themselves; it seems that efficient learning comes when such a skill is divided into its components and each component is mastered separately. Observation of training in the military shows use of these principles. The military trains large numbers of people to do both simple and complex tasks. Aiming a rifle is taught in one smooth action—coordination of a series of parts—whereas taking apart the rifle for cleaning is taught in a series of tasks, each of which is to be mastered before the next can be approached.

Next, all teachers know that simple ability to demonstrate a skill ignores the problem of demonstrating the skill at a certain level of quality. Teachers have standards; they want to help pupils to do *and* do *well*. For this reason, teachers ought to provide pupils with standards of performance. Pupils can know not only that they have successfully done what was to be done, but also know that the doing has been of the proper quality.

When a learner is to be brought to a certain level of ability in performance, it is better for her to have a description of how far she is from the standard ("Your essay would be at standard if you would not make that spelling error you always seem to make") than for her to know just the general standard. This is perhaps particularly important when the pupil is practicing a task. If she is practicing it incorrectly or below the level of expectation, the practice will merely help her fail. The old adage about practice making perfect is true only if that practice is accompanied by the best and most accurate feedback.

Learning and Related Theory Concerning Reinforcement, Rewards, and Punishment

A large body of theory has come out of behavioral research that attempts to show how one not only can bring a horse to water, but also *can* make him drink. According to the behaviorists, human actions (doing and not doing things) are based on various contingencies in the environment. In the first type of contingency, if a child, for instance, hears a loud noise and then is slapped and these two events are associated over and over again, soon the little fellow will link the loud noise with the slap (which makes him cry). Ultimately, he will begin to cry when he hears the noise even if the slap doesn't follow. When the stimulus (a loud noise) occurs, the child cries. In the other type of contingency, our example might be a young man who calls up a girl and asks her out on a date. If the girl says yes, the young man is likely to try again the following week; his efforts have been rewarded. According to the behaviorists (who are linked in many people's minds with social conditioning, teaching machines, and so forth), these contingencies are operating on us all the time. A wise teacher will attempt to manage these contingencies to the advantage of the pupil.

A *reinforcer* is something that follows an action and increases its strength or likelihood. If a teacher wants a pupil to read a chapter of history, he is likely to reinforce the student who reads the chapter. The problem, of course, is to find something that will act as a reinforcer, something immediate and of the right sort. We are all familiar with the universal reinforcers that seem to have the power to touch all humans—money, food, power, and so on—but if all humans are unique individuals, humans will tend to differ insofar as what will reinforce an action. Therefore, what is reinforcing can only be discovered by careful observation of individual pupils. Some pupils respond very well to praise, while others find getting correct solutions to problems reinforcing. Still others need a very tangible external reinforcer like money or a token that can be exchanged for a desired object. In this regard, it must be pointed out that the variety of possible reinforcers is much larger than what traditional educational thought has usually permitted. Teachers must decide for themselves how far they are willing to depart from the traditional educational reinforcers. For example, a particular school situation might make paying the students (with real money) an effective way to reinforce studying. A teacher who holds views about virtue (in this case virtue = study) being its own reward, might not be able to condone the paying of pupils. But the definition of reinforcement leaves the nature of the practice open-ended. In a classroom the playing of games, reading a comic book, talking with a friend, listening to a record of the pupil's choice, or even looking out a window might be discovered to be effective reinforcements for various pupils. If the teacher cannot imagine permitting a pupil to read a comic book even though the comic book has been observed to be reinforcing, then the teacher ought to look some more until he can reconcile effective reinforcements with his or her conception of what is appropriate. In addition, the reinforcer to be educationally sound should have some *real* connection with what is being reinforced. For example, we might find that students will do their math if they can thereby get hamburgers. If there is no real relationship between hamburgers and math ("What do math and hamburgers have in common?"), the student will soon figure out ways to get hamburgers without doing the math.

A *preferred activity* can be used to reinforce a less preferred activity. This is called the Premack Principle. A ten-minute break (preferred) can be used to reinforce the reading of a chapter in the history book (less preferred). It must be remembered at all times that the Grandmother Rule is in force. The Grandmother Rule states: "*First* you eat your green beans and *then* you can go out and play." The reinforcement ought to depend upon the successful completion of the less preferred activity. "We will read the chapter in history for the next twenty-five minutes and then we will take a ten-minute break." Warning: the nature of what is preferred is not fixed. Pupils may prefer to read the history chapter than to go outside, especially if it is cold and rainy. Reinforcement depends upon sensitive and imaginative application on the part of the teacher.

Reinforcement is most effective for maintaining a desired behavior if it occurs in a variable ratio to the actions being reinforced. Research has found that if reinforcement of an action is, for example, a piece of candy, the reinforcement that comes after, say, three performances, then after five more, than after ten, and then after two, is more effective than the reinforcement that comes regularly or every third time. Just think about the attractions of gambling. The reinforcements come at highly irregular times, but people who gamble find that uncertainty very reinforcing and keep on gambling. (Developing a new behavior, of course, may require consistency in reinforcement until the behavior is well established.)

Some Notions about Reinforcers

- Novelty or something out of the ordinary may serve as a reinforcer. "After math, we are going to the swimming pool to watch the new water polo team practice."

- Reinforcements that touch the actual needs of an individual (see also the Sixth Idea later in this chapter, the section on needs and motivation) are very powerful. A lonely little girl may need recognition by an admired adult. The smile or nod of approval by a teacher may be a more potent reinforcer than a thousand dollar bill.
- Reinforcement is a kind of information. The piece of candy tells the pupil that the task has been done according to the teacher's expectation. Teachers ought to think about the information that reinforcements bear. Information that tells a pupil his work is satisfactory may be effective reinforcement. In an experiment, it was found that positive comments on student papers ("Good work," "Keep it up," "Way to go") brought about improvement on the next set of tests.
- Reinforcement should depend upon *actual performance.* A teacher should reinforce only what has been *done,* not what is promised. If a task is too difficult for a pupil to do, then it might be broken down into parts so that the pupil can be reinforced for an approximation of the correct performance. If the student says, "I c-can't translate the sentence," you might prompt, "Can you tell me the meanings of the words?"
- Reinforcement ought to match the task. A student who gets an A on a spelling test should not be taken on a Caribbean cruise. A rule of thumb is that the smallest possible reinforcement is the most effective reinforcement. In fact, it seems that the simple fact that reinforcement will come is enough.
- Reinforcement is usually positive in tenor. Punishment seems to be a poor reinforcer because it is often difficult to decide what is actually being reinforced. In the well-known example of the pupil who won't read the chapter in history, punishment may be actually reinforcing the pupil's desire for attention. (See the chapter on Control.)

ACTIVITY
Examine your classroom and list what appear to be reinforcers. What is your repertoire of reinforcers? How large is it? Can you make a list

of them that is longer than five, ten, twenty? Does each pupil have an opportunity to be reinforced? Remember the song about "different strokes for different folks." Can you think of reinforcements you give that you may not have been aware of? A teacher of our acquaintance had a good deal of trouble keeping the level of hilarity within limits when he first started teaching. The most serious lesson would dissolve in laughter. A friendly colleague helped the young teacher to discover the cause of the problem. "When someone cuts up, *you* smile," she said. "You're rewarding them." It is possible to reinforce behaviors unconsciously.

Helping Students Get the Most out of Studying

In providing students with an opportunity to learn, teachers are anxious to help students do things that will make the effort pay off. It is an article of faith that if students "know how to study" they will be more successful in academic tasks. Although no one has yet designed a universally applicable and effective set of rules for study, some hints as to what effective study is come from what successful students report as being helpful.

1. Successful study is systematic. The teacher can help students to be systematic by providing clearly outlined tasks: (a) provide goals for each assignment, (b) provide models of the end products of the assignment—a model essay, set of math problems, and so on, (c) show students how to outline and provide outlines of difficult material, (d) make charts and use blackboard effectively, (e) teach in a systematic and orderly way, i.e., develop ideas and principles step by step, (f) remember the principle of clarity (see First Idea).

2. Successful study is positive and cooperative. Successful students seem to be willing to make the effort to be interested in the work at hand. The problem of motivation will be dealt with at greater length in the Sixth Idea below, but as has already been suggested, teachers can help students be interested (emphasis on the word "help") by showing or explaining to them how it is to their advantage, by being clear as to goals and means, by being variable, that is, using a variety of educational methods, media, approaches, and so on. That successful study tends to be cooperative needs some explanation. First, it does not necessarily mean that successful students study in groups. Research indicates that group study works only if it is directed toward things that are already known. Group practice might be appropriate for students who know how to conjugate French verbs ending in -*ir*; but when the task at hand is to learn correctly unknown material, study is perhaps better done alone. Cooperative here means that the pupil feels comfortable talking over with the teacher the difficulties and implications of the material to be learned. The teacher might help in this by encouraging students to come in to talk about schoolwork, by providing a time when pupils can reach him, and by providing a reason for pupils to talk over schoolwork. Besides giving assignments, a teacher might provide extra challenges in the form of puzzles or interesting open-ended questions that encourage pupils to go beyond information. The teacher might also cooperate with parents or might bring the parents into the study situation. In Oakland, California, in the fall of 1977, the parents were asked to sign a contract whereby they agreed to provide a quiet place and time for their children to study—a time without TV, radio, and so on. An effort might also be made to encourage pupils to get enough rest and to eat properly.

Homework

Much study that pupils do is assigned under the guise of "homework." Once again, the state of our knowledge does not confirm the common belief that lots of homework helps pupils improve their academic performance. Successful pupils claim that they do an hour or so out-of-school work each evening, but it is difficult to make a causal relationship between success and homework.

We would suggest that teachers who are concerned with homework ask themselves some questions about the why's of their assignments. Is the homework that is assigned simply busy work? Has the teacher been clear as to the why the work is given? Is it corrected after it has been handed in? Remember the importance of feedback. Is there any variety in it or is it always "the first five problems"? Is there a clear connection between the homework and the work being covered in class? Are the pupils provided with models of the homework properly done?

Finally, we might suggest that teachers consider their own experience in regard to the homework that is assigned. There may well be pupils in the class, perhaps even a majority of the pupils, who will not have a time or a place to do homework. In this case, giving over some class time for individual work might save much frustration for both the teacher and pupil. In the classroom the pupil has an opportunity to get help that might be needed to successfully complete the work.

Tests

We have talked about the importance of statements of educational goals. In many ways, when teachers give tests they are not only giving pupils a change to get feedback, but they are giving themselves a chance for feedback as well. First, what sort of feedback on tests seems to help pupils? Earlier we mentioned that there is some indication that positive feedback, as expressed by brief positive comments, acts to improve subsequent test performance. Recall, too, that feedback ought to be informative in showing pupils where they succeeded and where they did not. Simply to mark a test item as incorrect might not be as helpful as making some indication about the difference between the pupil's response and the teacher's standard. For example, a student might get a wrong answer because of an error in computation. On the other hand, the pupil might get a correct answer by a wrong method. The feedback on the test or quiz should give the pupil this sort of information.

Which is more effective, strict grading or easy grading? What little research has been done in this area seems to indicate that the *presence* of a grade is more important than its strictness or easiness. First, strictness is a relative quality. Common sense would seem to say that the strictness of grading ought to be related to the pupils' ability levels, previous learning, and so on. Some research suggests that there should be a consistency in grading. Pupils ought to understand and be able to predict the teacher's standards. Common sense suggests that the standards which the teacher wishes to apply ought to be in force from the first day of school. It is poor psychology to grade easily and then "get tough" after two or three assignments. It behooves a teacher to make clear to both pupils and herself the grading criteria to be used. Surprises are often pleasant, but not on grade cards. Feedback on tests and quizzes should also provide pupils with a realistic picture of how well they are doing.

The level of strictness probably influences the anxiety with which pupils approach academic work. Some stress is necessary, of course, just as it is with building muscles; however, the teacher ought to bear in mind that while anxiety seems to have some helpful influence on performance of simple tasks, the more complex tasks are actually inhibited by higher levels of anxiety.

Finally, it ought to be noted that grades seem to have some influence over pupil attitudes toward material learned in school. Good grades seem to go along with positive attitudes toward a subject, and apparently getting a good grade card can change a negative attitude into a positive one.

ACTIVITY
Make a list of your goals for a particular lesson and put it aside. When the unit is over and the pupils have been tested, look over the tests and quizzes given. Which questions or activities on the tests correspond with which of the initial goals? Were there any goals that did not appear on the quizzes or tests? What sort of variety was there in types of tests and activities? It might be suggested that just as a variety of teaching methods goes along with effective teaching, a variety of testing methods also might be of value. Some pupils will do better on essay type questions and others may have good command of the multiple-choice test. Are all

of the questions of the "regurgitation" variety, that is, do pupils repeat the material as it was presented in class? Are there opportunities for pupils to speculate on the information, on its implications, on other possible meanings of it?

FIFTH IDEA: EFFECTIVE TEACHERS WHOSE GOALS INCLUDE A DESIRE TO HAVE THEIR STUDENTS GAIN IN ACHIEVEMENT TEND TO BE BUSINESSLIKE AND WORK-ORIENTED.

There is a growing body of evidence that student gain, as measured by tests, is related to the amount of time students are *actively engaged* with material to be learned. A classroom in which the pupils are actively engaged with material seems to be characterized by some of the following factors:

> The teacher is the dominant leader who decides what will take place.
> The teacher's manner is warm, convivial, and businesslike.
> The goals of the lesson are well-known to the pupils.
> Pupils spend relatively little time in unsupervised activities, games, play rehearsals, and the like.
> Students work alone or in groups supervised by the teacher.
> Teaching materials tend to be structured and to provide immediate feedback.
> Teacher and workbook questions tend to be narrow and direct (there is a single correct answer) (Rosenshine and Berliner, 1978).

If this sounds like the description of a dour and somewhat unpleasant classroom atmosphere, we would add that recent research also seems to indicate that teachers who help students gain academically also have students who have positive attitudes toward school and good self-concept. Learning *can* be rewarding.

We would further suggest that being businesslike is not necessarily in conflict with "being interested in" or "enjoying oneself." If a classroom is the pupil's window to the world, then learning—whether it be in the language of mathematics, science, literature, or physical movement—ought to be an exciting and engaging prospect.

ACTIVITY

Some questions to ask: Do my plans give enough structure and direction to my classroom? That is, do I have a clear idea (and an appropriate plan to put the idea into operation) of the relationship of the various classroom activities to my educational goals? Are my pupils given enough time to concentrate on the task at hand until it has been mastered to my (and their) satisfaction? Do my pupils have an opportunity to see the relationship between the parts of the classroom activities and some goal which they can identify as a personal goal? Human beings seem willing to work very hard when it is clear that they are accomplishing something. Have your pupils done or accomplished something: can they write a good sentence, solve a math problem, fold an origami bird, catch a ball?

SIXTH IDEA:
THE EFFECTIVE TEACHER RECOGNIZES THAT PUPIL MOTIVATION IS RELATED TO THE PERSONAL NEEDS OF THE PUPIL

The first five ideas in this chapter are based on research into teacher effectiveness. This sixth idea is based on research into the nature of the learner.

Teachers make every possible effort to do those things in the classroom that will enhance pupil achievement. They search out the information that will help students to academic and personal success. But all teachers know that even after making material clear, being enthusiastic, using a variety of methods, providing pupils with the opportunity to learn, and being businesslike, some pupils still seem unresponsive.

As one teacher noted in his diary:

> One of my biology students has apparently become my cross to bear. Never have I had such a belligerent, obnoxious, stubborn, indifferent, and lazy student. In his science last year he made all A's—so far in biology he's managed F's. This student is not in-

competent, only extremely lazy with a very poor attitude toward school.

A teacher phrase that might sum up this pupil is "lack of motivation." If pupils are not motivated, then no matter how well the lesson is planned, nothing will happen. To complicate matters, the notion of motivation is connected in the mind with notions of personal success. If teachers care about what they do in the classroom, they probably believe that what pupils learn is going to help them in their future lives. Therefore, it is more than a matter of personal pride that pupils enter wholeheartedly into classroom activity.

What is Motivation?

Motivation is an inner drive, not an external one. When a pupil is motivated to watch a film and to answer questions about it after, she has not been driven to watch it by an outside force, such as the quality of the film or the teacher's ability to motivate. She has watched the film because wanting to watch came from inside. She motivated *herself* to watch. Watching met some inner needs, in other words.

Motivation, then, refers to a drive or a reason for doing something that originates with internal needs. Thus it is probably incorrect to speak of a film as being motivating. There is nothing intrinsic in a film, a book, or an activity, that will motivate pupils to attend to it. If the film, book, or activity deals with a topic of interest to pupils—how to ask for a date, say—there may be a high *probability* that pupils will pay attention, *if* they are curious about asking for dates and dating.

Needs arise from two sources in the human being. First, some needs are *physiological or innate* and therefore universal among humans. For example, all humans need to eat, to satisfy thirst, and to sleep. One of the factors that characterizes humans when compared with other creatures is the relatively small number of physiological needs. Generally speaking, the higher up the chain of creation we go, the greater the number of *learned* needs. Newly hatched chicks, for instance, automatically run for shelter when the shadow of a hawk passes over them. The chicks do this before there has been any opportunity to learn about hawks. In fact, newly hatched chicks can even recognize and discriminate between the shadow of a hawk and that of a harmless bird like a pigeon. Human children, on the other hand, need to learn when to run and when to stand. It is the learned needs that affect pupil (and teacher) behavior. Learned needs are sometimes referred to as *social* or *psychogenic* needs. Abraham Lincoln's drive to education was learned, just as was the alleged need that George Washington had to never tell a lie. Since these needs are learned, we might suspect correctly that they differ for each human since the learning experience (life experience) for each is different. One person might have a very strong need to succeed in school. For him, grades represent the measure of his success and therefore he tries very hard to ensure that his grades will be good. Another might see success in terms of fast cars. Satisfaction of the need comes in a drag race; grades mean little or nothing to him.

What are these needs? That is a difficult and as yet unanswered question. However, several researchers and theorists have created lists of needs that seem to be supported by observation of humans. One list of 28 needs was created by Murray (1938). Murray's list includes those needs which are alleged to be common to all humans, although as Murray points out, the same need can be satisfied in a variety of ways. Murray claims that humans have a need for acquisition, the gaining of possessions and property. In some of us this will be manifested as normal collecting of property: a house, a car, a television set. In others, the same basic need will become hoarding and avarice. In short, even if we know the basic needs of humans, we must be careful to recognize that the expression of the needs will be as diverse as human beings.

Maslow's Hierarchy of Needs

Another description of human needs is that of Abraham Maslow. Maslow's system is appealing because it is more than a simple list of needs. Human beings are dynamic, that is, ever-changing, and Maslow's hierarchy of needs is dynamic as well. According to Maslow, humans are striving to achieve the greatest potential. Each of us has a need to become free and autonomous. In order to reach this lofty goal, we must climb a ladder of needs. Before we can pass to the next level, the needs of the lower level must be satisfied. It works this way:

First, each human has *physiological* needs like hunger and thirst. Unless these survival needs are met, the organism will cease to exist. Because they are survival needs, a human cannot focus on any other activity until these needs are satisfied.

After the basic survival needs have been met, the human attempts to ensure his *safety*. A man lost on a desert island, Robinson Crusoe fashion, will find himself something to eat and drink and then climb a tree to sleep safe from any wild animals on the island. Only when these needs for survival and safety have been met can the human move up in the hierarchy. We might pause to speculate about what happens to learning in classrooms where pupils are hungry, fearful, or both. Fortunately, in general our society provides for the needs of survival and safety. There is more problem with the higher needs.

Next, comes the need for *affiliation,* to belong to a group and to feel loved. Once this need is met, we can begin to feel esteem for ourselves. Our self-concept is based largely on whether or not others (or we feel that others) feel we belong to their group.

Each level in the hierarchy measures a degree more of independence for the individual. Satisfaction of each set of needs really is a process of freeing the individual from those needs. At the very top of the hierarchy, the individual is free to develop her personality to meet her greatest potential. Self-development (what Maslow terms "self-actualization") demands that the individual exercise curiosity and explore the environment. School philosophies seem to put school activities into the highest of Maslow's levels. In a practical sense, then, the teacher's task might be to ensure that within the environment of the classroom as many needs of the pupils can be met so that the pupils are truly free to be curious and explore.

Some Practical Notions Relating to Pupil Needs and Motivation

- Different pupils have different needs and hence different motivations or drives. For example, the motivation of boys and girls seems to be different by the time of junior high, though it was the same when they began school. If an eighth grade boy sees spelling as not meeting his needs (maybe he sees it as a girl's task), how can a teacher arrange spelling lessons so that spelling does meet the boy's needs? Needs may be related to social class as well. Consider the learning of needs for a child growing up in a large, poor family. Needs may relate to cooperation and emotional support for one another. In a small and prosperous family the needs may be related to being competitive, and emotional needs may express themselves in material things. A teacher may find that grades are "motivating" (that is, "needs meeting") to the eldest son of the local doctor, while supportiveness and emotional warmth are more motivating to the fifth of eight children of a poor farmer.

- Motivation does not change very rapidly. It is unlikely that a teacher can expect to see much change in the ways that pupils satisfy needs in six weeks or even in a semester. Patience is a virtue for teachers. The ways that needs are satisfied do change; it just takes time.

- All organisms (this means you too) need stimulation and seem to seek it out. The more stimulating the environment (its richness, its variety, its uniqueness), the more likely it is that it will be sought. Recall the third teaching effectiveness principle, concerning variety. If stimulation is in fact something good in the sense that it attracts, then nonstimulating environments are bad. Nonstimulating environments even seem to cause a slowing down of mental activity. Perhaps they bring about changes in attitudes as well. In an experiment in the 1920's, a group of subjects were set to doing boring, repetitive, and unstimulating tasks. Not only did they become tired and bored quite quickly, but they began to show hostility to the experimenter and thought of a lot of other things they had to do instead. To complicate matters, though, we must recall that an environment that is stimulating and that encourages exploration and curiosity *may not* be stimulating to a child whose world is neither warm nor predictable. All of those neat games and toys and opportunities for free choice activity may actually inhibit the frightened child into what appears to be apathy or boredom. New experiences, then, might be available to pupils only after they feel free from threats. We might suggest that while stimulation of the environment might be a good motivating force, the degree of stimulation presented ought to be adjusted to the ability of the pupil to respond to it.

Some Suggestions About Motivation

Look at your classroom and ask yourself the following questions about the things you ask your students to do. Think of conditions you can create so that you can say "Yes" to these questions.

First, in what ways does the task meet a pupil's level of experience and previous learning? Can a connection between the task and the pupil's own life be seen by the pupil?

Second, is there an opportunity for pupils to help plan how the educational goals will be met?

Third, is there a way that pupils can bear responsibility and accountability for their own language?

Fourth, does the task enable each pupil to achieve some sort of success?

Fifth, does each pupil have an opportunity to receive some sort of success? (Berelson and Steiner, 1967; Thompson, Prater, and Poppen, 1974)

Some Ways to Think about Motivation

In thinking about motivation, do you see it outside-in or inside-out? Outside-in thinking seeks external things that are "motivating." If the teacher can find the right "things"—the really interesting books, relevant films, and worthwhile topics—then pupils will be motivated to learn about what the teacher knows must be learned. Inside-out thinking, on the other hand, assumes that "what is worthwhile examining" does not dwell in the things of the world but in the minds (and hearts) of those doing the examining. A movie is not "relevant" in an absolute sense. A movie about the drug culture is relevant, but a film about dance during the English Renaissance might also be relevant. Relevance depends on the needs of the individual. Perhaps the best strategy for teachers interested in motivating pupils is to approach the problem with the inside-out thinking. A teacher will try to see pupils in terms of individual motives, of needs, and realize that pupils attend to that which appears to meet their needs. This does not reduce the teacher to a waiter who merely takes pupil orders and then delivers up the appropriate dishes. A teacher is a trained, sensitive, and aware adult who knows more than the pupils about many things. The teacher might be able to connect a need for manipulation (demonstrated by a fascination with automobile engines) into the accumulated human knowledge about the physical properties of mechanical things. Begin with basic needs (as viewed by the pupil) and move on to show the connections between those needs and the larger, common world where all people live together.

SEVENTH IDEA:
IT IS POSSIBLE FOR TEACHERS TO GO BEYOND INFORMATION; TEACHERS CAN HELP THE PUPIL-PERSON TO GET THE MOST OUT OF SCHOOL

Teachers are concerned with the personal growth and development of pupils. They know that pupils are not simply minds that are to be filled, like so many pitchers, with information.

> My problem today involved the play cast. They had an unusually bad rehearsal and I really couldn't think of anything to say to them. We still had an hour of rehearsal time left, so we decided to do some theater games and work on those techniques which were really poor. Now I like theater games and I believe in their ability to disinhibit and strengthen physicalization, but it seems that when we dwell on an emotional level, the students become personally involved and will often break out in tears or scream at one another. So, in actuality, what I have is an encounter group session. I have a hard time handling these sessions, but usually when it is over the cast will work together more, maybe because they understand each other better. Well, the problem is do I continue to use the games and hope that nobody ever really flips out, or do I discontinue the games and ruin a performance?

Let's go back to a problem that was presented in Chapter 1. Though it is different in its circumstances, its theme is the same: How can teachers help pupils to deal with life beyond information?

> One of my students who has never really tried very hard in the past has recently been doing all her homework and classwork and seems to be working to the best of her ability. Today was test day and she failed. When she turned in her paper she appeared most pleased with herself for having done her best. We are told to treat students as individuals. If I were to do this and pass her with a low grade, the other students would accuse me of being unfair. And

don't think they don't know each other's business. However, if I don't pass her, she will believe all her work was in vain and go back to not caring.

It would be pleasant to be able to present a formula about being a helpful teacher. The fact is, of course, that such a formula is an impossibility. Very little is known about human beings and we cannot describe any medicine that will solve problems like the ones quoted above.

One writer who has tried to find the qualities of teachers who *seem* to have good relationships with pupils—that is, who seem to be able to help pupils grow and flourish—has identified five qualities of these teachers. Such teachers tend:

1. To have positive and upbeat attitudes toward life and other people.
2. To see other people as friendly and worthy with good motives.
3. To have the ability to see things from the other person's point of view.
4. To be more democractic in classroom management.
5. To see pupils as capable of doing things for themselves once they feel trusted, respected, and valued. In short, helping teachers do not do things *to* pupils or *for* pupils; they help pupils help themselves. (Don Hamachek in Mohan and Hull, 1975, p. 245)

To this we would add some common sense notions drawn from the classic writers on teaching—Quintilian, Rabelais, Montaigne, Rousseau, and the like. After all, human beings have been teaching other human beings for thousands of years. It would be foolish to ignore the cumulative wisdom about teaching.

Know yourself. You are part of what you teach. It is important that your own values and attitudes be clear to you and your pupils. For example, can you describe how you see your role as a teacher? (If you have a quick answer to this question, you are perhaps not really answering its spirit. It is a very difficult question and one that needs to be reanswered every day of your life.)

Communicate clearly. Our relationships with others depend on our ability to communicate. This means listening as well as talking. Write yourself a letter telling why you think it is important for your pupils to learn what you teach. Read the letter critically. If it is difficult to tell yourself, imagine how hard it is for your pupils to understand. Write your letter again.

Be a teacher in all you do. When you ask your pupils to do their work carefully, have you taught them how by doing yours carefully? Are your habits a fit model for your pupils? In short, are you a good model? Really?

Make it worthwhile. Your pupils spend a portion of their lives in your classroom. Do they get a good return on the investment? Kill ignorance, not time.

Look at your pupil. Remember people are not all like you.

The Three Roles of the Helping Teacher

First, the teacher is a model. There is no way out of this role. A teacher in contact with pupils must serve as a model. The pupils learn all sorts of things from teachers. They learn how the teacher handles frustration (is he patient or hot-tempered), how the teacher organizes her life (is she prepared or ill-prepared and disorganized), and how the teacher relates to others (is he warm and outgoing or is he reserved). It is probably difficult for a health teacher to make good points about drugs and tobacco when his clothes are reeking of stale cigarette smoke. Combs, Avila, and Purkey (1971) use the example of an adult stopping a fight by roughly and angrily hauling the kids apart. The adult has shown the kids about adult aggression by modeling a good (bad) example of it.

Next, the teacher is a reinforcer. (Recall that a reinforcement is something which, when it occurs with another event, increases or intensifies the event reinforced.) The teacher must be acutely aware of his or her own behavior so that it is possible to reinforce what is desirable. A teacher might reinforce the pupil's dependence on the teacher when the teacher really wants to reinforce the pupil's independent behavior. The teacher must also be a sensitive observer of his pupils to understand what is reinforcing and what is not.

Finally, the teacher acts as an extinguisher, one who helps the pupil extinguish behaviors that are undesirable. In all learning, feedback is crucial. The teacher can provide the pupil with information that says: "No, that's not right. Why don't you try again." Generally speaking, psychologists see punishment as a dangerous or at best questionable technique. Behavior that is not rewarded or reinforced generally disappears. In providing feedback, the teacher is making a series of decisions as to what is felt to be good and what is not. It is therefore imperative that the teacher be clear about his own values and standards.

Finally, it is not what the teacher does that will bring about positive change in pupils; it is how the pupil feels. The teacher can help the pupil to feel:

1. *Unthreatened.* It won't hurt to change. Since change implies trying new habits or ways of doing things, it also implies the possibility of failure. In creating the atmosphere for change, the teacher needs to show the pupil that failure is part of learning and not a final experience.
2. *Able.* The pupil needs assurance that desirable change is within his ability. The teacher may do this by making the precise nature of the desired change clear: "I want you to not interrupt others when they are speaking," rather than "I want you to be good."
3. *Encouraged.* The teacher must give some of the spirit needed to energize the change.

4. *Satisfied with the action of change.* Change must be perceived as being beneficial to the changer. (Combs, Avila, and Purkey, 1971)

SOME THINGS TO THINK ABOUT

First, how do you think that you can best help your pupils to personal success? If you value your subject matter, for example, and don't feel comfortable attempting to take time from it for "discussions," then you may well be of most help to your pupils by sticking to teaching your subject.

Second, how well do you communicate your values and how well do you listen to what others are saying to you? If you often feel frustrated because pupils "just don't listen," you might examine how you are saying what you say. Is there agreement between what you want to *say* and your actions? Remember the old saw about actions speaking louder than words?

Third, does your classroom provide support for positive changes in pupils? Are errors punished or are they seen as feedback for learning? Is your classroom a safe place for pupils to learn? After all, a pupil who has not had a successful time in school may approach even a supportive classroom as though it were a pool filled with hungry sharks. The pupil will need a lot of realistic encouragement as well as evidence that success is possible.

SUMMARY

The problems that teachers face in the realm of student success are truly daunting. It is hoped that this chapter has helped to clarify the nature of the problem. We have also provided information about what is known about teaching and learning so that solving problems in student success may seem a little more possible.

GETTING A HOLD ON PROBLEMS OF STUDENT SUCCESS

1. Make decisions about what you mean by success. List your goals. Explain them to yourself. Explain them to your students.
2. Listen, watch, pay attention to the feedback you are getting about what you are doing. Teaching is an interactive process. Are the pupils able to understand you? Attempt to see yourself as your students see you.
3. Take advantage of what is known about teaching and learning. The Seven Ideas about effective teaching are based on what is known from empirical studies of real classrooms and real pupils:

Effective teaching is *clear* teaching.

Teaching is an interactive process. Effective teachers seem to involve themselves enthusiastically.

The classroom is a center of diversity. Effective teachers tend to use a variety of teaching styles, educational materials, and so on to meet this diversity.

Effective teachers provide students with the opportunity to learn the material covered in the course.

Teachers whose goals include a desire to have their students gain in achievement tend to be businesslike and work-oriented in their classrooms.

What interests pupils and what they want to learn are closely related to the personal needs of the pupils.

It is possible for teachers to go beyond information. Teachers can help the pupil-person to get the most out of school.

To be effective this information must be applied with sensitivity and imagination. There are no foolproof cookbooks for producing student success.

4. Be your own investigator of teacher effectiveness. Use the information presented in this chapter experimentally. Seek the best ways for you to apply it to your classroom.
5. Be patient. Be patient with your pupils; whatever is worth learning takes time. Be patient with yourself; your profession is a difficult one for there is no end to the subjects it deals with. It might well be that the more you know about it and the more skillful you become in practicing it, the more difficulties and problems you will see. It is as a wise man said once, "The teaching of others teacheth the teacher."

RELATED READINGS

Berelson, Bernard, and Gary A. Steiner. *Human Behavior,* Shorter Edition, New York: Harcourt, Brace & World, 1967 pp. 159-73.

Bloom, Benjamin S., and others (eds.). *Taxonomy of Educational Objectives: The Classification of Educational Goals, Handbook 1: Cognitive Domain.* New York: McKay, 1956.

Bush, Andrew and others, "An Empirical Investigation of Teacher Clarity," *Journal of Teacher Education,* XXVII, no. 2 (March-April 1977), 53-58.

Brophy, Jere E., "Reflections on Research in Elementary Schools," *Journal of Teacher Education,* XXVII, no. 1 (Spring 1976), 31-34.

Combs, Arthur W., Donald L. Avila, and William Purkey. *Helping Relationships: Basic Concepts for the Helping Professions.* Boston: Allyn & Bacon, 1971.

Dickens, Charles. *Hard Times* (Geneva, Switzerland: Heron Books, Edito-Service S.A.), pp. 8-9.

Frazier, Alexander. *Teaching Children Today.* New York: Harper and Row, 1976.

Gage, N.L., and David C. Berliner. *Educational Psychology.* Chicago: Rand McNally, 1974.

Garrison, K.C., and R.A. Magoon. *Eductional Psychology*. Columbus, Ohio: Charles E. Merrill, 1972.

Grigson, Geoffrey. *The Cherry Tree*. New York: Vanguard Press, 1959.

Highet, Gilbert. *The Art of Teaching*. New York: Random House, 1950.

Jackson, Phillip W. *Life in Classrooms*. New York: Holt, Rinehart & Winston, 1968.

Lamm, Zvi. *Conflicting Theories of Instruction*. Berkeley, Calif.: McCutchan Publishing Co., 1976.

Maslow, A.H. *Motivation and Personality*. New York: Harper & Bros., 1954.

——. *Toward a Psychology of Being*, 2nd ed. Princeton, N.J.: Van Nostrand Reinhold, 1968.

Medley, Donald. *Teacher Competence and Teaching Effectiveness*. Washington, D.C.: AACTE, 1977.

Mohan, Madan, and Ronald E. Hull (eds.). *Teaching Effectiveness: Its Meaning, Assessment, and Improvement*. Englewood Cliffs, N.J.: Educational Technology Publications, 1975.

Murray, Henry A., (ed.). *Explorations in Personality: A Critical Experimental Study of Fifty Men of College Age*. New York: Oxford Univ. Press, 1938.

Quintilianus, Marcus Fabius. *Institutes of Oratory*, trans. H.E. Butler (Cambridge, Mass.: Harvard University Press, 1953), pp. 213-15.

Robinson, Francis P. *Effective Study*, 4th ed. New York: Harper and Brothers, Publishers, 1970.

Rosenshine, Barak. "Recent Research on Teaching Behaviors and Student Achievement," *Journal of Teacher Education*, XVII, no. 1 (Spring 1976), 61-64.

Rosenshine, Barak, and David C. Berliner. "Academic Engaged Time," *British Journal of Teacher Education*, 4, no. 1 (January 1978), pp. 3-16.

Rosenshine, Barak, and Norma Furst. "Research on Teacher Performance Criteria." In B.O. Smith, (ed.), *Research in Teacher Education*. Englewood Cliffs, N.J.: Prentice-Hall, 1971.

Thompson, Charles, Alice Prater, and William A. Poppen. "One More Time: How Do You Motivate Students?" *Elementary School Guidance and Counseling,* vol. 9, October 1974.

Ulich, Robert (ed.). *Three Thousand Years of Educational Wisdom.* Cambridge, Mass.: Harvard University Press, 1975.

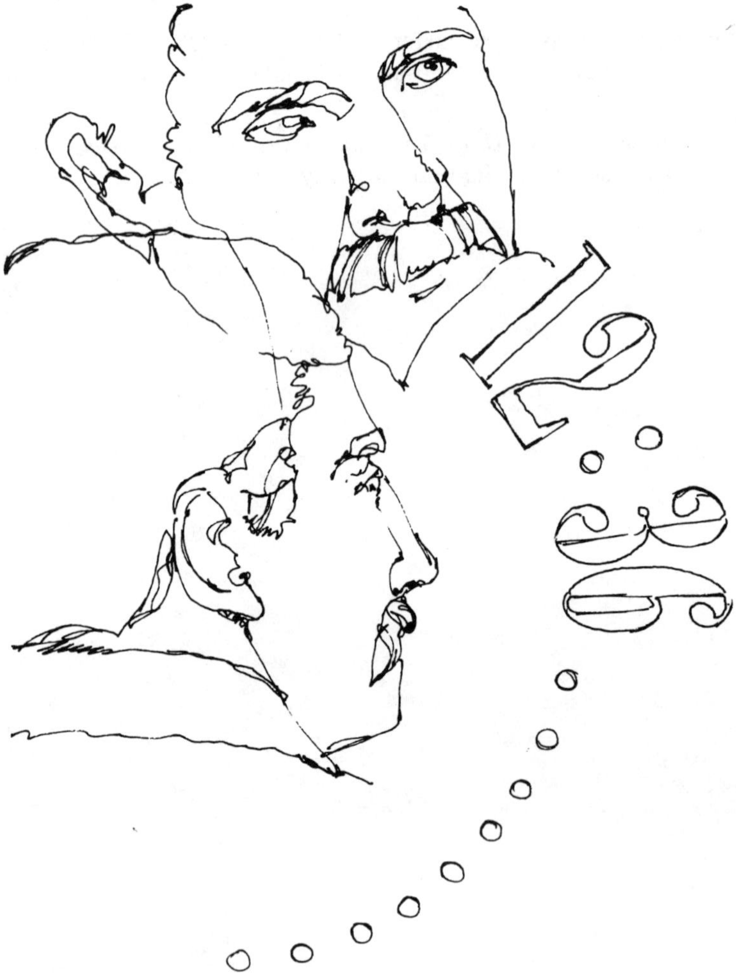

chapter 9

time
JANE APPLEGATE

Chapter 9 Outcomes: *As a result of reading Chapter 9 you should be able to:*
—understand why time can be a problem for teachers,
—examine and value the ways you use your time,
—identify principles of time management for teachers,
—elaborate on each principle,
and
—plan new strategies for using your time more effectively.

If only I had the time . . . I could get to know my students better; I could know more about what I'm teaching; I could plan better lessons; I could help slower students more; I could really get to know my colleagues; I could come to understand the parents and the community. There are so many things I could do. If only I had the time. . . .

THE PROBLEM

We teachers often feel plagued by time. It represents to us a major constraint. It keeps us from doing the things we'd like to do and forces us to do things we don't want to do. Often we feel like the teacher who writes, "Time—why isn't there more of it? It is always a struggle to get all of the work done that must be completed. At times I get very upset at school. Thank goodness there are weekends and vacations."

Though we don't understand the nature of time, we do know that it seems to make demands upon us. It guides our daily activities. It structures our work environment. It reminds us of work uncompleted, friends ignored, responsibilities not fulfilled. When we feel unable to direct our lives, we look at time as a thief of our freedom, our autonomy, our professional dignity. We show our displeasure by blaming time for our own inability to get done the things we'd like to do.

Often we'd like to protest the way our lives are scheduled and directed by the clock. We swear off wrist watches; we do away with bells; we take the clocks out of the classrooms. Yet old sayings stir our thoughts: "Do not squander *time,* for that is the stuff life is made of." "A stitch in *time* saves nine." "*Time* and tide wait for no man." "*Time* is money." We are constantly reminded of the importance of time. Though we are not quite sure what it is, we know that directly or indirectly it exerts control over us. We would like to be effective managers of our personal and professional lives, but time often interferes. We want to control the use of our time and not let time control us.

THE CULTURE AND THE SCHOOL

The American anthropologist Edward T. Hall has looked carefully at the significance of time in our culture (Hall, 1959, 1976). He has made us aware of the structure and meaning of time systems and time intervals by pointing to the different kinds of time with which we operate. Hall notes that time may even indicate the importance of an occasion. He states that Americans tend to think of time as something which is fixed in nature. For that reason we highly prize an individual's ability to keep track of his or her time, to schedule it. Children learn this early when they are put on feeding schedules as infants and bathroom schedules as toddlers. It is an insult in our culture to be asked to do something at the last minute. Americans expect and value advance notice. We continue to stress the importance of schedules throughout schooling by operating upon fixed time intervals and having particular amounts of time assigned for reading, or spelling, or arithmetic. As a result, when we become adults we are expected to be able to schedule time and we look upon those who don't as inefficient. For us time is talked about as a commodity—we earn it, save it, spend it, use it, abuse it, and waste it. We value it. We have a need to be goal-directed. Americans never question that time should be planned. We look ahead to results—immediate results which must be obtained as the evidence for our planned time.

Promises to meet deadlines and appointments are taken very seriously in our culture. It is a violation of time code to keep changing schedules or appointments or to deviate from a preestablished agenda. Hall points out that Americans tend to specify how much time is required to do everything. The overriding pattern with us is that once you have scheduled the time, you have to use it as designated, even when that plan turns out not to be the best one. Schools operate as agents of cultural traditions. As you think about the way you function in relation to time in school, you will see how much of the cultural attitudes toward time are taught through the structure of the school.

> The analysis of one's own culture simply makes explicit the many things we take for granted in our everyday lives. Talking about them, however, changes our relationships with them. We move into an active and understanding correspondence with those aspects of our existence which are all too frequently taken for granted or which

sometimes weigh heavily on us. Talking about them frees us from their restraint. (Hall, 1959, p. 166)

GOALS

This chapter aims to help you become more aware of your own uses of time and to help you learn to use your time more wisely. As teachers our lives appear to be directed by the clock, the bell, the class period, the grading period, the vacation periods, and the school year. We have many responsibilities, some that are given us because we have chosen to be teachers and some that we choose for ourselves. Many of us don't know our own limitations so we take on more projects and make more commitments than we can hope to complete. This chapter has been designed to help you understand more fully your own uses of time and to provide you with some common sense suggestions for improving your use of time if you so desire.

ORGANIZATION OF THE CHAPTER

If you are not satisfied with how you are now using time, this chapter should be beneficial to you. The next eight divisions are organized around time management principles in what are termed "Time Capsules." They are:

1. Know yourself—your values, needs, beliefs, attitudes, and habits.
2. Know what you want to accomplish—set goals.
3. Know your work environment.
4. Plan.
5. Know your support system—or you can't do it all.
6. Concentrate on what you want to do.
7. Act—don't procrastinate, don't delay.
8. Follow through—finish.

The capsules contain practical suggestions for self-knowledge and self-improvement in the area of time management.

When you complete the chapter you should have more control over your use of time. Good luck.

TIME CAPSULE 1: KNOW YOURSELF—YOUR VALUES, NEEDS, BELIEFS, ATTITUDES, AND HABITS

Do you understand yourself?

Do you know your own view of time?

Do you consider your health, your sleep, your exercise when you manage your time?

Identify Your Needs

The first step toward understanding the ways you use your time is to look closely at yourself. Time is a relative phenomenon; it is what you want it to be. You need to understand what your own values and beliefs are in order to understand why you use time the way you do. Look at the ten statements listed below. Rank them from 1 to 10, placing a 1 beside the item on the list that is most important to you and a 10 beside the item that is least important.

___ Acquiring a new house, car, or other important personal possession.

___ Being precise, neat, and organized.

___ Accomplishing something difficult.

___ Being respected.

___ Being able to lead or direct others.

___ Being able to identify and empathize with others.

___ Being different, unique.

___ Having and maintaining friendships.

___ Behaving well, obeying the law, avoiding criticism by others.

___ Avoiding tension.

Each of the above statements describes a basic human need. All human beings want these things but the degree to which they use their time to attain them is a personal matter. What does your ordering of these statements tell you about your needs? How do your needs affect your use of time? Think about your ordering of needs. Would a person who knows you well know that, for example, it is important for you to accomplish something difficult? Do you take on difficult projects like using your time to create individual activities for each child in your class? If a discrepancy exists between your needs and your use of time, it may point to a source of your personal or professional frustration. Ask yourself what is most satisfying about teaching. Is that how you use your time?

Explore Your Own Time Perspective

Think for a minute about the life events you consider most important. Have they already happened to you? Are they happening to you daily? Are you looking ahead to the future as the source of your fulfillment? Thomas Cottle (1976) suggests that people have different perspectives of time which may affect their behavior. One way to explore your own time sense is to think about your relationship to your own life experiences.

Psychologists describe personality types based upon individual perceptions of time. For example, a person who focuses primarily upon the *past* may see the meaning of events through memory. The past may direct present behavior by building upon and relating each event to something which has come before. A past-focused person might, for example, enjoy collecting things, keeping diaries, or telling stories.

If you judge yourself as being a *present*-focused person you are more likely to believe that what you are doing *now* is of most importance. You are concerned with the immediate. You probably have the ability to understand the impact of current events and experiences. Your quick responses to requests makes you superbly equipped to deal with crises and emergencies. You would like things to go your way; you are not one to wait.

If you judge yourself to be a *future*-focused person you may believe that your life is continuously evolving. Your major life activity may be to prepare for what is ahead. You might be keenly aware of the future as a reality and you probably let your vision direct your present behavior. You are concerned with possibilities as you dash from one thing to another. You are probably active and an idealist but not a perfectionist. You are more of a starter than a finisher.

Regardless of your perspective on time, we know that time and your perception of it does play a role in guiding and directing your actions.

Know Your Personal Time Needs

While we all share the same view of the standards of time established long ago—a minute, an hour, a day, a month, a year—we differ in perception of personal time. How long is "in a while" or "sometime" or "soon"? We also somehow develop different personal tempos and rhythms which may change our behaviors.

Think for a few minutes about your personal tempo and rhythms. What time of the day is best for you? Are you a "morning person" who jumps out of bed at the crack of dawn, bright, cheerful, ready to go, but who winds down about 1:00 P.M. and can't wait to get home for a nap after school? Or are you a "night person" who can barely crawl out of bed after the alarm has rung five minutes, can't remember your first two classes in the morning, but about noon starts to come alive and can go easily until the early hours of the morning? Productivity can be heightened if you understand your periods of high and low. You do not turn on automatically at 9:00 A.M. and off at 3:30. Learning to work with rather than opposing your own readiness will help you accomplish more and be less fatigued. By knowing your daily rhythms and integrating them into your life plan, you will be able to use your alert times for the more demanding tasks.

Use Your Time Well

Do you know how much sleep you require? Most adults average between 7 and 7½ hours of sleep per night, but for many 5 to 6 hours is plenty. To find out how much sleep you require you might want to experiment with different sleep lengths. Try sleeping 6 hours per night for two weeks and see how you function. If you feel drowsy and are unable to concentrate, then increase your sleep. Follow the two-week testing procedure until you find the amount of sleep that is right for you. You might be able to add an additional hour to your waking day. Sleep needs vary within the individual from day to day. More sleep is needed during periods of unusual stress or illness. Differences in sleep requirements seem to be related to metabolic differences, temperament, and the amount of enjoyment you derive from your daytime activities. Whatever you require to maintain your health and vitality is right for you.

Do you exercise? We can all give many reasons for not keeping in shape, but we often fail to consider the benefits accrued from a consistent routine of physical exercise. Being in good physical condition can increase the percentage of your high-powered working hours. If you feel well, you will have less difficulty keeping up with your students and a rigorous school schedule. We tell ourselves that the pace of a school day is more than enough exercise. This may be true for some teachers who climb stairs between classes or who play with students during recess. The majority of us, however, might feel better if we spent 20 to 30 minutes during the day in jogging, tennis, swimming, cycling, or other vigorous sports. The aggressiveness with which you perform tasks throughout the day may be closely related to physical fitness.

Exercise is a good release for stress that builds during a school day. Good management of your time each day will permit you to use some of your time to get yourself into balance physically and mentally. Teaching is a stress-producing profession. Teachers feel pressured to produce more and more in less time. For that reason you may find yourself exhausted at the end of the school day. A realization that you make the decisions about how you will use your time and that you can plan each day for some personal time—time to read, meditate, exercise, relax, socialize, or sit in solitude—will help you establish a personal schedule which will consider your total person. For a teacher to maintain the pace that schools and students demand, he must be fit, must be able to sustain periods of stress, must be able to cope with tension. To do this the teacher needs to be mindful of himself—his values, needs, beliefs, habits —and consider them as he leads a life of giving to others.

What You Know Now about Yourself

What have you learned about yourself from this capsule? You have found out that your use of time can say a lot about your personal needs and values. You have also discovered something about your own personal behaviors, beliefs, and habits. You know now that you have a particular physical tempo and that sleep and exercise may affect your day-to-day functioning. If you have considered these points when reflecting upon yourself, you have learned a great deal.

TIME CAPSULE 2: KNOW WHAT YOU WANT TO ACCOMPLISH—SET GOALS

Do you know what you want?
Have you examined your goals recently?
Are you satisfied with the direction your life is taking?

Accepting Responsibility for Your Goals

Teachers frequently find themselves caught between what they want to accomplish that will be fulfilling in their professional roles, and what the school or other people feel they should be and do. Knowing what *you* want to do and why *you* want to do it are your first steps toward getting done those things which you will find personally and professionaly rewarding. In Time Capsule 1 you thought seriously about yourself and your relation to time. You are now ready to do some life planning and to see how your goals affect the way you use time at home and at school.

Few of us ever take the opportunity to think about what we want or about how much control we have over the things that happen to us at home or at school. We prefer to think that events or activities just happen to us and the best we can do is react to situations. Sometimes we think our own direct and purposeful action makes no difference. The fact is that we do make things happen for ourselves and for others; we create our own realities by knowing and understanding ourselves. Simply stated, we *can* have control over our lives.

Examine Your Goals
Alan Lakein writes:

> In one way or another, whether you have been aware of it or not, you have been thinking about your lifetime goals almost as long as you have been alive. However, thinking about your goals is usually quite a different experience from writing them down. Unwritten goals often remain vague dreams while written goals tend to be more concrete and specific, helping you to probe beyond the surface of the same old ideas you've had for years. Once committed to paper your goals can be examined more closely. They can be analyzed, refined, changed, pondered. (Lakein, 1973, p. 31)

Take a few minutes now to commit your goals to paper. Get two pieces of paper. At the top of one write "Personal Lifetime Goals" and on the top of page two write "Professional Goals." On the first sheet, begin each statement with, "I want. . . ." Make your statements as specific as you can. For example, instead of writing, "I want to be happy," think about what makes you happy and write "I want a warm, loving relationship with another human being" or "I want to spend a month hiking to the top of Mt. Everest." On the second sheet, begin each statement with "As a teacher, I want . . . ." Give yourself about ten minutes to complete each list. The list you write today might not be the one you would have written five years ago or the one you might write in ten years, but it may give you some new perspectives about where you want to be headed.

Now put your two lists together side by side. Are some of your professional goals similar to your personal goals? Is your profession helping you to attain some of your personal goals? For example, you might have written:

Personal Lifetime Goals	*Professional Lifetime Goals*
I want to help other people learn and grow.	As a teacher I want to be sure that all my students in my classes have an opportunity to learn.
or	or
I want to enjoy what I am doing.	As a teacher, I want to be enthusiastic.

From this comparison you should be able to see that your professional goals and your personal goals are harmonious, that is, through teaching you are able to reach toward some of your lifetime personal goals.

However, if, for example, you find written under *Personal Lifetime Goals* "I want to be wealthy" and you see under *Professional Goals* "As a teacher, I want to continue classroom teaching for twenty years," you might find a goal conflict between your personal and professional desires. If you want to be relatively wealthy, you probably will not achieve that end as a classroom teacher. If you find many conflicts between your personal and professional goals, you probably should consider changing jobs or revising your goals since teaching is not fulfilling for you.

Reflect upon Your Goals

After you have compared your lists, ask yourself which of the goals are attainable within the next six months. Which of them do you think you could accomplish within the next year? Five years? Which of them are out of your reach and provide a constant source of frustration? Consider this junior high school teacher's problem:

> Today's schedule was turned around to accommodate achievement testing and early dismissal. This confused everyone and made for a very hectic day. All of my classes are at different places because of omitted classes and early dismissals. This makes it very hard to know where each student is and makes for further delays. The students' attention in classes was not good because of all the changes. All in all the confusion of the day made for a very poor learning experience in the classroom.

What seems to be the teacher's goals?

1. The teacher wants school activities to go as scheduled.
2. The teacher wants all his classes to move at the same pace.
3. The teacher wants to know how each student is progressing.
4. The teacher wants students to pay attention in class.
5. The teacher wants a good climate for learning in his classroom and in the school.

Which of these goals are easily attainable? Probably with some readjustment to the lesson plans, the teacher could restructure some classroom activities to get all the students back on schedule. This might be the only goal which the teacher alone can control.

Which of these goals should the teacher consider unattainable? The answer to that question would depend upon how much he values each goal and how much time and energy he is willing to use to resolve the conflicts inherent in the other goals. For example, maybe the principal is unaware of the problems that testing and early dismissal create for teachers. Possibly a simple conference with the principal about the problem would help him to be more considerate in announcing deviations from the schedule. On the other hand, the principal may feel that the teacher is expecting too much from the administration to ask for all school events to be prescheduled and he may ignore the teachers's request. Then what can the teacher do? He might learn to live with hectic days occasionally, or take the problem to the local teachers' organization for arbitration.

Be Realistic about Your Goals

Remember that the price of perfection may be prohibitive. So what if you don't become Teacher of the Year? Think about the teacher who set his goal to reach every child. He worked hard and became frustrated when everyone in the class did not reach perfection on the weekly spelling test. He worried so much about what he was doing wrong and yet his goal was never reached. He was never satisfied with his performance as a teacher. Consider, too, the students who benefited from the teacher's extra effort. Because the teacher set high goals for himself, he was able to help some students achieve more. Though internally he was frustrated, by another's standards he was successful.

The attainability of larger goals requires more effort with a touch of realism. You always must weigh the advantages of goal attainment against the disadvantages of frustration or disappointment. Only you can decide what goals are worth your time. Feel good about the ones you have chosen. They reflect you.

What You Know Now about Goals

What have you learned about goal setting from this capsule? You have learned that goals arise from your needs and values. Knowing what you really want out of life is half of attaining it. You now have considered and clarified your direction. You have accepted control for your use of time. You have examined your present aspirations and have reflected upon them. As you accept your goals, you accept yourself and feel comfortable with your decisions to move toward particular ends. As a result, you really will be able to make better use of your time.

TIME CAPSULE 3: KNOW YOUR WORK ENVIRONMENT

What is the temporal structure of your school?
What is the schedule?
How does it affect your use of time?
What amounts of time within the school day do you have control over?
How do you use your time then?
How do you deal with interruptions?

Relating to School Time

For the teacher, the school is the work environment. Because much of your environment is time-governed or time-bound, it is important for you to know which aspects of school life and school time can and cannot be controlled. In school you spend at least seven hours every day, five days every week, approximately nine months every year. Most American schools operate on the assumption that every hour, every day, and every month of human life is pretty much like every other. You and your students are conditioned by the bells and routines of school to ignore personal tempo. What is appropriate class work at 8:30 in the morning should be equally suitable for the 2:30 P.M. class. The school year and the school day are fixed by rigid time boundaries which are usually set by administrative convenience in accordance with policies developed by local boards of education and state departments of education. There is very little you as a classroom teacher can do to change the length of the school day or school year.

The uniformity, predictability, and neutral nature of clock time shape and direct your work environment. The daily schedule is given to you at the beginning of each school year. You know precisely when to teach, when to plan, when to eat lunch, when to go to the bathroom, and when to stop. The clock is a central symbol in each classroom. The school work environment rarely recognizes the random timing of human needs, and knowing this is part of understanding your work environment.

Teachers seem to have few problems coping with clock-time standards. They accept the temporal aspects of the school year, the grading period, the school week, and the day. Regularity and predictability seem to provide a rather secure kind of framework within which to function.

Teachers believe that aspects of school time which are preestablished cannot be changed. Regardless of their desire to have 35-minute periods rather than 50-minute periods, or to have two 30-minute planning sessions a day rather than one 60-minute session, teachers seem to feel powerless to change the temporal setting. However, in some schools teachers are finding that time boundaries are changeable.

In some schools where teachers work together in teams, they may be given complete control over time during the school day and may be encouraged to break up the day into more flexible intervals. Still other schools utilizing the computer for individual instruction are allowing students more time to work on their own. These changes in school time have come about largely as a result of teachers' efforts.

Would you like to have shorter periods or longer ones? Would you like to begin or end the school day earlier or later? Would you like a different time arrangement for the distribution of grade cards? Would you like to have your planning time at the end of the day or at the beginning? Do you know why your school time is scheduled the way it is?

Think for a few minutes about the temporal aspects of your work environment. Which of them are you comfortable with? Which of them would you like to change? What support can you give for change? How might the change benefit the school as a whole? Who should you contact in your school to have impact upon the way your school time is scheduled? Though you have felt that teachers must or should accept these time aspects of their environment, this may not be the case. Think about it.

Eliminate Interruptions

In spite of the administrative or governmental constraints placed upon you, class time is primarily under your control. Whatever amount you have is entrusted to you to use wisely. However, a frequent concern of teachers is the number and unpredictable nature of interruptions. Recall this teacher's story from Chapter 1.

> The day was filled with interruptions. Morning classes were shortened because of homeroom meetings. The guidance counselors called kids out of the already shortened periods to register for next year—kids were coming and going in my classes all day. Then the intercom broke in three or four times during the day to announce things that didn't pertain to my classes. Afternoon classes were supposed to be shortened so we could have an assembly—a vocal group who didn't show up. After I changed my lesson plans for the afternoon and had gotten halfway through the first class doing something different than I had originally planned, it was announced that classes would run full length after all. With so many ill-timed interruptions I didn't have enough time to accomplish anything....

Interruptions are all in the course of a teacher's day. They can't be eliminated but they can be understood and can be reduced. If, for example, the intercom is a frequent irritation to you, you might want to let your principal know that for every classroom interruption by the intercom there is a "down time" or restlessness in the form of students' getting off their learning tasks. If the registration for next year's classes by the counselor has been an irritation, you might suggest that the counselor try to register students by taking ten minutes of one class rather than causing a day of interruptions or you might suggest registration during study halls. When you know in advance that a day or class period will be lengthened or shortened, plan activities to allow students to practice skills rather than trying to introduce new concepts or materials. (See Time Capsule 4).

Use Uninterrupted Time to Its Full Advantage

Assume that you are going to teach an uninterrupted lesson. During the next 40 minutes there will be no fire drills, no one will come to your door with a message for a student, no student will arrive ten minutes late for class, no one will be called to report to the attendance office or bookroom or principal's office, there will be no emergency assembly or yearbook collections. You will have complete control of the next 40 minutes. How will you use your time? Look at Ms. Gregory's seventh grade math class. The first ten minutes were used for getting out the materials she needed for teaching a lesson on how to use a compass. She had nothing planned for her students to do during this time so they carried on informal conversation with one another. When she finally got the materials distributed she struggled to gain the attention of her students. Settling the class took another five minutes. Already a planned 40-minute lesson would have to be crammed into 25 mintues. Ms. Gregory began the lesson by asking students not to pay attention to the materials she had distributed, but to watch her as she demonstrated at the board how to draw a circle. During her demonstration the chalk broke and she had to leave the room to find more chalk. In the meantime, students busily experimented with the materials on their own. The bell signaling the end of the period rang before the students had the opportunity to practice the skill she had demonstrated or before she had taken time to give assignments or collect materials. What fixed features of time could Ms. Gregory have been more aware of? How did she choose to use them or ignore them in her teaching? What other time boundaries did she set for herself and her class? What did her use of time say to her students? What advice could you give her to help her use her time more effectively?

Think now about your own classroom. Try making an

audio tape of one of your lessons. As you listen to yourself, consider how you used the time features of beginning and ending your class. What other time indicators did you give to your students? Did you set time limits? Did you say "Finish soon," or "Time's about up," or "let's do this quickly," or "Take all the time you need"? What did your use of time say to the students? What advice would your principal, supervisor, or a fellow teacher give you about your own use of time?

What You Know Now about School Time

What have you learned about time and the school environment from this capsule? You know now that the time element in schools is central to the functioning of the classroom and that time also dictates many unnatural events in the course of a school day. You know that some time constraints within a school are fixed while others can be changed. You know that the time you have most control over at school is classroom time but even that may be disrupted and interrupted many times in the course of a day. You have gained new insights into your work environment which you can use to enhance your use of time.

TIME CAPSULE 4: PLAN

Do you know your priorities? Can you say "No"?
Do you have a master plan?
How do you incorporate your life goals? Your daily goals?
Do you set deadlines for yourself?
Can you follow your plan once you have made it?

The Problem of Planning

Throughout your teaching life you have been told to plan. As an undergraduate in teacher education you were taught formats of planning, components of planning, and systems of planning. Planning for teachers means establishing a record of your expectations including those you have for your students. A plan is tangible evidence not only that you have thought ahead and considered what you will teach, but that you have thought about how you will teach it and how you will know when students have learned. As you have gained in teaching experience you have probably become more skilled in planning for teaching. However, planning as it relates to wise use of time remains a problem for many teachers. Consider the following teacher's problems.

> For first period my plans were as follows:
>
> 1. Check the homework papers and work any problems the students want to see.
> 2. Review some of the rules for working with exponents and introduce some new ones.
> 3. Do an assignment of 50 problems.
> 4. Record the rules in their notes.
>
> The whole group was through in 25 minutes. What to do with them for the next 20 minutes was a problem since I didn't want to give the students any new information or busy work. I don't know what to do when my class needs only half of a class period to complete all that I have planned.

This teacher was having trouble judging the pace and skill level of her students. Can you tell what her goals are from reading through this plan? Does the teacher expect too little from her class? How does the teacher know that the students have the concepts and skills she expects them to acquire? How does the teacher expect her class time to be used? What suggestions might you offer to her about planning? Do we know from her plans how she taught the lesson or what the students learned? What does she mean by "busy work"? More practice? Is "busy work" necessarily bad?

Another teacher expressed a planning problem in a different way:

> Today is Friday. Each Friday the periods are shortened by ten minutes so that an activity period can be added. With dressing time and shower time taken from our P.E. periods we are left with approximately twenty minutes on the floor. This is frustrating to students and instructors because the lesson just gets under way and it's time to quit. The last gym class also has to put equipment away, which leaves them with a little more than ten minutes for the activity. With so little time, the lesson becomes a farce and we can well understand why some students "hate gym." This seems like something we can do nothing about.

Changes in schedules and shortened periods do affect plans if the plans are made for regularly timed periods. Because this problem is a frequently occurring one (every Friday), it can be anticipated and overcome. Are there physical education activities which might not require changing into gym clothes or showering (a film on mountain climbing or an introduction to spectator sports or playing of table games)? Are there other ways to add time to the Friday classes? Does the activity period always have to come on Friday?

These two incidents are included to show that planning can create or solve time problems. When you plan, do you think about the students, the class period, the day, and the week? Do you consider the flow of activities and the integration of sets of goals into the larger picture of your life's goals?

Learn to Set Priorities

Before you plan, you need to understand your priorities. You need to know what is important to you, to your students, and to your school.

Teachers are busy people. Most of them seem to have more to do than can possibly be done. They make hundreds of decisions each day and each decision takes time and determines a teacher's use of time. In addition to a teacher's having a personal set of priorities, others in a teacher's life also have priorities which they try to bestow upon teachers. The principal has a school report to file with the central office and needs to know *immediately* how many pieces of movable furniture are in your classroom. Susan James' parents have decided to take Susan to Europe for a month and they need to know *immediately* what her assignments will be while she is gone. Sam Parker and Tom Bartho have just started punching each other and unless you take action *immediately* someone is going to be hurt. Your colleague and friend just came into the room and wants to know *immediately* if you'll play bridge after school tonight. As a teacher you must decide what your priorities are.

Say No When You Can

Setting priorities is a good way to begin to get work done. Central to your ability to set priorities is your ability not to take on more than you can handle. Saying no when necessary is important.

Once you have established priorities, you will not be able to follow through with them unless you learn to say no. Don't accept new responsibilities or volunteer for new projects without considering first your use of time. According to the Pareto Principle or, as it's sometimes called, the 80/20 rule, "If all items are arranged in order of value, 80% of the value would come from 20% of the items, while the remaining 20% of the value would come from the other 80% of the items" (Lakein, 1973, p. 71). What this suggests to teachers is that possibly in the classroom 20 percent of your students take 80 percent of your time, or 80 percent of your pleasure from teaching comes from 20 percent of your teaching responsibilities. This principle helps us realize that not all of what we do is vitally important and we need to be reminded to invest our time in those activities which provide us with the most personal and professional satisfaction. When you say NO to a request, know that you are doing it for the right reasons—*your* reasons. You are really saying YES to yourself.

Once you have established priorities and practiced saying NO, you are ready to build plans that will work for you. You know what is important to you and you know what you want. You are now able to integrate your plans with your life's goals.

Integrate Your Plans and Your Goals

On a full sheet of paper draw a pyramid larger than in Figure 9-1. Divide it into seven sections. Start at the base and write one of your life goals (see Capsule 2) on the left side of the base section. To the right note an activity which might lead you to that goal. On the next level think about a professional goal that might contribute to or might grow out of your life goal. Write it down. On the next level write a goal for the year which would grow from the professional goal you listed. As you proceed up the pyramid check to determine if each goal grows from the one written below. When you have finished, ask your-

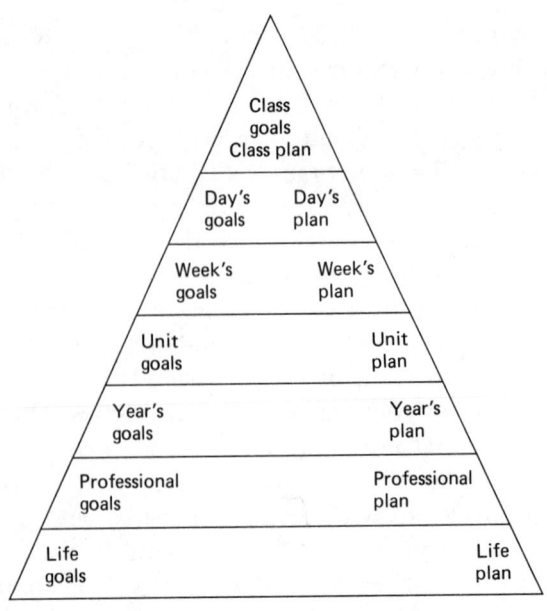

FIGURE 9-1.

self if each section grew from the one preceding it. Planning purposefully can really contribute to your personal and professional achievements.

How Plans Can Help

Though plans are not sacred and must be modified to meet the needs of the situation, planning is important. Without expressions of intent, you'll allow other people's actions to determine your priorities and you'll find yourself dealing primarily with problems rather than opportunities. Time management studies show that the more time spent in advanced planning, the less total time required for the completion of the project. In education, planning is a contributing factor to the organization of learning in the classroom and can affect student achievement (see the chapter on student success).

As you plan ask yourself exactly what you want to accomplish with the activity being considered. Is it really worthwhile for the students? Have you set a deadline for yourself? Is it realistic in terms of student ability and tempo? Have you considered the environmental factors which might influence your deadline (see Capsule 3)? How will you know when your deadline has been met? What outcomes will you look for?

Remember Parkinson's Law as you plan: "Work expands to fill the time available for its completion." If you give yourself a month to complete a particular unit of work, then you are likely to take a month to complete it. If you allow yourself two hours to grade a set of papers, then it will probably take you that long to finish. You can increase your own work effectiveness and possibly increase the effectiveness of your students if you give yourself and your class a deadline for each task and do your best to stick to it. A promise to yourself—a commitment you make because you believe it is important to finish what you start—will make vague wishes turn to action. If you are not good at keeping promises you make to yourself, then make them aloud to someone else. Tell your students that you will have their papers back to them by Friday or tell your spouse that you will bring work home from school only two nights a week. Then once your deadlines are set, do you best to respect them.

Time used for planning carefully is time used wisely. A good, flexible plan will encourage you to be effective in your teaching and your management of time. If you plan and follow through, you will be pleased with yourself and with the accomplishments of others whom you had the time to help.

What You Know Now about Planning Wise Use of Time

What have you learned about planning from this capsule? You have learned that good planning can prevent many problems. You know that for plans to be really beneficial they must relate directly to your personal and professional goals. You know that plans and time work either together or in conflict depending upon your ability to make judgments about the length of an activity or project. You are now ready to put your plans to work.

TIME CAPSULE 5: KNOW YOUR SUPPORT SYSTEM—OR YOU CAN'T DO IT ALL

Who can help?
How can they help?
Are you willing to let others help?

Don't Feel That You Have to Do It All

Traditionally teachers spend most of their working day in individual classrooms with students. The egg-crate approach to structuring schools has sustained the teachers' need for professional autonomy—so much, in fact, that teachers frequently feel there is no one within the school organization whom they can turn to for help or advice. Teachers believe that the work to be done must be done alone, that no one can manage the class as well, plan a lesson as well, or take care of a student's problem as well as they can. We all know teachers who come to school even when they are sick because they are certain that no one on the substitute list could accomplish the work planned for the day in the way the teacher would like.

How many teachers who teach the same subject or the same grade level never share with one another their approaches to teaching particular content? How many times have the same lessons been prepared by different teachers? How often do teachers wish they had someone who would listen to teaching problems, empathize, suggest alternatives without being condescending or judgmental? It appears to be one of the unwritten rules in many schools that sharing and supporting one another is taboo. Teachers develop the "I must do it *all*" syndrome. Too frequently teachers observe their colleagues' activities to see how they deal with particular problems, but don't offer support. This is not to say that teachers don't want to help one another, because they do, but they don't want help or advice to be interpreted as "Do things *my* way," or "You're not doing your job well so I'll step in." So helpful, supportive teachers wait in silence to be asked for advice or assistance, eager to lend a hand but mindful of each teacher's desire for autonomy.

Identify and Use Support That Is Available

Some school systems, believing that collegial support can be beneficial to teachers and can lead to a wiser use of teachers' time, have instituted organizational patterns which encourage and promote the sharing of knowledge, ideas, materials, and students. Such arrangements have been termed team teaching, groups, house plans, or departments. Though there is no evidence from the research literature to suggest that teaming arrangements improve student achievement, teachers who participate in teams by choice do stress the impact that sharing information and ideas has had on their own sense of themselves as teachers (see Chapter 5, "Affiliation").

In other schools, some teachers are forming informal

groups for the purpose of sharing teaching ideas. Sometimes this sharing comes under the heading of in-service education. Teacher groups meet weekly to discuss particular problems with students or particular interdisciplinary projects they are interested in undertaking. A new national movement toward teacher centers is another way of providing support. Teacher centers are places where teachers can meet to work together, share ideas, develop new curricula, and talk about concerns and problems. Sometimes this sharing is instituted formally by the school counselor who brings a student's teachers together to discuss attitudes and behaviors in different classes. These teachers have recognized a need for support, are reaching out to one another, and are finding that collectively they can work for the good of the school and the students.

Students can also aid you with time management. Recently a teacher told this story:

> Today a girl became ill in class and I took her to the nurse's office. I left one student in charge of the classroom. This all happened just before classes changed so I had to tell one student to tell another student that he was in charge of the next class. The students took everything in stride. It's good to know that my eighth graders can behave so responsibly.

This teacher was able to call upon students to handle tasks while she was busy. Being assigned responsibility should encourage students to grow and enable them to assume decision-making roles that can help free more of your time. Remember, students too, by and large, want to help you when they can.

Create Your Own Support System

How do you deal with support? Do you provide it for others? Do others provide it for you? In considering your use of time, might you think that there are times when supportive teachers, secretaries, principals, students, or parents are essential to your personal and professional well-being? Now is the time to consider carefully your own support system.

Below is a set of hypothetical situations which might necessitate your calling on someone for support. Beside each question write the name of the person you would most likely go to. If you would solve the stiuation yourself, write *No one*.

1. Who would you go to if you had a particularly bad day at school and you needed to talk it out? _____

2. Who would you go to if you needed help grading papers?
   _____

3. Who would you go to if you needed to know more about a particular child in one of your classes? _____

4. Who would you go to if you needed to be cheered up?
   _____

5. Who would you go to if you were suddenly out of chalk?
   _____

6. Who would you go to if you needed a quick idea for a lesson?
   _____

7. Who would you go to if you had a disagreement with another colleague? _____

8. Who would you go to if your room needed more desks?
   _____

9. Who would you go to if you thought one of your students couldn't read? _____

10. Who would you go to if students in your fifth period class just wouldn't quiet down after lunch? _____

11. Who would you go to if the school librarian couldn't get you the set of books you need for next week's special project?

12. Who would you go to if a student had missed 15 days of this grading period?

13. Who would you go to if the unit you just taught was a masterpiece and you wanted to tell someone how well you and your students did?

14. Who would go to if you discovered that the textbook you were assigned to use was too difficult for your students?

15. Who would you go to if you needed five refrigerator cartons to build a learning center in your classroom?

Now review your responses. How many "No one" answers do you have? If you have more than four, you should take some time to review your personal support system. Remember, you are not the only one around who can or should do the job. Now note where you put a particular person's name. Is there someone you are depending upon frequently for most of your support? Are you reciprocating? Do you know who is dependable? Chances are, you are now more mindful of the support system you have working for you. Remember, you may be a part of someone else's system, too. When others give you their time, they may want your help sometimes, too. So set aside some time in your schedule to be of assistance to others who need you.

What You Know Now about Support

What have you learned about the support you can get at school from this capsule? You know that while support from your peers is readily given, it is rarely asked for. You know that many school systems recognize the value of providing teachers with support and have formally or informally instituted ways to help teachers get things done. You have learned through the questionnaire who makes up your own personal support system. You are now ready to utilize that support available to you in better managing your time.

TIME CAPSULE 6: CONCENTRATE ON WHAT YOU WANT TO DO

Do you have a place to work?
Do you plan for uninterrupted time?
How do you plan for getting paperwork done?

Concentration

Teachers with time management problems often are trying to do too many things simultaneously. It is not uncommon for teachers to be preparing a variety of lessons for different levels of students or in different content areas, to be serving on two or three school committees, and to be thinking about what to get at the grocery for supper. With so many different things floating around in teachers' minds, concentration can be a problem. The amount of time a teacher spends on a task, be it planning, grading papers, or whatever else, is not always what counts; what *can* be important to wise use of time is *uninterrupted* time. Time when you are not being bothered or distracted by people, objects, or events in a school setting is at a premium. Just as your students need uninterrupted time on tasks, so do you.

Make Space and Time for Concentration

Do you have a place at school and at home where you can work without being distracted? If so, use it. Many new schools provide teachers with work space in separate offices or cubicles away from classrooms and the social life of the teachers' lounge. If you are in one of those schools you are fortunate. If you are not in a school that can provide quiet work space, then you have to either create some for yourself or resign yourself to working in a quiet space at home. If you prefer to get most of your work done at school so that your home time is relatively free, then examine your schedule for the most likely times for uninterrupted work and look around the building for the most likely places to do it. Often, a vacant classroom will provide quiet work space. Coming to school an hour early each morning may give you an hour of uninterrupted time for work. You may create another uninterrupted hour by staying in the building an hour later in the afternoon. You may need only one additional hour a day for school work, or you may need two hours some days and none others. Whether you need the time now or not, it is good to know where and when you can have it when it's needed. Remember, a span of quiet uninterrupted time will allow you to use your time more effectively.

Sometimes teachers do have to work at home. That is one price you pay for a shorter (but more intense) work week and year. However, if you find yourself taking work home every night, it could be a sign that something is wrong; either you are trying to do too many things yourself or you might have failed to organize your time at school effectively. You may be trying to impress other teachers or your principal with how overworked you are. You may also be taking work home because you are assigning too much paperwork to students. Ask yourself if every assignment has to have a written product. Do you ever find yourself carrying books or papers out of the building from habit, when you really have no intention of looking at them at home? If so, make a conscious effort to leave them at school. Ask yourself as you walk out the door at the end of the day if you really are going to work on those plans or papers tonight. If the answer is no, then take them back into the school. You probably need to get away from your work at the end of the day both mentally and physically. Remember that time spent at home doing school work tends to drain your energies and may alienate friends and family. A great way to create stress in your personal life is to carry your work with you everywhere. Frequently teachers find themselves at home or in other social settings talking only about what happened at school that day or about what Jill Rousch's mother said during your parent conference. You owe it to yourself and your friends not to be a teacher twenty-four hours a day.

Whether you work at school or at home, your work space is important to consider in relation to effectiveness of time use. Take a look at your desk. It can represent your best kind of help or your worst enemy depending upon how the two of you function. Do you know what is in every drawer? Does everything have its place? Does your desk tell people around you that you are organized and efficient or does it reflect clutter and chaos? Clutter may be counterproductive to good classroom management; books and papers tend to get lost or misplaced on a desk where everything is stacked randomly and time must be used to find things when they are needed. Too many things on your desk may prevent you from concentration on the task at hand because the piles of work to be done or undone are constantly catching your eye. Piles of paper may foster tension, stress, and frustration, and feelings of loss of control may erupt. If there are piles of paper on your desk, resolve to clear them. Which belong to you? Which belong to students? Sort. Eliminate. Return. Throw away. For a week, try clearing your desk or at least organizing it each afternoon before leaving the building. It might make you feel each morning as if you are ready to control a new day.

Plan for Paperwork

Establish for yourself a routine that will allow you to get things done and maintain a healthy, happy outlook toward yourself and your role as a teacher. The routine should be flexible enough to allow for disruptions and interruptions (see

Capsule 3) without causing you undo frustration. Include a plan for handling your paperwork. Consider this teacher's plight:

> The event which caused me the most concern today was attempting to remember no less than eight forms which I either had to fill out and sign or merely to sign—and all of them due today. Some I had to delay filling out; others I received as recently as this morning. My problem was first remembering to fill them out, then finding time to fill them in, and then remembering to hand them to the right people. All in all the superabundance of paperwork coupled with a shortage of time made my day miserable.

Paperwork is a part of a teacher's work and should be planned for. Time each day should be set aside for dealing with requests and correspondence as a matter of routine. Teachers have to write letters frequently: they write to order materials, to communicate with parents, to thank volunteers. In addition, teachers get requests for many different kinds of written information: How many students' fathers work for the federal government? How many textbooks need rebinding? How frequently do you use AV equipment? This kind of paperwork can take many extra hours of work if you do not have a daily routine for handling it. Take the Mailbox Quiz to help you determine how prepared you are for handling papers.

As you look back over the Mailbox Quiz, are you able to assess what kinds of paperwork give you the most problems?

What You Know Now about Concentration

What have you learned about concentration and time use from this chapter? You know now that uninterrupted work time is more productive for doing planning and for dealing with paperwork demands. You know that you should establish a routine for working which will allow you to be efficient with the time you have. You know that carrying your work with you everyplace you go may cause affiliation problems. You know that your work space is important in helping you get things done. Now you have more ideas for how to use time wisely.

Mailbox Quiz. This morning when you arrived in school, you visited your mailbox and found the following items. In the space to the right of each item write *where* you would put this paper, *how soon* you would deal with it, and *how much time* you would use for this task. If you have to think about any item for very long, put a ? beside it and go to the next item.

Item	Where	How Soon	How Much Time
A bill for classroom materials you have purchased.			
Two new educational journals.			
A note from the principal asking you to attend a meeting of the PTA executive committee next Thursday at lunch.			
A unit plan from Ms. Smith, a fellow teacher, on a topic you were considering teaching next month.			
A letter from your supervisor asking for the names of potential volunteers from the community who might be interested in donating some time to the school. (This letter went to everyone in your department.)			
A form letter from the central office administration noting changed phone numbers.			
A memo from the social committee asking if you would be attending the faculty picnic Sunday and what you would be bringing.			
A brochure from a textbook company advertising a new text.			

TIME CAPSULE 7:
ACT—DON'T PROCRASTINATE,
DON'T DELAY

Do you put things off?
What are your best procrastination devices?
What do you fear about direct, positive action?

Procrastination

Procrastination is a frequent time use problem. When tasks present themselves, do you try to find something else to do? If a set of papers needs to be graded, do you think that you'd better type up next week's dittos first? Maybe a short break in the lounge would put you in the right frame of mind to grade papers. . . .

Watch for Common Procrastination Devices

Lakein, noted time-management expert, points to seven common escapes for not doing what we probably should do (Lakein, 1973 pp. 143–45). As you read through them, think about those which *you* do.

1. *Indulging yourself:* You escape from your work by first doing something you enjoy. When you are at school, this may mean a visit to the lounge for a Coke or a trip out of the building during your planning period—to the bank or to the grocery or to a nearby restaurant for lunch. When you are at home you might take a nap, watch TV, sew, read a new book, or go out for the evening. Whatever your indulging activities, you can be sure that those papers won't be graded or those parents won't have been called.
2. *Socializing:* It is always good to have someone to talk to. At school, the people not in class are easy marks when you need companionship. Students, secretaries, counselors, and principals will take their time for you when you want to chat. At home, there is always the telephone. Making small talk every chance you get will shorten the time you have to spend on your work.
3. *Reading:* Around school and in your desk are always unread papers and periodicals just begging for your attention. When reading is not

something you have to do to prepare a particular unit plan or for a course you are taking, the reading can be both pleasurable and time-consuming.
4. *Doing it yourself:* There is no one who can do it better, is there? (See Capsule 5.) Those 209 letters for that new bulletin board must be cut out by you. Taking detailed notes from a text rather than photocopying the pages must be done by you. Baking your own bread or spending your time worrying about how you will get all your work done—all these escapes use the time you set aside for your Urgent and Important tasks.
5. *Overdoing it:* There are some activities which require inordinate amount of time and they keep you from doing other things. Sharpening all the pencils in your desk to exact points, taking out the drawer linings in your desk and replacing them with new clean ones, lining up all the dictionaries on the window sill until they are exactly even, dusting the chalk trays—all may be convenient ways to keep you from doing other jobs.
6. *Running away:* If you're in your classroom, make up some reason to go to the office; if you're in the office, make up some reason to go to the classroom. Take a long coffee break or hurry through a unit plan to get to another when your students haven't learned the material. All these running devices keep your work from getting done the way you want.
7. *Daydreaming:* It's easy to let your mind wander, to think about what you're going to do when school is out or where you will go over Christmas break. The daydream provides a rest from routine but sometimes people get carried away and let the dreams become not merely a rest but an escape.

Remember that all these procrastinating devices can be beneficial to you and sometimes they are needed. They can be assets in that they are things you want to do, but they become troublesome when you do them to avoid other tasks.

Don't Fear Failure

Sometimes we put things off or put them aside because there are no guarantees of success or happiness at the end of the project. We may even fear embarrassment, rejection, or failure.

Just as our students want to succeed and feel good about what they are doing, so do we. You may find that you hesitate to act because you are unsure of the consequences of your actions. You hesitate to call parents because you don't know how they will respond.

You may find yourself focusing upon the "What if's" rather than on the "of course I can's." Think for a few minutes about your fears. How often do they determine your course of behavior? Ellis and Harper (1970) have outlined what they believe to be some basic irrational ideas which keep us from acting the way we would like to act. As you read through the list, ask yourself which of these ideas most influence your desire to procrastinate:

1. I must be loved or approved by everyone for virtually everything I do (or, if not by everyone, by persons I think are important to me.)
2. I can't stand it when things are not the way I would like them to be.
3. When I am unhappy it is because something external to me such as persons or events causes me to be that way.
4. Although I want to face difficult situations and self-responsibilities, it is easier for me to avoid them.
5. In order to have a feeling of worth, I should and must be thoroughly competent, adequate, intelligent, and achieving in all possible respects.
6. Something that once strongly affected me will always or indefinitely affect me.
7. I don't have much control over my emotions or thoughts.
8. I should rarely confront other people or assert my own thoughts or feelings about another person because people are fragile and are hurt easily. I don't want to hurt anybody.
9. Most of the time I will please other people even if I have to forego my own pleasure.
10. I am happiest when I just remain inactive and passive.

It is Ellis's theory that man is a rational being who can have control over emotions and behavior, and that it is our own perceptions, attitudes, or internalized fears about events outside us that affect us most. If, for example, a student says to you, "Mr. Zebb, you are the worst teacher I've ever had," and if you hold the first belief mentioned above, you may try to win the disgruntled student over to approving you. You may put off other activities to do those things you know the student will like so that he in turn will like you. Ellis recommends that when one or many of these irrational beliefs interfere with what you want, you should ask yourself: What is the worst possible thing that could happen? Is that a realistic possibility? It is up to each of us to learn to challenge, contradict, and ultimately replace those thoughts, ideas, or beliefs that do not serve our best interests. By doing so, we can gain control over our emotions and behaviors and will not have a need to put off those tasks which involve risk taking because we will have confidence that we have behaved and acted reasonably.

If you are avoiding a job because it looks too big, list in writing the small steps involved in getting it done. Then tackle them one by one. Think about what you can look forward to if you get the job done. Ask yourself what is positive about the task. Instead of looking at the job as something that has to be done, look at it as something you want to do. Think about what you can learn from each task or about how you might approach an old job in a new way. Start each day with a "To Do" list and immediately do something on the list so that you can prove to yourself that you "Can Do." A positive approach to any task can make the task easier. Your time will be better spent when you come away from school each day looking at your accomplishments.

What You Know Now about Procrastination

What have you learned about procrastination from this capsule? You now know several common methods of putting work off. You also know which of those methods is your downfall. You know, too, that sometimes procrastination is necessary and healthy, that you can't or shouldn't expect yourself to be task-oriented all the time. You also know that fear of failure can interfere with your ability to do what you have planned. If you think through your fears, you may be able to conquer them and accomplish those dreaded tasks after all.

TIME CAPSULE 8:
FOLLOW THROUGH—FINISH

Do you meet your goals?
Do you check up on yourself?
What does being "finished" mean?

Finishing

Do you assign homework and forget to collect it? Do you tell students you are going to keep track of each person who speaks out and forget to write it down? Do you tell your department chairperson that you'll attend a meeting after school and then remember that you promised the counselor you'd go on a home visit with him? If you are not consistent or do not follow through on your commitments, you may be wasting your time and that of others. On the other hand, if you have established a pattern of following up every assignment by checking students' work, or if you carry through your expectations for student behavior, you are doing a good job of finishing what you started.

People are well intentioned. We mean what we say and we'd like to finish what we start but sometimes we don't. Perhaps the special unit that was planned about the effects of energy conservation on the environment wasn't completed because you lost interest in it; the twenty instructional packets you started are in pieces because grades had to be sorted and then permanent records had to be sorted. You *meant* to finish but other things interfered, so you say "I just didn't have time." Many of the teacher problems discussed in this chapter are a result of not being able to finish what was started. When teachers say they don't have enough time to prepare or they don't have enough free time or they don't have enough time to teach and do everything else that schools expect teachers to do, what teachers mean is they didn't use their time to meet the goals that they value most—others' priorities interfered with them, and planning or teaching wasn't completed as well as they would have like.

Look Positively upon What You Have Completed

Take a few minutes now to consider the tasks you *have* been able to finish, the goals you have been able to meet. Take a piece of paper and make three columns. Head the columns, Accomplishments, Reasons and Time Management. In the column labeled "Accomplishments" list five things you have finished recently. Beside each of your accomplishments, in the column labeled "Reasons," write down the reason(s) your wanted to do each task. In the third column, write a few words about how you managed your time in order to get these things done. Are there particular reasons that are motivating you to accomplish what you are doing? Are there time management techniques that seem to work for you frequently? Keep these things in mind as you begin to tackle new ventures.

Your own will power, when used to turn away from procrastination techniques (see Capsule 7), can be your best tool for finishing what you start. Lakein (1973, p. 149), time-management consultant, says that will power is most needed to:

1. Plan when you're feeling harried and overwhelmed.
2. Keep yourself involved in a project even though some of the instant tasks you try lead to a dead end.
3. Avoid your favorite kinds of procrastination when you have important tasks to do.
4. Maintain a positive attitude.
5. Do something every day to lead toward your life goals.
6. Overcome fears, real or imagined.
7. Resist doing a very easy (but important) task that is right in front of you.

Build upon Past Experiences

Most teachers think about each new school year as a clean slate, an opportunity to start afresh with new students, new goals, new ideas, and new plans. Each year represents a different set of challenges and a chance to redesign curricula to meet personal and professional needs which somehow were passed by the year before. Unfortunately, we often reinvent the wheel. New books are explored, new tests are devised, new plans are made, new units are developed which seem to stress the skills you now deem important. Over the summer you have pushed into the back of your mind the experiences of the year before, and the boxes and files and cabinets containing the materials, projects, and plans are pitched out or carried to the attic or put into the closet. You vow to begin fresh, to do a better job, to teach more stimulating lessons.

But what about all those things you did right last year? What about all those good ideas that worked, all those lessons the students loved? Will they be forgotten too? If you manage your time wisely, your good ideas won't be lost. They will be preserved, built upon, and restored. This is not to say that once you have taught a year, you have mastered the teaching role and year after year after year you will teach the same way. No. What to do instead is take time to reflect upon what you have done and use your past experiences to provide a foundation for your professional growth.

Acquire Self-Discipline

Acquiring more self-discipline is not easy. One technique that may help you to stick to a task is to start with small steps. A large task seems harder to complete than three or four or five small ones. When you have a large task to complete, like making out grades for 183 students, break it down into small units such as class groups and give yourself a small reward for each group you finish. Soon you will have all the grades completed and you will feel great.

Another technique often suggested for when you're having

trouble finishing what you've started is to think for a few minutes about why you are having trouble. Analyze your procrastination. Think about what you will achieve when you get the job done. Be sure to include that feeling of relief that comes with finishing a project.

Not finishing what was started can become a habit. We all know people we might call "idea" people; they are great starters —enthusiastic, go-get-'em types—who begin worthwhile projects that somehow are never fully realized. Habits are hard to break, especially those that have been nurtured successfully for years. If you have the Unfinished Habit, make up your mind that as soon as you finish reading this chapter you will finish some small unfinished piece of business. Make a list of intentions and tomorrow finish one of them. Finish another the next day. You will find that the pleasure you find from being able to finish will support you and and encourage you to finish something else.

Most people don't start projects they believe they can't finish. Belief in outcome is good, but belief alone will not get the work done. Good prior planning will prevent you from committing yourself to projects that you might lose interest in or might not complete.

If you develop the habit of finishing what you start, you will not waste time on tasks that you will only give up later and you will not have to spend time retracing your actions or reviewing something you stopped in midstream. Once you can think of yourself as a finisher, you will come to respect yourself more. Furthermore, your students', fellow teachers, and school administrators will know that when you say you're going to do something, you do it.

What You Know Now about Finishing

What have you learned about finishing what you start from reading this capsule? You know now that it is all too easy not to finish, but you know too that being able to finish is a valuable asset. You know that it is important to look at past successes for encouragement in getting tasks completed. You know four techniques for helping yourself acquire more self-discipline, and you know that you have taken a step forward in learning to use your time wisely because you have finished reading the time capsules.

SUMMARY

Time problems will always be a part of teaching, but the resolution of many of them will become easier for you if you apply what you have learned. Your use of time is personal. No one else may see or use time exactly the way you do. To make the ideas in this chapter work for you, you must personalize them, integrate them, make them a part of you. Ultimately to be able to use your time wisely, your use of time must be satisfying. Once you know what you want to accomplish and have considered the constraints of your school and your role, you will be able to set priorities and plan realistically to accomplish your goals. The information and exercises in this chapter were intended to enable you to do just that.

Throughout your reading you have been encouraged to be reflective, to think about what has worked for you in the past and how that relates to your present goals. You have also been encouraged to reflect upon the people in your school who can help you get your work done in a less frustrating way. You have taken a few minutes to think about your work space at home and in school and have considered the usefulness of several techniques which can aid you in concentrating upon the tasks at hand. You also have thought about your procrastinating idiosyncrasies and have determined those barriers which prevent you from completing work.

Borrowing from Hall's statement at the beginning of this chapter, you have made explicit many things you have taken for granted in your teaching life. You have moved into an active understanding of your relationship with time and through this you are now better prepared to make changes in your time-use patterns. The choices to be made are yours. Putting into practice each of the eight principles offered through the capsules will require firm determination. Now when you find yourself saying, "I just don't have time," it will be because you have decided not to use your time in a particular way. It will be through a conscious evaluation process that you have concluded that a particular task or activity would not be beneficial to you.

As you finish reading this chapter, be mindful of the old saying, "Rome wasn't built in a day." Your present problems with using your time wisely are products of several years of time-use habits. If you are now determined to change an old unproductive routine, do it slowly. Don't make commitments to yourself and others that may be impossible to keep. Don't expect to suddenly find large amounts of free time because you are trying out new behavior and management styles. Be rewarding to yourself. Think positively. In spite of the interruptions and changes in school life, eventually you will become more satisfied with your relationship with time.

RELATED READINGS

Bliss, E. *Getting Things Done: The A.B.C.'s of Time Management.* New York: Scribner's, 1976.

Cottle, T. *Perceiving Time.* New York: John Wiley, 1976.

Ellis, A., and R.A. Harper. *A Guide to Rational Living.* Englewood Cliffs, N.J.: Prentice-Hall, 1970.

Fraisse, P. *The Psychology of Time.* New York: Harper & Row, Pub., 1963.

Hall, E. *The Silent Language.* New York: Doubleday, 1959.

———. *Beyond Culture.* New York: Doubleday, 1976.

Hennings, D. *Mastering Classroom Communications.* Pacific Palisades, Calif.: Goodyear Publishing Company, 1975.

Lakein, A. *How to Get Control of Your Time and Your Life.* New York: New American Library, 1973.

Luce, G. *Body Time: Physiological Rhythms and Social Stress.* New York: Pantheon, 1971.

Reinert, J. "What Your Sense of Time Tells About You." *Science Digest,* 69 (1971) 8-12.

part III

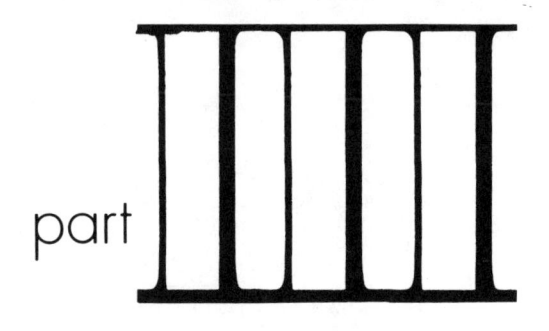

TEACHER PROBLEMS AND TEACHER PERSONALITY

The final chapter enables us to compare ourselves with other teachers who have similar problems. It is interesting to find out to what extent we are like them *and what our problems may tell us about ourselves.*

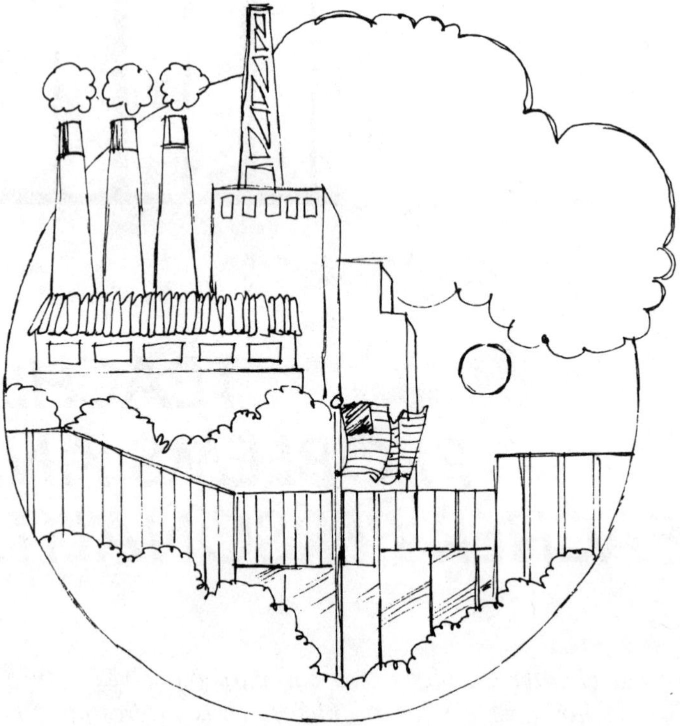

chapter 10

relationships between classroom problems and personality or place of work

BETTY MYERS

Chapter 10 Outcomes: *As a result of Chapter 10 you should be able to:*
— *describe teacher personality characteristics which appear to be related to teacher problems,*
— *describe socio-demographic or situational characteristics that seem to be related to teacher problems, and*
— *understand that although relationships between teacher personality characteristics and teacher problems exist, these relationships are complex and often difficult to interpret.*

Do you believe that your teaching problems are related to the kind of person you are? Do you believe that they are related to the kind of school and neighborhood in which you work? A study has been done in order to determine the answers to these questions (Myers, 1977). Since you know what your teaching problems are, you will be interested in the study and the results.

A total of 432 Ohio teachers of grades 7–12 took part in the study. They completed a Teacher Problems Checklist, the Edwards Personality Inventory, and in addition supplied other information about themselves and their schools. The form of the checklist used was different from that of the TPC in Chapter 2 in that it asked teachers to indicate both how *frequent* and how *bothersome* a problem was.

The teachers' responses to the Teacher Problems Checklist indicated that the problems fell into the five areas of concern we have been dealing with in this book: affiliation, control, parent relationships, student success, and time.

In the sections that follow, profiles of teachers are presented for each of the five problem areas.

PROFILES OF TEACHERS WHO REPORT THAT THEY HAVE AFFILIATION PROBLEMS

Recall that affiliation problems are related to the teacher need to establish and maintain good relationships with others in the school.

Teachers in the study who reported that they *frequently* had such problems tended to believe that they are *seen by others*, as leaders, persistent, articulate, virtuous, efficient planners, neat dressers, self-confident, and considerate but above all else, hard workers. In addition, they tended to believe that they were seen by others as unconcerned about making good impressions and not shy but above all else not angry and not self-critical. The same teachers reported that they were dissatisfied with teaching and dissatisfied with the school in which they worked.

Following are definitions of the above-mentioned personality characteristics adapted from the Edwards Personality

Inventory of teachers who reported that they had frequent affiliation problems.

- *A leader.* This kind of teacher is probably found in both appointed and elected positions of leadership. Department chairmen and teacher organization representatives as well as faculty spokespersons could be like this.
- *Persistent.* This kind of teacher works long hours without being told. He keeps on trying to solve problems even after others would have given up. It is common for these kinds of teachers to become so involved in work that they forget about time and sleeping.
- *Articulate.* This kind of teacher is able to express her thoughts clearly and summarizes discussions well. She can keep a discussion going easily, even with strangers or when the topic is of little interest to her.
- *Virtuous.* A teacher like this believes that others attribute to him all virtues to the highest degree.
- *Plans work efficiently.* These teachers are businesslike in that they plan in detail what they want to do and then waste no time in doing it. They are able to work at more than one task at a time, and do not let their attention wander from the task at hand.
- *Neat in dress.* This kind of teacher is very concerned about his appearance and is always neat. He takes care of his clothes and finds buying new clothes satisfying.
- *Self-confident.* A teacher who is self-confident would seem to be one who is most likely to depend more on herself than on others for getting things done. She probably neither requests nor offers help either individually or by volunteering to serve on committees.
- *Considerate.* These teachers are tolerant of others and even recognize good points of others who disagree with them. They feel affection and warmth for others and possess few authoritarian attitudes. They can criticize without offending.
- *A hard worker.* Teachers who are hard workers take their work very seriously. They can't leave a job only half done and, in fact, spend time when they're not at school doing school work. Having decided to be teachers, they put all their energy into doing the things they believe are necessary for teaching well. Having a lot

of work to do doesn't discourage these teachers, and if they can't find work to do they become bored.
- *Does not worry about making a good impression on others.* This kind of teacher would probably be unaware that he makes any impression at all on others. He probably lacks feeling for collegial relationships and therefore is not depended upon for support by others. He is probably unaware that his behavior impacts on other teachers either positively or negatively.
- *Not shy.* This kind of teacher is at ease with others even with those she knows only slightly. She belongs to many organizations and does not feel timid in social gatherings.
- *Does not become angry.* These teachers don't become upset or shout if others oppose them, keep them waiting, or take advantage of them.
- *Not self-critical.* These teachers do not doubt that they are as competent as any teacher or that they will be successful. They may overestimate their abilities and not recognize their limitations. They have confidence generally, and feel they have good personality traits.

Teachers who reported frequent affiliation problems seemed not to be the kind who attended seriously to others to any extent. Many of their characteristics were related to work and accomplishing tasks; some were related to their abilities to get others to accomplish tasks; but few were related to any sense of dependence on, alliance with, or rapport with others for personal reasons. Given these related variables, how can the occurrence of these affiliation problems be explained?

One explanation could be that these teachers seem to feel unusually competent and therefore act self-assured. They may consider themselves, and others also may consider them, to be "superteachers." They show up well when teaching: they don't ever appear to be inept. They believe they are good teachers and indeed they do appear to do many things well. These teachers may alienate their colleagues by being too good. What they do, they do thoroughly. It's what they don't do that may cause them affiliation problems. For example, these teachers are characterized as "considerate," and that seems odd. Why would teachers who "treat others with affection and warmth" perceive frequent affiliation problems? One explanation may lie in their infrequent interaction with others. If these teachers are so busy with tasks, then that must limit their opportunities for interacting with their colleagues and students. As teachers perhaps they are businesslike and systematic, and these qualities could make others perceive them as aloof. In any event, it seems that the many characteristics which are related to having and achieving goals may interfere with even considerate teachers' abilities to avoid frequent affiliation problems.

A somewhat different explanation could be that these teachers expect their relationships with other teachers and students to be as successful as their task-related accomplishments are. What they may not realize is that their success in this area is dependent on the complex interactions of many variables, only some of which an individual teacher can control.

It is interesting to note that in spite of all the other ways in which these teachers are successful, they are not satisfied with teaching or their schools. It seems noteworthy that this was the only group that was dissatisfied. Because of the way the data was collected and analyzed, it is not possible to determine whether the social-demographic characteristics—the dissatisfactions—describe the same group of teachers as the personality characteristics do or whether they describe a different group.

If this is a different group of teachers then we might say, okay, here are some teachers who don't like teaching or their schools and it's no surprise that they have frequent affiliation problems. These teachers may not feel part of the school community *because* they don't like teaching. On the other hand, if these teachers are the same ones described by the personality characteristics, then how can their dissatisfaction by explained? They do so much, so well, and seem to be most strongly motivated toward doing those things, that it seems as if there could be no basis for their dissatisfaction. Perhaps, in spite of the apparent power of task-related goals for these teachers, it's possible that affiliation problems are indicators that these teachers want to develop closer relationships with others than they have been able to.

Teachers in the study who reported that they were *bothered* by affiliation problems *tended to believe that they are seen by others* as not making friends easily, not virtuous, not articulate, not logical, desiring recognition, not considerate, angry, and self-critical. In addition, they tended to report that they were satisfied with the school in which they worked (which was most likely in a rural or suburban setting), they had little teaching experience, they were young, and notably, they were satisfied with teaching.

Following are definitions of these characteristics of teachers who reported that they were bothered by affiliation problems. They are also adapted from the Edwards Personality Inventory.

- *Does not make friends easily.* This kind of teacher is a person who is difficult to get to know. He doesn't enjoy meeting others or making many friends. He has few friends.
- *Not virtuous.* A teacher like this does not believe that others consider her a better than average person.
- *Not articulate.* This kind of teacher tends not to be able to express his thoughts clearly or to be able to summarize a discussion well. He also has difficulty keeping a conversation going, especially with a stranger or when the topic is of little interest to him.
- *Not logical.* She does not value logic about personal feelings. Her judgments may be biased and she tends to make decisions impulsively.
- *Desires recognition.* These teachers are ambitious; they would like to accomplish something of significance and receive recognition for it. More specifically, they want their accomplishments to be unique and their recognition to be national or, even, better, international.
- *Not considerate.* These teachers tend not to be tolerant of others and have difficulty recognizing good points of any who disagree with them. They possess authoritarian attitudes and feel little affection for others. Others are offended by their criticism.

- *Becomes angry.* Teachers like this become upset and shout when others oppose them, keep them waiting, or take advantage of them.
- *Not self-confident.* This kind of teacher is reluctant to depend mainly on himself for getting things done. Instead he prefers to work with others, individually and in committee.

Such personality characteristics provide many reasons for expecting affiliation problems to occur. Taken together, they represent many characteristics not uncommon to new, young professionals. Their untried knowledge gives them a sense of confidence, which probably is the characteristic that tends to heighten the other characteristics associated with these problems. This explanation gains increased validity from an examination of the social-demographic characteristics.

The picture that emerges does describe a group of teachers who are young and inexperienced. They teach in suburban, neighborhood schools and they are satisfied with teaching and with their schools. None of these characteristics seems incompatible with the tendency of these teachers to be self-centeredly confident. For them, affiliation problems may be perceived as the main flow in their otherwise nearly perfect performance or situation. We might speculate that resolving these problems is analogous to a maturation process; that is, experience and age will be more effective than anything else.

To summarize, when the question is asked, "What kinds of teachers tend to perceive affiliation problems?" the answer seems to be at least two or three different kinds. For some teachers, frequent affiliation problems are reported; others report being bothered by them. You might ask yourself which dimension of this problem area had the greater influence on your perception of problems. Perhaps examination of the associated profiles and interpretations will help you to understand why you have these problems.

A caveat! This research provides information about groups; specific *individuals* may or may not conform to the group results.

PROFILES OF TEACHERS WHO REPORT THAT THEY HAVE CONTROL PROBLEMS

Recall that control problems are related to the teacher need to have pupils behave appropriately.

Teachers in the study who reported that they *frequently* had such problems *tended to believe that they are seen by others* as avoiding arguments and especially that they are easily influenced. The same teachers tended to report that they had structured classrooms, few years of teaching experience, that they were satisfied with their school, and especially that they were satisfied with teaching.

Following are definitions of the two above-mentioned personal characteristics of teachers who reported that they had frequent control problems.[1]

- *Avoids arguments.* These teachers avoid discussing controversial topics because they don't like to express opinions which they know will be contrary to those of others. They tend to agree with others and will go out of their way to stay away from an argument.
- *Easily influenced.* These are teachers who have difficulty presenting and maintaining a position opposed by others and who yield to another point of view quickly. One reason these teachers give in to others is that they are easily fooled by others' arguments; they tend to believe whatever they're told.

Teachers who reported *bothersome* control problems also *tended to believe that they are seen by others* as avoiding arguments and being easily influenced. Similarly, they reported that they had few years of teaching experience and that they were satisfied with their school and teaching.

In addition to the characteristics they shared with teachers

---

[1] This listing and all listings of personal characteristics in this Chapter are derived from the Edwards Personality Inventory.

reporting frequent control problems, the bothered teachers reported that they were *perceived by others* as liking a set routine and wanting sympathy. Further, they reported they were female and young.

Following are definitions for liking a set routine and wanting sympathy.

- *Likes a set routine.* These teachers tend to be upset by change. They get a schedule established and, left to themselves, do not deviate from it. They feel unable to work without a routine; when their plans don't work out, they are upset.
- *Wants sympathy.* These teachers feel that their work is unappreciated by others, that they are criticized unnecessarily, and that they never had a chance to show what they can really do. They don't trust others and feel that others don't like them.

Thus the profiles of teachers reporting either frequent or bothersome control problems tend to have several things in common. The significance of these observations is that teachers who perceive frequent control problems will tend also to be bothered by them.

The two commonly shared personality characteristics, avoiding arguments and being easily influenced, present a fairly consistent, albeit lopsided, characterization. The question is, what kinds of people, or teachers, have needs to be agreeable and not to oppose others? One response is that new teachers could be expected to feel like that. If the social-demographic characteristics are examined, these teachers are indeed seen to have fewer years of teaching experience. Such teachers may still be trying to win acceptance and are concerned with how their students and others regard them personally. It seems reasonable that these teachers would be reluctant to test their authority over their students but instead would attempt to influence them. Recall that control problems occur because teachers want students to behave in some ways and not in others. Because they are in the weaker position, being so concerned with gaining their students' acceptance, these teachers might be more easily influenced by their students than their students are by them. Having a relatively highly structured classroom is also typical of new teachers because they tend to worry things will get out of control. These teachers' satisfaction, both with teaching and with their schools, also might be the consequence of their newness; they have been preparing for four years and now, at last, they have their own students. They finally won the prize!

Recall that two additional personality variables—likes a set routine and wants sympathy—are associated with being bothered by control problems. They suggest that bothered teachers possess certain additional behaviors and attitudes.

When these two characteristics are added to those from the frequency characterization variables, then we must consider what kind of teacher *this* is. These new variables seem to contribute mainly by fleshing out somewhat more the still lopsided portrait we have of teachers with control problems. Liking a set routine goes very well with establishing a classroom whose organization is described as structured. Wanting sympathy also fits in. These teachers have control problems in spite of having tried so hard to please. The associated social-demographic variables provide even more information. We had already inferred that these teachers would tend to be young because they had few years of teaching experience. However, they also tend to be female. That's not surprising since many studies have indicated that female teachers seem to have more control problems than male teachers have. (Perhaps men are just more reluctant to admit that they have control problems.) All the teachers are satisfied with teaching and with their schools. Again, whatever the explanation, having control problems doesn't seem to be what makes teachers dissatisfied.

PROFILES OF TEACHERS WHO REPORT THAT THEY HAVE PARENT RELATIONSHIP/ HOME CONDITION PROBLEMS

Parent relationship and home condition problems are related to the teacher need to relate and work well with adults who are important in the lives of students.

Teachers in the study who reported that they *frequently* had such problems *tended to believe that they are seen by others* as cooperative and not as perfectionists. Most of all they do not think others perceive them as being misunderstood. Definitions of these personal characteristics follow.

- *Cooperative.* These are teachers who enjoy working on projects with others, who take pride in group accomplishments, and who willingly carry out group decisions. These teachers also respect those who have authority over them, tend to ask them for suggestions, and usually agree with their opinions.
- *Is not a perfectionist.* This kind of teacher does not pay much attention to minor things so is willing to let a lot of things remain undecided or undone. He does not care if his work or that of others is not done perfectly; as long as something is approximately as he means it, he is willing to let it pass.
- *Does not feel misunderstood.* These teachers don't feel that their work goes unappreciated, that they are criticized unnecessarily, or that they have never had a chance to show what they can do. They don't feel mistrusted or disliked by others.

These characteristics seem to describe teachers who don't have very strong self-images. They desire to blend into a mass and do not want to stand out from others. They are not accustomed to acting and assuming others' support for their actions. When it comes to how they establish contacts with parents, it seems unlikely that teachers such as these will find frequent need to do that. They simply do not initiate. Thus their parent contacts which cause problems probably are initiated by parents, and it's unlikely that parents will do that unless they are concerned about something. Since this kind of teacher (not being any more independent that he is) is probably not a very good problem solver, he perceives a parent's concern as a problem. Since the teachers described seem to be unable to exert control in their contacts with parents, perhaps they act similarly when teaching. If so, parents have many reasons to be concerned and this kind of teacher might expect to have frequent parent relationships problems.

Teachers in the study who reported that they were *bothered* by parent relationship/home condition problems *tended to believe that they are seen by others* as easily influenced, not articulate, and, like their frequency counterparts, not perfectionists. Descriptions of the two unshared personal characteristics follow.

- *Not articulate.* This kind of teacher tends not to be able to express his thoughts clearly or to be able to summarize a discussion well. He also has difficulty keeping a conversation going, especially with a stranger, or when the topic is one of little interest to him.
- *Easily influenced.* These teachers have difficulty presenting and maintaining a position when others oppose it and tend to yield to another's point of view quickly. One reason these teachers give in to others is that they are easily fooled by others' arguments; they tend to believe whatever they're told.

Although only three characteristics describe these bothered teachers, they do seem to provide a meaningful portrait. Here is a teacher who does not attend to details and therefore may not be effective at explaining the circumstances of a problematic situation to parents. In addition, he doesn't approach a meeting purposefully or bring to it abilities which could produce a satisfying resolution of a problem. It seems as if bothered teachers might be somewhat careless about their relationships with parents and perhaps even regard them as relatively unimportant, at least until they encounter problems.

Although these frequency and bothersome profiles can be interpreted, such interpretations are offered tentatively, especially when so few characteristics constitute the profiles. If you believe you possess these characteristics, don't hesitate to consider alternative interpretations and then ask if your own interpretations provide a better explanation for your parent relationships problems.

PROFILES OF TEACHERS WHO REPORT THAT THEY HAVE STUDENT SUCCESS PROBLEMS

Student success problems are related to the teacher need to help students succeed academically and socially.

Teachers in the study who reported that they *frequently* had such problems *tended to believe that they are seen by others* as not having cultural interests, not easily influenced, not persistent, not enjoying the center of attention, and especially avoiding arguments and not being perfectionists. The same teachers reported that they teach students of low socioeconomic status (SES) in cities.

Following are definitions of the above-mentioned personal characteristics of teachers who reported that they had frequent student success problems.

- *Does not have cultural interests.* These teachers tend not to do or be the things associated with having cultural interests. That is, they don't read widely, tend not to have a wide range of interests, and tend not to visit museums or attend musical events.
- *Not easily influenced.* Teachers characterized in this way don't have more than the usual difficulty presenting and maintaining a position opposed by others. They do not yield to another's point of view quickly, at least partly because they don't give more creddence to other's arguments than to their own.
- *Not persistent.* This kind of teacher does not work for long hours on her own. She is not motivated to continue to try to solve a

problem any more than an average teacher. Such a teacher does not become so involved in her work that she forgets about time or neglects to sleep.
- *Does not enjoy being the center of attention.* This kind of teacher dislikes doing things that call attention to himself. This does not seem to be due simply to modesty but is an active shunning of attention. He tends to tell amusing stories or to speak loudly.
- *Avoids arguments.* These teachers avoid discussing controversial topics because they don't like to express opinions which they know will be contrary to those of others. They tend to agree with others and will go out of their way to stay away from an argument.
- *Not a perfectionist.* This kind of teacher does not pay much attention to minor things so is willing to let a lot of things remain undecided or undone. He does not care if his work or that of others is not done perfectly; as long as something is approximately as he means it, he is willing to let it pass.

Recall that student success for teachers means helping students to be successful academically and socially. It seems doubtful that teachers would mention any of the characteristics above, with the possible exception of Not Easily Influenced, if they were asked to identify personal characteristics which help them to be successful with students. The point is that teachers who tend to have frequent student success problems don't themselves possess characteristics which indicate that they ever had any firsthand experience with such success. While teacher experience is not requisite for helping students learn some things, student success is such a global goal that modeling may be a necessary way of learning it. Even if it is not, a teacher's not having had some of the specific experiences still seems to be an obstacle to achieving this goal. How can a teacher who admits to not being widely read stimulate students' interest in reading widely? If these are teachers who don't pursue dreams and who have not developed interests beyond those needed for survival, it is hard to believe that they will be able to help their students develop such interests. The social-demographic characteristics add to their problem.

Most teachers are middle class, and even those with cultural interests, more often than not, are ignorant or unappreciative of lower-class cultural interests, so they lack common cultural interests from which they could encourage wider interests. It is widely accepted that some teachers of low SES students and some teachers in inner-city schools hold lower expectations for their students than teachers generally hold for other students.

A somewhat different interpretation suggests that these teachers not only hold goals which they are ill-prepared for achieving, but that they may be unaware of being ill-prepared for achieving them.

Teachers in the study who reported that they were *bothered* by student success problems *tended to believe they were perceived by others* as not wanting sympathy and not feeling misunderstood. The behaviors and attitudes which designate these characteristics are described below.

- *Does not want sympathy.* These teachers don't need more assurance than the average teachers that what they are doing is right. They don't tell their problems to friends or others in order to gain sympathy. They don't expect friends to feel sorrier for them than for others when they have failures.
- *Does not feel misunderstood.* These teachers don't feel that their work goes unappreciated, that they are criticized unnecessarily, or that they have never had a chance to show what they can do. They don't feel mistrusted or disliked by others.

Although, as was the case with some other profiles, these two characteristics don't give a full picture of the teachers, they do seem to describe one aspect and perhaps that is the most important one with respect to explaining why teachers are bothered by student success problems. Unlike teachers who reported frequent student success problems and who seem to possess few if any of the "success" attributes themselves, these teachers could be exactly the reverse. They are neither asking for sympathy nor blaming others for their problems. While we don't know to what extent they possess the characteristics which the other group lacked, we do know they don't lack them to the same extent. Consider the following interpretation of this profile as one possibility. Maybe these teachers are relatively successful, independent, and competent themselves. Because they are like this, their expectations for their students are also high; they believe limits are there to be stretched. When they try to help a student to do this and don't succeed, that bothers them. This interpretation is actually more an extrapolation and certainly is arguable. The evidence for it is negative. Does it seem likely that a teacher who did not feel competent and who did not strive, usually successfully, to help his students achieve success would be characterized by this particular pair of variables? The absence of related social-demographic characteristics might be interpreted as additional support for this argument. These teachers' feelings of success and competence are relatively independent of external variables; they feel as if they do affect student learning.

PROFILES OF TEACHERS WHO REPORT THAT THEY HAVE PROBLEMS WITH TIME

You will recall that these problems are related to teachers' inability to find enough time for accomplishing both personal and professional things.

Teachers in the study who reported that they *frequently* had such problems *tended to believe that they are perceived by others* as hard workers. They also tended to teach (1) large classes, (2) work in suburban or rural areas with (3) high socio-economic status (SES) students, and (4) be satisfied with teaching.

The single personality variable associated with frequent time problems is "hard working." It is defined below.

- *Hard workers.* Teachers who are hard workers take their work very seriously. They can't leave a job only half done and, in fact, spend time when they're not at school doing school work. Having decided to be teachers, they put all their energy into doing the things they believe are necessary for teaching well. Having a lot of work to do doesn't discourage these teachers, and if they can't find work to do they become bored.

The four characteristics of the school and students seem to describe a setting where (a) a teacher would have a lot of pressure to work hard and (b) a teacher who did work hard would probably feel successful. In other words, the setting provided the potential for success. An example of this potential is the high SES of the students. Research has shown that high SES correlates with high student achievement at school, and hard-working teachers seem to work in achievement-oriented schools; perhaps they seek out these kinds of schools. The opportunity the school offers for student success motivates these teachers to spend a lot of time at their work. Unlike many of the other problem areas, solutions for frequent time problems are relatively simple. Teachers could decide to limit the amount of time they will spend on work. Those who perceive time problems seem instead to decide to accomplish some amount of work regardless of the time needed. They are generally satisfied with their schools, so having time problems may be less important to them than not accomplishing the work they believe they should do. Perhaps if these teachers took a hard look at what they do and how they organize to do it, they might find it possible both to accomplish what is most urgent and important and to have more time.

On the other hand, teachers in the study who reported that they were *bothered* by time problems *tended to believe that they are seen by others* as anxious about their performance, feeling misunderstood, wanting sympathy, and especially, as avoiding problems and being absentminded.

The same group of teachers reported that they were satisfied with teaching and especially with their school.

Following are definitions of the above-mentioned personal characteristics of teachers who reported they had frequent time problems.

- *Anxious about performance.* These teachers worry about how well they are doing and become anxious if they believe their performance is to be compared with that of others. They think they should be able to answer all their students' questions and are concerned that students won't think they are as good as other teachers.
- *Feels misunderstood.* These teachers feel that their work is unappreciated by others, that they are criticized unnecessarily, and that they have never had a chance to show what they can really do. They don't trust others and feel that others don't like them.
- *Wants sympathy.* These teachers need reassurance that they are doing what is right and tell their friends and anyone else who will listen about their problems in order to gain sympathy. They expect others to feel sorry for them when they have failures.
- *Avoids facing problems.* Teachers having this characteristic tend to put off making difficult decisions or unpleasant tasks. They don't want to think about things that cause them anxiety.
- *Absentminded.* Forgetting to return what they borrow such as books or pencils is characteristic of absentminded teachers. Generally they forget names, appointments, dates, and where they put things.

Teachers who are bothered by time problems and who possess these personality characteristics might be described as living in a world of their own making. They find much to worry about and little that is rewarding. Their motivation seems to be to avoid responsibility and what they perceive must follow it—blame. They are so overwhelmed by problems that they would be unlikely even to notice a successful outcome. These surely are the pessimists of teaching. These teachers' time problems may be more a function of their own personalities than of their teaching role.

Social-demographic variables indicate that teachers who are bothered by time problems are satisfied with teaching and with their schools. Given the above personality characteristics, these results are indeed surprising. Possible explanations could include the following:

1. This is a different group of teachers than those described by the personality characteristics.
2. For some teachers, being anxious does not decrease job satisfaction.

Other explanations may also exist.

If you have time problems, ask yourself: Am I like any of the teacher groups described above? If you think you are, can you understand better now why you may have those problems? Remember that although you will probably be able to think of instances when any given characteristic would have described you, you are only "like" a given profile if *most* of the characteristics are *typical* of you.

Remember that the evidence for the relationships discussed above was obtained from one exploratory study and must be regarded as extremely tentative. The interpretations are suggested because speculating about what relationships mean can be productive for increasing understanding. More evidence supporting these findings would be needed before they are accepted with confidence. They are being shared with you partly because they are provocative and also because, if you recognize yourself in them, they might help you to understand better why some problems are more important to you than are others.

RELATED READING

Myers, Betty. "An Empirical Investigation of the Relation of Teacher Perceived Problems to Teacher Personality Variables and Social-Demographic Variables." Doctoral dissertation, The Ohio State University, 1977.

part **IV**

SUPPLEMENTS

The last section of the book contains two supplements. Supplement 1 provides sets of practice problems for each of the five areas of teacher concern. Supplement 2 presents a description of how the Teacher Problem Checklists used in Chapter 2 was developed.

1 supplement

some problems of practice
DONALD R. CRUICKSHANK

Following is a set of vignettes for each of the five areas of teacher concern. They are presented to you as they were written by classroom teachers. They have not been edited. You may find them interesting and especially useful as catalysts for discussion if this book is used in in-service education or college classes.

Vignettes Related to Teacher Goal of Affiliation
1. I get very angry at a coach on our staff who doesn't like to teach. He never talks about anything but sports and he uses foul language. Today in the lounge he said, "I'm not a good teacher, but I'm really not interested in that sort of thing." I am concerned about his attitude and about his relationship with his students and with us.
2. The freshmen in Environmental Design are coming up with great proposals for altering the school and proposals that are immediately realizable, but the administration is notorious for letting faculty-student initiated programs die from inaction. How can I tell an enthusiastic group of freshmen that a good, inexpensive, well-

planned and conceived idea is being ignored, and then expect them to care about their school?
3. One teacher who works in our department assumes credit for every idea. She brags about her accomplishments to other teachers who view her in great awe. The people in our department know that she is bragging. Many times she exaggerates and sometimes she even lies. She is looked upon as super creative when, in reality, she has stolen the ideas from people in our department.
4. I worry about being evaluated. Whenever the principal comes in my class I get extremely nervous. Last week he came in while we were having a class discussion. I found that I couldn't listen to the students' answers and even forgot my next question. I quickly made a reading assignment.
5. Today Sandy seemed very withdrawn again. I thought I had been making real progress in establishing a good relationship with her. Yesterday she had done poorly on a quiz and I felt really disappointed for her. She seemed crushed. How can I reestablish this relationship?

Vignettes Related to Teacher Goal of Control

1. In homeroom, my student council representative is a minor discipline problem. He continues to talk out loud during announcements and makes smart remarks during homeroom business. If I reprimand him, he tries to look innocent like he couldn't do anything wrong.
2. Upon entering my fourth hour class I encountered a student writing on her desk and in her book. She flatly denied that she did it. We have a rule about writing on desks and in the school books.
3. I had to take a boy to the office today to see the principal. He had been loud and abusive most of the year, but today he tried to mimic me and I will not tolerate this disrespect. The boy has no parents (he lives with his relatives) and we would like to keep him in school. The problem is, How much should I overlook to help keep him in school? It is my belief that any student who behaves in the manner of this student should be helped, but not at the expense of other students in the class.
4. I covered for a junior high shop teacher in his study hall today. I'm not accustomed to "baby-sitting." My regular study hall is older and more mature. I could hardly keep my temper with the antics of

these younger kids. I didn't do anything but discipline the entire period. Usually I get some of my own work done, but not today. I also do not believe in browbeating students, but at the time there seemed to be no other recourse. I feel that my time as well as theirs was wasted.
5. The biggest problem today was the children's attitudes toward each other. The bigger children really take delight in picking on the smaller ones. This upsets the smaller children and disrupts the learning atmosphere. It seems that the boys with the more negative attitude always want to dominate the "quiet" boys.

Vignettes Related to Teacher Goal of Parent Relationships

1. I have the problem of parents not backing school rules. I teach food service management in a vocational school. The students *must* follow hair care and hygiene rules strictly. One or two students' parents only wring their hands and say they hope I can get their children to follow the rules as they cannot.
2. I teach a senior distributive education program. The students are required to work in a retailing business. One mother worried herself into a frenzy if her daughter (age 18) was 15 minutes late getting home from the job. She was always sure that her daughter was meeting men, getting high, etc. Her daughter was one of the nicest students that I have had. I talked at length with her mother. It seems the girl had an older sister who got pregnant, hence the mistrust on the part of the mother. The mother insisted that her daughter quit her job.
3. I had been working quite intensively in helping a senior high boy find a job. It was quite difficult because the boy was retarded and needed quite a bit of assistance in initiating job contacts. After getting the boy a job, I got a phone call from his stepmother at about 11:00 at night. She was abusive, swearing, and talking so funny that I thought she was drunk. She accused me of keeping some of the boy's job money. I couldn't reason at all with her so I hung up on her. It's the first and only time I have ever treated a parent this way, and I felt very guilty about doing this. The stepmother did call back and apologize the next night, but I don't think I ever convinced her that her son received all the money that was due him.
4. In my school community there are more college-educated parents

than noncollege-educated ones. The *average* amount of completed years in school is about 14 or 15. So you can see that many parents are extremely well-educated. As a result, parents often take the attitude that they know more than the teachers—which may be true in some cases. They have a rather arrogant attitude, in some cases, about what the teachers do wrong.
5. At the school where I teach the attendance is poor. The daily absence report takes up four columns, single-spaced, both sides of an 8½ X 14 sheet of paper. Often the reasons given are that the child was needed to baby-sit, or the family went to visit relatives for six weeks, or the child didn't want to come. The school is low in the parents' priorities and they seem to take no interest in the children's schooling. As a result it is difficult to get cooperation or even to get the parents to come for conferences. They don't even support the PTA.

Vignettes Related to Teacher Goal of Student Success
1. Without failure whenever there is a chemistry lab, there is a distinct lack of following directions, even though directions are precisely, logically, and clearly stated in the lab sheets. I always go over the lab the day before with explanations and hints on procedure, questions to be answered, data needed and so forth. Yet when the lab is actually done a million questions will be asked of me as to "what shall be done." Nine out of 10 times my answer is "refer to the instructions." By the end of the second quarter there should be some slight semblance of independence in lab work—at least in doing exactly what the instructions dictate. But alas, that requires effort by the student. It seems easier to ask the teacher and get an oral reply than to read. Frustration! Somewhere teachers have failed to teach thinking and independence.
2. The problem that caused me the greatest concern was the total unresponsiveness of my first period class. There are many students in the class who are underachievers and read below their grade level but usually there are a few who are enthusiastic and participate. Today they decided to let me do all the work, and although they weren't disruptive, they acted completely indifferent to what was going on.
3. The marking period closed on Friday and today everyone wanted his marks. The difficulty I had was in defending my marking system and

in convincing students that the system is fair. One student was so vocal about his mark that I had to discipline him. I have found that my students are very grade conscious.
4. A lab day, and the problem is a fairly normal one. The students do not apply what they know and have learned to laboratory situations. They can work problems on a quiz or test, but when they are in the laboratory and encounter an identical problem it is as if they had never seen it before. For some reason they can't transfer their knowledge from one environment to another. I find this most discouraging since it implies that the students will not be able to transfer knowledge from the classroom to their lives outside school.
5. Today my appointed group work backfired. I do not seem to be able to motivate this class to accomplish much during a group activity. They just seem to waste time. The alternative to group work seems to be in large part a teacher-centered activity. This is what I would like to get away from. But my attempts to do so have not succeeded.

Vignettes Related to Teacher Goal of Time

1. I work in an interdisciplinary center, and there are so many bureaucratic meetings which last such a *long* time and occur so often. Also, we have reports for each student that must be written three times a year (by a deadline, of course) that take about five hours *per* student.
2. Essay type questions should be given more often than I am able to. It is impossible to grade 153 tests if essay type questions are given. Children are unable to express themselves when writing even though they may actually know the answer.
3. This was a Monday, the first school day after the end of the quarter, and the previous week had been a difficult one with most teachers giving quarter tests. Usually Monday is a productive day, but it wasn't this time. The students were restless and excited and didn't want to work. They were enjoying a feeling of relaxation. In chemistry I had set the period aside to check my grade book with them for missing lab reports and other discrepancies. While I did this they were free to talk quietly; it was a wasted period in a way, but probably necessary. In biology I tried to have them do a seat-work assignment, quite unsuccessfully. They weren't in a working mood.
4. This has been a day of scurrying about attempting to get all tests and compositions graded because averages must be computed and report

cards filled out. It is the kind of a day in which men convert to machines in order to complete tasks which often seem to amount to "much ado about nothing." In an attempt to grade as objectively as possible, one feels that he must rip away all concerns for the student that he may have and look only at the facts staring back from the mark book.

5. I think you'll get the point if you listen to the schedule for today.
   1st period—cut 15 minutes because of yearbook collection
   2nd period—okay
   3rd period—fire drill (5 minutes but enough to finish things)
   4th period—okay
   5th period—cut 10 minutes because of assembly
   6th period—cut 10 minutes because of assembly
  The day was slow to start but slower to end!

2 supplement

the development of the Teacher Problems Checklist

DONALD R. CRUICKSHANK AND BETTY MYERS

The Teacher Problems Checklist (TPC) is a new instrument available for use in identifying teacher concerns. Many teachers—elementary and secondary; urban, suburban, and rural; experienced and inexperienced—have submitted their problems and have responded to earlier checklists in order to make this one possible. (See Related Readings, Chapter 1.) The TPC has fewer items and more clearly focused problem areas than any of the earlier versions, and for these reasons it is better. The purpose of this Supplement is to describe briefly the most recent history of how the TPC was developed.

The 60 problems which constitute the items of the Teacher Problems Checklist (TPC) were derived from an analysis of hundreds of teachers' responses on two other instruments—the Teacher Problems Checklist for Elementary Teachers (TPC-E) and the Teacher Problems Checklist for Secondary Teachers (TPC-S). The 66 items on the TPC-E were responded to by 538 teachers in grades K-6. Similarly, the 80 items on the TPC-S were responded to by 432 teachers in grades 7-12. Each instrument assessed both the frequency and bothersomeness of the problems.

In order to identify *areas* of problems, factor analyses were performed. Altogether four sets of responses were analyzed: (1) TPC-E frequency responses, (2) TPC-E bothersomeness responses, (3) TPC-S frequency responses, and (4) TPC-S bothersomeness responses. Each factor analytical solution resulted in the identification of five analogous factors which were labeled Affiliation, Control, Parent Relationships, Student Success, and Time. These factor areas provided one source of items for the TPC in the following way.

The five highest loading problems on each of the four factor solutions were tentatively retained. Because 39 of the resultant 100 problems were among the top five on both TPC-E and TPC-S factors, there were actually only 61 problems from this source. Within the TPC-E and the TPC-S, many more items were common to both the frequency and bothersomeness factors. The consequence was that the *total* number of problems provided from this source was 43.

Individual problems which achieved statistical significance with respect to their importance for either frequency or bothersomeness, or both, but which did not have high loadings on any factor, provided a second source of items for the TPC. Each item from the TPC-E and the TPC-S was tested for significance ($p < .01$). A total of 26 items from the TPC-E and 37 items from the TPC-S met the established criterion. Of this number, 22 items were identical, so there were only 41 different, statistically significant items to be added to the TPC from this source. Of these 41 problems, however, 22 had already been included in the first group of 43 problems because they had high factor loadings. Thus, a total of 19 items were added from this source.

Adding the statistically significant individual items to the items obtained from the factor analyses made a total of 62 items for the new TPC. They were related to the five problem areas as follows (a) 7 items were related to Affiliation; (b) 11 items were related to Control; (c) 10 items were related to Parent Relationships; (d) 26 items were related to Student Success; and (e) 8 items were related to Time. After these items were examined individually, four of them were eliminated, either because they were complex (two problems presented as one) or because their relationship to the problem area was unclear. Two of the dropped items were from the problem area of Parent Relationships and two were from Student Success. Then, in order to facilitate responding and scoring, two new items were constructed so that one item was added to each of the problem areas of Affiliation and Control. The following section includes an item-by-item display which shows why each item was selected for inclusion on the TPC.

SOURCES OF THE 60 PROBLEM STATEMENTS INCLUDED ON THE TPC

TPC Number	Problem Statement	Reason for Inclusion*	Related Problem Area
1	Liking my students.	F	Affiliation
2	Getting students to participate in class	S	Student Success
3	Maintaining order, quiet, or control	F,S,	Control
4	Improving life for my students by correcting conditions both inside and outside schools.	F,S	Parent Relationships
5	Having enough free time.	F,S	Time
6	Getting my students to feel successful in school.	F,S	Student Success
7	Getting students to behave appropriately.	F,S	Control
8	Gaining professional knowledge, skills, and attitudes and using them effectively.	F	Student Success
9	Controlling and using my professional time in the most functional, efficient way.	F,S	Time
10	Understanding and helping the atypical or special child.	S	Student Success
11	Getting cooperation and support from the administration.	F	Affiliation
12	Helping students who have personal problems.	F	Student Success
13	Keeping my students away from things and people which may be a bad influence.	F	Parent Relationships
14	Planning instruction in different ways and for different purposes.	S	Student Success
15	Responding appropriately to improper behavior such as obscenities.	F	Control

The Development of the Teacher Problems Checklist 333

TPC Number	Problem Statement	Reason for Inclusion*	Related Problem Area
16	Developing and maintaining student rapport, affection, and respect.	F	Affiliation
17	Assessing my students' learning.	F	Student Success
18	Soliciting appropriate student behavior.	F,S	Control
19	Improving conditions so that students can study better at home.	F	Parent Relationships
20	Having enough preparation time.	F,S	Time
21	Extending learning beyond the classroom.	F,S	Student Success
22	Controlling aggressive student behavior.	F,S	Control
23	Getting my students to achieve competence in basic skills such as expressing themselves effectively in both writing and speaking.	S	Student Success
24	Completing the work I have planned.	F,S	Time
25	Promoting student self-evaluation.	S	Student Success
26	Getting the understanding and sustenance of teachers and administrators so that I feel efficient and professional.	F	Affiliation
27	Helping students adjust socially or emotionally.	S	Student Success
28	Establishing good relationships with parents and understanding home conditions.	F	Parent Relationships
29	Getting my students to value school marks and grades	S	Student Success
30	Enforcing considerate treatment of property.	F,S	Control
31	Establishing and maintaining rapport with students and staff.	F	Affiliation
32	Helping students improve academically.	F,S	Student Success

TPC Number	Problem Statement	Reason for Inclusion*	Related Problem Area
33	Enforcing social mores and folkways such as honesty and respect for teachers.	F	Control
34	Encouraging parental interest in school matters.	F,S	Parent Relationships
35	Having enough time to teach and also to diagnose and evaluate learning.	F,S	Time
36	Providing for individual learning differences.	S	Student Success
37	Getting students to use their leisure time well.	S	Control
38	Getting students to enjoy learning for its own sake.	S	Student Success
39	Avoiding duties inappropriate to my professional role.	F	Time
40	Getting every student to work up to his or her ability.	F,S	Student Success
41	Being professional in my relationships with staff.	F	Affiliation
42	Creating interest in the topic being taught.	S	Student Success
43	Holding worthwhile conferences with parents.	F	Parent Relationships
44	Having students present and on time for all classes, rehearsals, games, etc.	S	Student Success
45	Maintaining student attention.	F,S	Control
46	Establishing and maintaining rapport with administrators and supervisors.	F	Affiliation
47	Learning to use alternative methods of instruction.	F	Student Success
48	Eliminating inappropriate student behavior.	F,S	Control
49	Understanding the conditions of the homes and community in which my students live.	F	Parent Relationships

TPC Number	Problem Statement	Reason for Inclusion*	Related Problem Area
50	Using time wisely to get both professional and personal things accomplished.	F,S	Time
51	Guiding my students to do the things which will help them succeed in school.	S	Student Success
52	Removing students who are sources of frustration.	S	Control
53	Knowing how to differentiate between student learning and psychological problems.	S	Student Success
54	Teaching too many students or large classes.	S	Time
55	Vitalizing my students' interests in learning and improving their achievement.	F,S	Student Success
56	Developing confidence in my colleagues.	R	Affiliation
57	Overcoming a student's feelings of upset or frustration with himself.	S	Student Success
58	Assisting parents having difficulty with their children.	F	Parent Relationships
59	Overcoming student apathy or outright dislike.	S	Student Success
60	Teaching self-discipline.	R	Control

*There are three possible reasons for including an item: (1) it had a high factor loading (F) on a problem area identified by the elementary and/or secondary teachers? (2) it was statistically significant (S) for elementary and/or secondary teachers; or (3) it facilitated responding or scoring by the respondent (R).

Self-Scoring Answer Sheet
TEACHER PROBLEMS CHECKLIST (TPC)

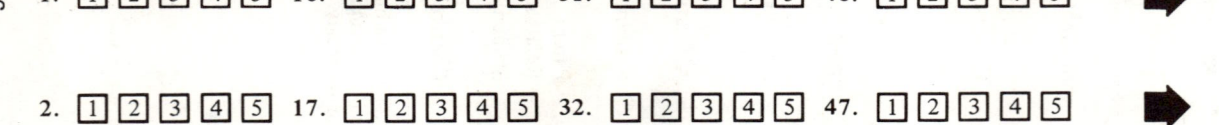

1. [1] [2] [3] [4] [5]	16. [1] [2] [3] [4] [5]	31. [1] [2] [3] [4] [5]	46. [1] [2] [3] [4] [5]
2. [1] [2] [3] [4] [5]	17. [1] [2] [3] [4] [5]	32. [1] [2] [3] [4] [5]	47. [1] [2] [3] [4] [5]
3. [1] [2] [3] [4] [5]	18. [1] [2] [3] [4] [5]	33. [1] [2] [3] [4] [5]	48. [1] [2] [3] [4] [5]
4. [1] [2] [3] [4] [5]	19. [1] [2] [3] [4] [5]	34. [1] [2] [3] [4] [5]	49. [1] [2] [3] [4] [5]
5. [1] [2] [3] [4] [5]	20. [1] [2] [3] [4] [5]	35. [1] [2] [3] [4] [5]	50. [1] [2] [3] [4] [5]
6. [1] [2] [3] [4] [5]	21. [1] [2] [3] [4] [5]	36. [1] [2] [3] [4] [5]	51. [1] [2] [3] [4] [5]
7. [1] [2] [3] [4] [5]	22. [1] [2] [3] [4] [5]	37. [1] [2] [3] [4] [5]	52. [1] [2] [3] [4] [5]

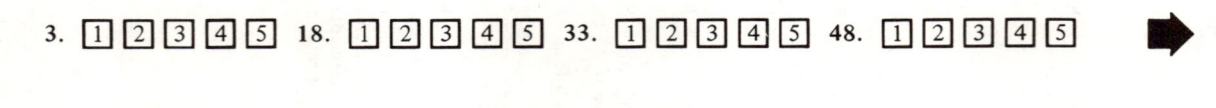

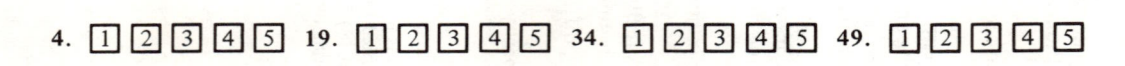

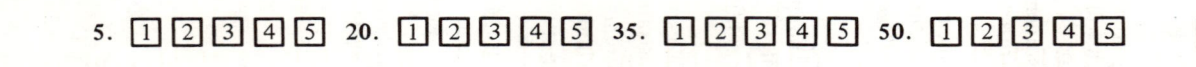

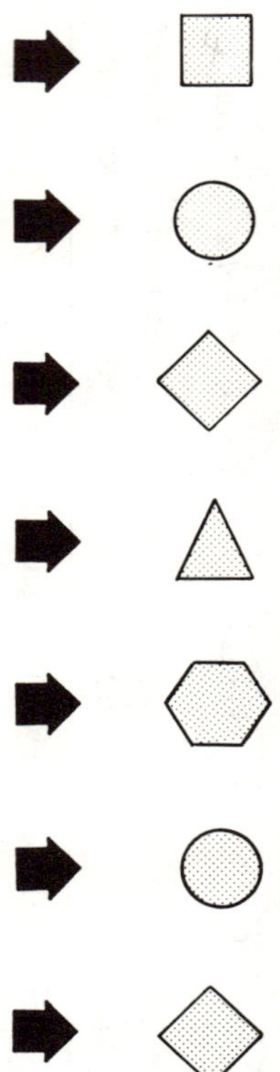

↑ □   ↑ ○   ↑ ◇   ↑ ◁   ↑ ⬡   ↑ ○   ↑ ◇

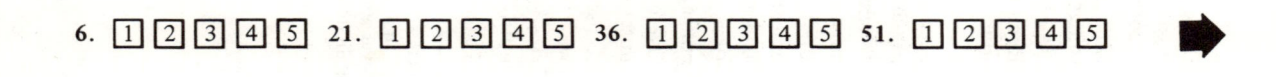

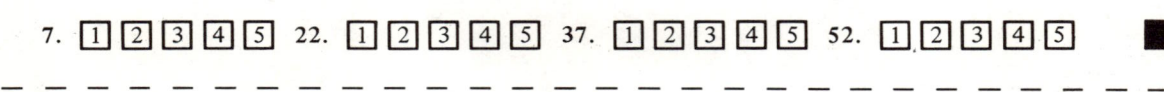

Answer Sheet

#	1	2	3	4	5
8.	□	□	□	□	□
9.	□	□	□	□	□
10.	□	□	□	□	□
11.	□	□	□	□	□
12.	□	□	□	□	□
13.	□	□	□	□	□
14.	□	□	□	□	□
15.	□	□	□	□	□
23.	□	□	□	□	□
24.	□	□	□	□	□
25.	□	□	□	□	□
26.	□	□	□	□	□
27.	□	□	□	□	□
28.	□	□	□	□	□
29.	□	□	□	□	□
30.	□	□	□	□	□
38.	□	□	□	□	□
39.	□	□	□	□	□
40.	□	□	□	□	□
41.	□	□	□	□	□
42.	□	□	□	□	□
43.	□	□	□	□	□
44.	□	□	□	□	□
45.	□	□	□	□	□
53.	□	□	□	□	□
54.	□	□	□	□	□
55.	□	□	□	□	□
56.	□	□	□	□	□
57.	□	□	□	□	□
58.	□	□	□	□	□
59.	□	□	□	□	□
60.	□	□	□	□	□

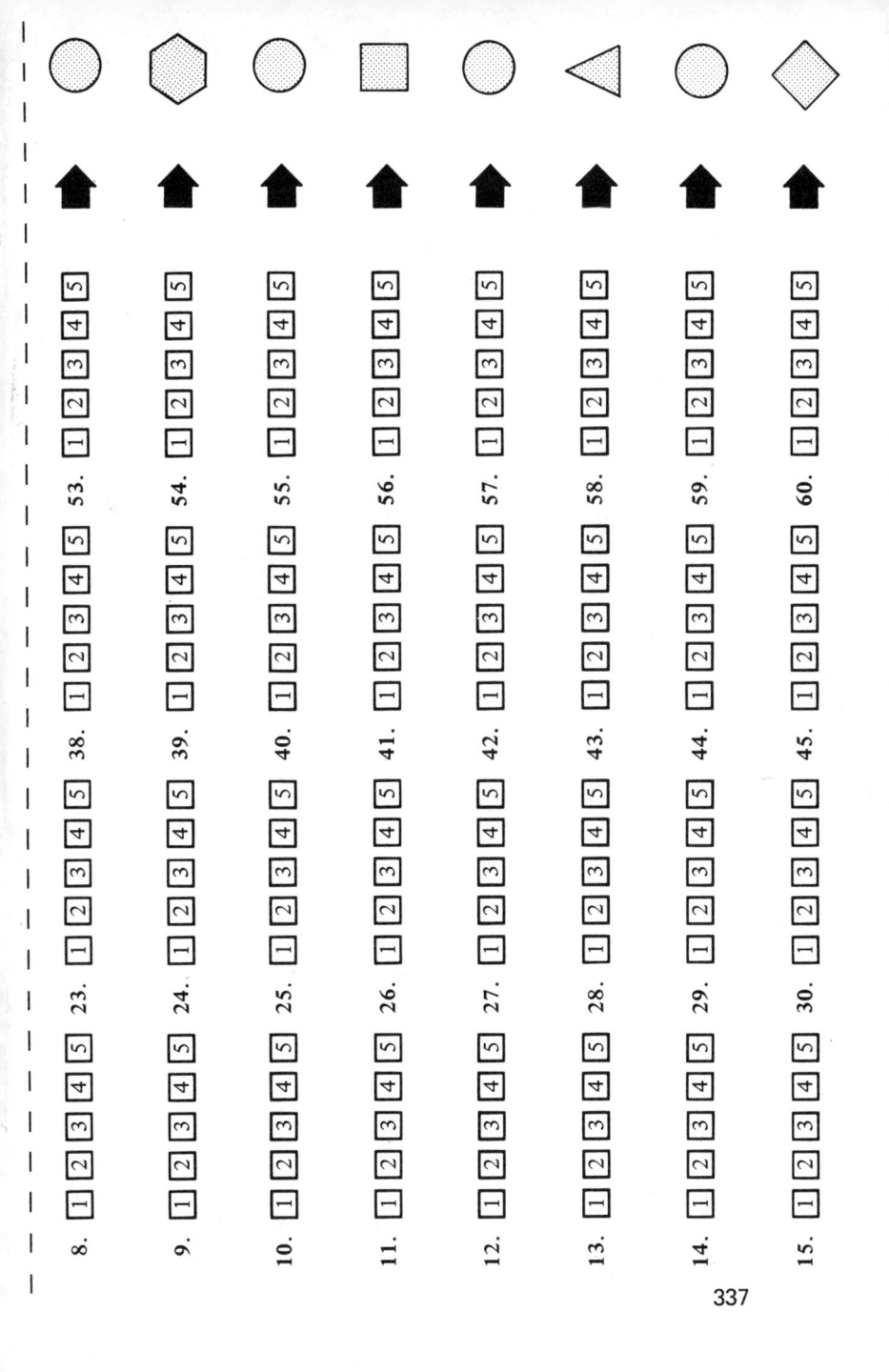

index

Accountability, 135-36
Action zone, 97-98
Active listening, 132-133, 137
Activity rewards, 127, 128
Adams, R. S., 97, 98
Affiliation, 16-17, 31, 75-109, 243, 281
  defined, 75-76
  examples of, 78-79
  group interaction, 99-108
  importance of, 76-77
  nonverbal communication, 95-99
  personality of teacher and, 304-9
  significance of, 77
  social interaction, 93-95
  teacher-administrator expectations, 89-92
  teacher-student expectations, 79-83
  teacher-teacher expectations, 83-89
  vignettes related to, 324-25
Anti-intellectualism, 86
Applegate, Jane, 257-99
Argyle, Michael, 101
Attention, 226-29
Attention-seeking behavior, 124-26, 133
Autonomy, 85
Avila, Donald L., 249, 251
Ayllon, T., 119

Bandura, A., 131
Beadle, George Wells, 205
Becker, W. C., 124
Berelson, Bernard, 246
Biddle, B., 97, 98
Bloom, Benjamin, 223, 224
Bloom, R., 121
Bourne, Geoffrey Howard, 76
Breed, G., 97
Brophy, J. E., 116
Broudy, Harold, 73-74

Brown, A. F., 90
Browning, Robert, 68
Bruner, Jerome, 216-17
Bush, Andrew, 210
Businesslike behavior, student success and, 239-40
Butler, H. E., 204

Cause-and-effect relationships, 144-45
Central liking structure, 104
Challenge arousal, 136
Child development, 215-18
Choice of problem solutions, 54-56, 69, 70-71
Clarity, student success and, 209-11, 235
Classroom arrangement, 97-99
Classroom Meeting, 133-34, 137
Cohesiveness of groups, 103-4
Colaiuta, N., 97
Combs, Arthur W., 249, 251
Compensation, 216
Competence, 182
Concentration, 285-88
Conferences, 187-92
Consistent punishment, 140
Consistent reinforcement, 130
Control, 16, 17-18, 31, 113-50
  as area of teacher concern, 114-15
  defined, 114
  identifying obstacles, 120-22
  kinds of problems, 115-16
  personality of teacher and, 310-12
  positive management techniques, 122-37
  punishment, 50-51, 102, 137-44, 231, 234, 250
  pursuing appropriate and important goals, 117-20

rewards, 50–51, 102, 122–32, 231–35
self-control, 144–49
vignettes related to, 325–26
Cottle, Thomas, 262
Cruickshank, Donald R., 1–3, 7–27, 31–43, 63–71, 84, 210
Cuing, 225
Cynicism, 86

Dickens, Charles, 201
Diffuse liking structure, 104

Edwards Personality Inventory, 304–5, 308
80.20 rule, 277
Ellis, A., 292–93
Enactive mode of information processing, 217
Enthusiasm, student success and, 211–13
Environmental impediments to problem solving, 11–13
Esteem needs, 114
Evaluation, 58, 71
Evertson, C. M., 116
Exercise, 264
Expectations (*see* Teacher-administrator expectations; Teacher-parent expectations; Teacher-student expectations; Teacher-teacher expectations)
Eye contact, 96–97

Facilitating forces, 49–51, 68
Failure, fear of, 291–92
Feedback, 12, 102, 229, 250
Finishing tasks, 294–98
Formal operations, 216
Frustration-related problems, 132–33

General human needs, 14, 15
Glasser, W., 133, 137
Goals, 11, 12, 14–20, 117–20, 265–70
Gordon, T., 133, 137
Grading, 237–38
Grambs, Jean, 100
Grandmother Rule, 233
Group alerting, 135–36
Group discussions, 133–34
Group interaction, 99–108

Hahn, Emily, 76
Hall, Edward T., 258–60, 298
Hamachek, Don, 248
Hard Times (Dickens), 201
Hargreaves, D. H., 85–86
Harper, R. A., 292
Hierarchy of needs, 76, 243–44
Highet, Gilbert, 200, 213

Hill, Warren G., 1
Holland, J., 77
Holton, John, 199–253
Home and community conditions (*see* Parent relationships and home conditions)
Home visits, 187–92
Homework, 236–37
Hull, Ronald E., 248

Iconic mode of information processing, 217
Identification of problems, 31–43, 46–47, 63–67, 120
Implementation of problem solutions, 56–58, 71
Improving Teacher Education in the U.S. (ed. Elam), 74
Information processing, 217
Infrequent contact, 90
Inside-out thinking, 246
Institutional needs, 15
Interaction (*see* Affiliation; Parent relationships and home conditions)
Interaction potential, 182
Interruptions, 272–73
Intrinsic rewards, 127, 129

Jackson, Phillip W., 204
James, William, 200
Jersild, Arthur, 3

Kennedy, John, 210
Koser, L., 124
Kouning, J. S., 134–35, 136

Lakein, Alan, 266, 277, 290, 295
Lateral thinking, 51–53, 68
Leadership, 91, 102–3
Learning, definition of, 222–23
Lee, Victor, 101
Levine, C. S., 145
Liking structure, 104
Linguistic mode of information processing, 217
Loyalty, 85

Madsen, C. H., Jr., 124
Mager, Gerald, 153–96
Mailbox Quiz, 288–89
Marcus Fabius Quintilianus, 203–4, 248
Maslow, Abraham, 76, 114, 243–44
Mediocrity norm, 86
Memory, 227–28
Michelangelo, 207
Mnemonics, 228
Modeling, 131–32, 249

Mohan, Madan, 248
Momentum, 135
Montaigne, Michel de, 248
Motivation, student success and, 235, 240-46
Multiple solutions to problems, 11-12
Murray, Henry A., 242
Mutual support, 156-60, 167-76, 194
Myers, Betty, 210, 303-21

National Institute of Mental Health, 185
Needs, 14-15, 76, 114, 241-44, 261-62
Ninth Annual Gallup Poll of the Public's Attitude Toward the Public Schools (1977), 185
Nomothitical needs, 15
Nonverbal communication, 95-99, 212
Norms, 102, 166-67, 194
Novak, Charles, 113-50

Obstacles, 48-51, 58, 120-22
Outside-in thinking, 246
Overgeneralization, 10
Overlappingness, 135

Paperwork, 287-88
Parent conferencing, 187-92
Parent education, 184-86
Parent relationships and home conditions, 16, 18, 31-32, 153-96
  conferences and home visits, 187-92
  influence of neighborhoods, 155
  influence of parents, 154-55
  mutual support, 156-60, 167-76, 194
  optimal home conditions, 160-62, 176-80, 195
  parent and teacher roles, 163-66, 193
  parent education, 184-86
  personality of teacher and, 313-15
  role negotiations, 175-76
  school community norms, 166-67, 194
  teacher-parent expectations, 172-75
  vignettes related to, 326-27
Parents Are People, Too (NIMH), 185
Pareto Principle, 277
Parkinson's Law, 279
Past-focused person, 262
Personal impediments to problem solving, 10-11
Personality profiles, 303-21
  affiliation and, 304-9
  control and, 310-12
  parent relationship/home conditions and, 313-15
  student success and, 315-18
  time management and, 318-21
Physiological needs, 14, 15, 76, 241, 243

Piaget, Jean, 215-16
Plager, E., 124
Planning, 274-80
Poppen, William A., 246
Positive control management techniques, 122-37
Power structure, 84
Prater, Alice, 246
Preferred activity, 233
Premack Principle, 233
Present-focused person, 262-63
Pressure, problem solving and, 12-13
Priorities, setting, 276-77
Private power, 58
Proactive teaching, 134-35
Problem-solving process, 45-60, 117, 134, 148
  analysis of situation, 48-54, 70
  choice of solutions, 54-56, 69, 70-71
  evaluation, 58, 71
  identification and ownership, 46-47, 63-67, 120
  implementation of solutions, 56-58, 71
  practicing, 63-71
  value clarification, 47-48, 70
  (*see also* Affiliation; Control; Parent relationships and home conditions; Student success; Teacher Problems Checklist; Time management)
Procrastination, 290-94
Profanity, management of, 121-22, 132
Punishment, 50-51, 102, 137-44, 231, 234, 250
Purkey, William, 249, 251

Rabelais, Francois, 248
Rasmussen, E. R., 90
Recall, 229-30
Reciprocation, 182
Reinforcement, 122-32, 142-43, 231-35, 250
Rejection, fear of, 102
Relationship-oriented leadership, 91
Response cost, 140, 141-42, 143
Reversibility, 216
Rewards, 50-51, 102, 122-32, 231-35
Roberts, M., 119
Role-derived needs, 15
Role negotiation, 175-76
"Role of the Foundational Studies in the Preparation of Teachers, The" (Broudy), 73-74
Room arrangement, 97-99
Rousseau, Jean-Jacques, 248

Safety needs, 76, 243
Schmuck, 104

School community norms, 166-67
Science, 204, 206
Self-actualization, 114, 244
Self-concept, 82, 243
Self-control, 144-49
Self-Directed Search inventory, 77
Self-discipline, 296-97
Self-evaluation, 84-85, 146-48
Self-fulfilling prophecy, 82
Self-knowledge, 261-65
Sleep, 264
Smoothness, 135
Social competence, 94
Social interaction, 79, 93-95
Socialization, 14
Social leader, 102-3
Social needs, 242
Social pressure, 102
Social promotion, 19
Social rewards, 127, 128-29
Socioeconomic status (SES), 183-84, 218-19, 315, 317, 318
Sociogram, 105-8
Socio-psychological needs, 14, 15
Sommer, 97
Staff organization, 84-85, 86
Steiner, Gary A., 246
Strum, Shirley C., 76
Student success, 16, 19, 32, 68, 117, 199-253
  businesslike behavior and, 239-40
  clarity and, 209-11, 235
  defined, 202-3
  enthusiasm and, 211-13
  five barriers to, 201-8
  helping relationship, 247-51
  homework, 236-37
  human nature and, 205
  knowledge about teaching and, 203-4
  motivation and, 235, 240-46
  nature of schools and, 205-6
  opportunity to learn, 222-39
  personality of teacher and, 315-18
  tests, 237-38
  variability and, 214-22, 245
  vignettes related to, 327-28
Super, Donald E., 77
Support system, time management and, 280-85
Symbolic mode of information processing, 217

Taba, Hilda, 102
Tangible rewards, 127
Task leader, 102-3
Task-oriented relationship, 91
Taxonomy of Educational Objectives, 223, 224
Taylor, P. H., 79
Teacher-administrator expectations, 89-92
Teacher centers, 282
Teacher-parent expectations, 172-75
Teacher Problems Checklist (TPC), 32-43, 67, 76, 115, 304
  development of, 330-35
Teachers' lounge, 85-86
Teacher-student expectations, 79-83
Teacher-teacher expectations, 83-89
Tests, 237-38
Thomas, D. R., 124
Thompson, Charles, 246
Time management, 16, 20, 32, 257-99
  concentration and, 285-88
  finishing tasks, 294-98
  goals and, 265-70
  personality of teacher and, 318-21
  planning and, 274-80
  procrastination and, 290-94
  self-knowledge, 261-65
  support system and, 280-85
  vignettes related to, 328-29
  work environment and, 270-74
Time out, 140-41, 143
Tokens, 127-28
Tracey, Katherine, 75-109

Value clarification, 47-48, 70
Variability, student success and, 136, 214-22, 245
Vertical thinking solutions, 51

When Teachers Face Themselves (Jersild), 3
Withitness, 135
Work environment, time management and, 270-74

Yee, A. M., 104

DATE DUE

MAR 17 1986		
MAR 17 1986		
FEB 28 1986		
AUG 12 1986		
AUG 1 6 1986		

DEMCO 38-297

NORTHERN ILLINOIS UNIVERSITY

3 1211 01758774 8